A BASKET OF FRAGMENTS

ROBERT MURRAY M'CHEYNE

D0774203

CHRISTIAN FOCUS PUBLICATIONS

CHRISTIAN FOCUS PUBLICATIONS
Henderson Road
Inverness IV1 1SP

A Basket of Fragments
First published 1848
First Christian Focus Publications Edition 1975
Reprinted 1979
© Copyright 1979

ISBN 0 906731 03 8

Contents

FOREWORD   vii

1   THE WORD MADE FLESH   1
John 1:14

2   A FAITHFUL MINISTRY   6
2 Corinthians 4:1-6

3   MINISTERS AMBASSADORS FOR CHRIST   9
2 Corinthians 5:20, 21

4   THE TRUE AND FALSE SHEPHERD   12
John 10:1-6

5   CHRIST THE DOOR INTO THE CHURCH   16
John 10: 7-10

6   THE HIRELING AND THE TRUE SHEPHERD   20
John 10:11-15

7   THE FREE OBEDIENCE OF CHRIST   24
John 10:17, 18

8   THE MARKS AND BLESSINGS OF CHRIST'S SHEEP   28
John 10:26-30

9   THE SALVATION OF GOD   33
Isaiah 55:6-9

10   THE IMPROVEMENT OF AFFLICTION   37
Job 34:31, 32

11   ADOPTION   40
1 John 3:1

12   ELECTING LOVE   44
John 15:16

13   THE TRANSFIGURATION OF CHRIST   48
Luke 9: 28-36

14   THE HEAVENLY BRIDEGROOM AND BRIDE   52
Ephesians 5:25-27

15   BELIEVERS NOT ASHAMED OF THE CROSS OF CHRIST   56
Romans 1: 15-18

16   THE ARK   69
Hebrews 11:7

17   A GOSPEL MINISTRY THE GIFT OF CHRIST   74
Ephesians 4:11-13

18   THE CALL OF ABRAHAM   79
Genesis 12:1-3

19   THE QUARREL BETWEEN ABRAHAM AND LOT   84
Genesis 13:7-13

20	HIGH TIME TO AWAKE OUT OF SLEEP *Romans 13:11*	88
21	THE SAVIOUR'S TEARS OVER THE LOST *Luke 19:41, 42*	92
22	CONVERSION *Zechariah 3:1, 2*	97
23	GRIEVE NOT THE SPIRIT *Ephesians 4:30*	101
24	THE TRUE PLEASANTNESS OF BEING A CHILD OF GOD *Psalms 16:6. Proverbs 3:17*	106
25	THE PILGRIM'S STAFF *Hebrews 13:5*	112
26	THE OFFICE OF THE RULING ELDER *1 Timothy 5:17*	116
27	THE MIGHTY CONQUEROR *Revelation 19:12*	121
28	APOSTACY *Hebrews 6:4-6*	128
29	THE SPIRIT COMMITTED TO GOD *Psalm 31:5*	131
30	CHRIST THE LIFE *John 5:40*	135
31	FAITH'S VIEW OF CHRIST *John 20:20*	141
32	THE LORD'S DEALING WITH HIS PEOPLE· *Isaiah 46:3, 4*	145
33	FUTURE PUNISHMENT ETERNAL *Mark 9:44*	148
34	GOD'S RECTITUDE IN FUTURE PUNISHMENT *Psalm 11:6, 7*	155
35	THE ETERNAL TORMENT OF THE WICKED, MATTER OF ETERNAL SONG TO THE REDEEMED *Revelation 19:3*	162
36	THE MENTAL AGONIES OF HELL *1 Corinthians 9:27*	168
37	PAUL, A PATTERN *1 Timothy 1:16*	174
	HYMNS	188

Foreword

An account of the effect that the saintly M'Cheyne's preaching had upon those who heard him is preserved for us in the autobiographic notes of Duncan Matheson, the Scottish evangelist. He relates how, on one occasion, M'Cheyne preached at a communion season in Strathbogie. 'He preached with eternity stamped upon his brow. I think I yet can see his seraphic countenance, and hear his sweet and tender voice. I was spell-bound, and would not keep my eyes off him for a moment. He announced his text — Paul's thorn in the flesh. What a sermon! I trembled, and never felt God so near. His appeals went to my heart, and, as he spoke of the last great day in the darkening twilight, for once I began to pray.'

M'Cheyne died in 1843 — over one hundred and thirty years ago. But being dead, he yet speaks. The 'seraphic countenance' is lost to us; the 'sweet and tender voice' lies silent in the grave — yet still, still the fragrance of his memory lingers on; still his hallowed words ring down to us in his many printed sermons. Alexander Moody Stuart remarked: 'Many of M'Cheyne's hearers would have thought that the effect of his preaching was partly owing to a halo of interest attaching to himself and that his words would lose not a little when committed to print; but they are more powerful when read and when dissevered from all that was adventitious.'

It is with the recognition of the enduring worth of M'Cheyne's sermons that the publishers undertake to send this volume out into the world again. We feel sure that the reader will find an abiding power in these discourses. They are stamped with eternity; they are the expressions of one upon whose heart the weight of perishing sinners pressed; they are the yearnings of one who was 'deein' to hae folks converted'.

While, as one would expect from notes taken down by hearers, there is much that is imperfect, we have in these sermons the very dust of gold. Robert MacDonald of Blairgowrie wrote of M'Cheyne: 'He would sometimes say but one word, or quote a text; but it was blessed. I never got even a note from him that I could burn. There was always something in it worth keeping.' These words exactly express the feelings of the publishers, past and present, as regards this volume. We wish to 'gather up the fragments that nothing be lost'. It is our heart's wish and prayer that these sermons will, under the blessing of

God, bring sinners to tremble; that the affectionate appeals of the holy author will go to their hearts, and that they will begin to pray.

As stated in the prefatory note to the first edition of this work, it was published from notes of hearers, taken without the least view of publication. The publishers of this edition decided that it was in the interests of the public to remove such imperfections as could be removed without detracting from the original. The reader may therefore be assured that what he has here — apart from minor typographical, punctuation, and Scripture reference corrections — is the very same book as came from the press for the first time.

Ian R. Tallach
Perth.   1974.

SERMON I

THE WORD MADE FLESH

John 1.14. *And the Word was made flesh, and dwelt among us, (and we beheld his glory, the glory as of the only begotten of the Father) full of grace and truth.*

You remember, brethren, when Philip went down to Samaria, it is said that 'he preached Christ unto them, and there was great joy in that city.' You remember that the apostle Paul says, 'I determined not to know anything among you, save Jesus Christ and him crucified.' Now, brethren, it is really the case that the only object in the world that can give peace to your soul is 'Christ, and him crucified.' Those of you who are not awakened are in a great mistake in this matter; you think you have to find out something good in yourselves; you little know, dear friends, that you are seeking rest in the creature, which if you could find it, you would make out that Christ has died in vain. It is for this reason that I have chosen this text tonight, though it is so deep and full that I approach it with fear and trembling; yet certain am I that if anything will give you peace it is the getting a sight of his glory, 'the glory as of the only begotten of the Father, full of grace and truth.' It is just beholding his glory.

The first truth that is laid open here is the humiliation of the Son of God. It is laid down to us in two parts. First, 'The Word was made flesh.' Second, 'He dwelt among us.'

I. *The humiliation of the Son of God consisted in his being made flesh.* I do not stop to inquire why he is called 'the Word.' I would just remark that as the word of a man expresses the mind of a man, so Christ was revealed that he might express the mind of God.

Let us consider what is meant in his being made flesh.

1. What is not meant. 2. What is meant.

1. It is not meant that *he really took a body without a soul.* We know that Christ, as he dwelt among us, had not only a body, but a soul — a loving, human soul: John 12.27, 'Now is my soul troubled; and what shall I say? Father, save me from this hour; but for this cause came I unto this hour.' Now, brethren, I do not so much insist upon the word 'soul,' as upon — 'what shall I say?' Ah, this expresses the tenderness

of a human soul. Speaking with reverence, I would say, there seems to
be a holy perplexity in his mind. Matt. 26.38: 'Then saith he unto
them, My soul is exceeding sorrowful, even unto death.' And then the
next verse shows he had a human will: 'O my Father, if it be possible,
let this cup pass from me: nevertheless not as I will, but as thou wilt.'
From these passages, it is obvious that when it is said, 'The Word was
made flesh,' it is not meant that the Godhead was united to a human
body without a soul. Again, you are not to understand that it was a
sinful body. The word 'flesh' is often used in this sense, thus: 'The
Spirit lusteth against the flesh.' Some have thought so, but it has not
always this meaning; thus, in Ezekiel it is said, 'I will take the hard
and stony heart out of your flesh, and I will give you a heart of *flesh.*'
And, again, we know quite well from the Word of God that Christ was
holy. The angels said at his birth: 'That holy thing which shall be born
of thee, shall be called the Son of God.' And we know that in his
manhood he was holy, harmless, undefiled, and separate from
sinners. And we are expressly told that the one thing in which he
differed was that he was without sin; Heb. 4.15. And we are told that
in dying, 'He offered himself without spot to God.' Now, we know that
it was his human soul and body he offered up to God. So it is true that
his humanity was holy.

2. I come now to the real meaning of the words — that he who was
the second Person in the Godhead, became one with a holy human
soul, and with a body with our infirmities, such as thirst, pain, etc.,
capable of tears, weariness, suffering, etc., for so much is implied in
the word 'flesh.' 'All flesh is grass.' This is spoken of our feebleness.
'The Word was made flesh.' Great is the mystery of godliness, God
manifest in the flesh. Perhaps some of you may ask why God was
manifest in the flesh. There were three great reasons.

The first was that *he might obey the law of God in the same nature
that had broken the law.* When the devil had got man to trample the
law beneath his feet, as if it had never been, he thought that the law
would never lift its head again. Now, the Word was made flesh that he
might obey it; and so it is said, 'God sent forth his Son, made of a
woman, made under the law, to redeem them that were under the
law.' I remember explaining this once before to you. First, that he was
made under the law that he might obey it. And then, he was made
under the curse of the law that he might endure it. Now, it is to the first
of these that I now speak, namely, that Christ might obey the law, and
do more honour to it, than if it had never been broken. This was one of
the great reasons why he became flesh. If it had not been for this he
might have visited the earth for an hour. But the reason why he had to
stop so long was to show that it was a good law. You know, brethren, if
you look across the world, and if you take God's holy law and shed the

light of it over the world, there is something overpowering to think how fearfully his law has been broken; think of all the Sabbath-breaking there is in the world, and all the thefts, swearing, adultery, etc., all of these streaming over the world, and blotting out, as it were, the law. And oh, brethren, it is sweet to think it was worth the condescension of the Godhead becoming flesh to obey the law, so as to show to men and angels and devils that God's law was so much more honoured, than if it had never been broken.

The second reason why the Word was made flesh was *that he might die* — that he might bear the curse of the law: Heb. 2.9, 'But we see Jesus, who was made a little lower than the angels for the suffering of death, crowned with glory and honour; that he, by the grace of God, should taste death for every man.' Verse 14: 'Forasmuch then as the children are partakers of flesh and blood, he also himself likewise took part of the same; that through death he might destroy him that had the power of death, that is the devil.' In these two verses it is distinctly said that the Word was made flesh in order that he might die. You know, brethren, if he had remained in the bosom of the Father he could not have suffered — for the divine nature cannot suffer; but in order that he might die he must be made flesh. The reason why he took upon him a body was that he might bear the curse. You know we are under the curse; now, Christ took upon him flesh, that he might bear the curse.

I would just mention the third reason why he was made flesh. It is *that he might have sympathy for men.* Heb. 2.17: 'Wherefore in all things it bchoved him to be made like unto his brethren, that he might be a merciful and faithful high priest in things pertaining to God.' Brethren, there are no persons that can have compassion, as those who have felt like us. You know God said to the Jews, 'You shall be kind to strangers: for ye know the heart of a stranger, seeing ye were strangers in the land of Egypt.' So God says to Christ, You know the heart of a man. This was one reason why he was made flesh. Those of you who are afflicted believers, you know what it is to have a friend that was tried in all points like as you are.

II. I come now to the other part of his humiliation, 'He dwelt among us.' In the Greek it is, 'he tabernacled among us, as in a tent.' It is believed by divines that there is here an allusion to the tabernacle in the wilderness. And just as the tabernacle was the meeting place with God, so Christ is the meeting place between a sinner and God. But further, it implies his going from place to place. You know this was the case with the tabernacle; so this was one of the parts of the humiliation of Christ. He was not only born, but born in a low condition, and his life was one of poverty. Why did he this? One reason was that he might sanctify affliction. Some say, 'I have not clothes to come to the church with.' My brethren, do you not know that Christ had not where to lay his head? Ah, my brethren, this is one reason why he dwelt among us as in a tent. Away with your excuses that you cannot come to the church because you have no clothes; Christ was poor, though he might have chosen a palace. But here we see the glory that burst through his humiliation. 'The Word was made flesh and dwelt among us (and we beheld his glory, the glory as of the only begotten of the Father), full of grace and truth.' Some may perhaps ask, When he became flesh, did he cease to be God? No, he did not. Then did he entirely veil his glory? No. Then did all see it? Oh, no, 'We beheld it.' True, his glory was seen by some that did not believe on him. Angels saw his glory, and you remember there was a star that appeared at his birth — outward, carnal eyes could see that star. And you remember as he sat in the temple disputing with the doctors, they were astonished at his words — all the world could see that glory. And you remember at the marriage of Cana of Galilee, he made the water into wine — outward, carnal eyes could see that. So with all his miracles. But this is not the glory spoken of here; at least it is not all the glory. What is this glory then? I answer, it was the glory of the divine perfections, divine wisdom, divine love, etc.

1.   There was the glory of the divine wisdom shining through him. Who could see it, but those whose eyes were open? Brethren, in all that he did he was bearing the sufferings of many. And oh, brethren, have you seen this glory? for this is the glory of the only begotten of the Father. Have you seen this glory? for this was the glory that shone through the Word made flesh. It was not only the star; it was not only the wisdom he showed in the temple; it was not his miracles; it was not these so much as the plan of redemption — the scheme he accomplished, when he said, 'It is finished.' It was *that* that showed his wisdom.

2.   There was the love of the only begotten of the Father. His very appearance in the manger at Bethlehem showed the love of the only begotten of the Father. Have you seen that love?

I would now begin to ask you the question, Have you beheld that glory? John says, 'We beheld it.' The first moment that a sinner is brought to peace is when he beholds a divine person bearing the curse due to him for sin. Then the soul says, 'Here will I rest.' Have you seen that glory? I know you cannot see it till your eyes are anointed.

Last of all, The provision laid upon in Christ: 'Full of grace and truth.' Perhaps some here are saying, If Christ is so glorious, I cannot come to him, I can only say with Peter, 'Depart from me, for I am a sinful man, O Lord.' If it is true that all the perfections that dwell in the Father dwell in Christ, then I cannot come to him — How can I come to him? There is but one answer to that: 'He is full of grace and truth.' I do not know if I can make it plainer; but the meaning is just this, that he is full of grace — grace for those that deserve wrath. Once he sat in Levi's house with publicans and sinners — how could they sit beside him? Ah! the reason was, 'He was full of grace.' Brethren, I think I could say that you could not imagine a Saviour so suitable to your soul as Christ is. Some of you would perhaps wish that he was not so glorious — that he was not so just. Ah! think you that you could come to him more easily if he were less just? Oh, brethren, you could not imagine a more suitable Saviour than he is. And then he is full of truth. 'The law came by Moses, but grace and truth came by Jesus Christ.' The law was a shadow, Christ is the substance. All that is in Christ is truth. The pardon he gives is true pardon. The peace he gives is true peace. Brethren, will you come to him? I would now invite all heavy laden sinners to come to him; and I would give you two reasons why you should come. First, He is full of grace. Second, He is full of truth. My brethren, you need a divine Saviour, and yet you need one full of grace. Brethren, what Saviour can you imagine to yourself if Christ does not do. How graciously does he invite you to come. 'Ho, every one that thirsteth, come ye to the waters, and he that hath no money; come ye, buy, and eat; yea, come, buy wine and milk without money and without price.' And if you will not come, then he comes to you and says, 'Behold, I stand at the door and knock; if any man hear my voice, and open the door, I will come in to him, and will sup with him, and he with me.' How full of grace he must have been who said, 'Unto you, O men, I call, and my voice is to the sons of men.' Consider how long you have lived without him, trampled on his blood, despised his invitations, and yet he has waited all that time. Consider how long you have provoked him since you were awakened, making him a liar by not believing his Word. Consider how long he has stood. Brethren, he is full of grace, though he is full of glory. Will you not let him save you? Is it much he asks of you? Will you not allow him to justify you? Ah, brethren, if you do reject so gracious a Saviour, 'How shall we escape if we neglect so great salvation?' Surely, brethren, an eternity in hell will not be too much for those who despise the blood of Christ. I beseech you, brethren, that you receive not the grace of God in vain. You do not know the guilt of that man who will go away to-night despising Christ. You do not know the guilt and danger of despising him who is so able, as well as so loving a Saviour.   Amen.

SERMON II

A FAITHFUL MINISTRY

2 Corinthians 4. 1-6. *Therefore, seeing we have this ministry, as we have received mercy, we faint not,* etc.

It is five years today, brethren, since I began my ministry among you in this place. It will be good for us today to stand up in the sight of God, and see how we have improved the years that are gone by.

I.   Let us observe, first of all, that *faithful ministers preach Christ Jesus the Lord.* Verse 5: 'For we preach not ourselves, but Christ Jesus the Lord.' Now there may be two things implied in preaching not ourselves.

1.   We *do not preach the fancies of ourselves, but the truth of Christ.* Many men preach themselves — they preach their own theories. Many before the days of the apostles did this — they taught their own fancies. But when the apostles came they took a very different manner. Witness John the Baptist — 'Behold the Lamb of God that taketh away the sin of the world.' So the apostles; they said, 'We are witnesses of all things which he did both in the land of the Jews and in Jerusalem; whom they slew and hanged on a tree.' And then you remember Philip when he went down to Samaria, 'he preached Christ unto them.' And this is exactly what John says in his 1st Epistle, 'That which we have seen and heard declare we unto you.' This is the very beginning, middle, and end of a gospel ministry. And looking back on the five years we have been together, I think I can lay my hand upon my heart, and feebly think this iş what I have done. And why should we do this? Because it is the most awakening truth in the world. One evening lately, I was passing by a building and I heard a man speaking, who seemed in earnest. I stopped and listened — he was preaching about laws and politics. I said that man may preach to the day of judgment, but he will never make the people holy. But we preach Christ Jesus the Lord, that you may be made holy.

2.   *We do not preach ourselves as the end, but Christ.* I believe that all worldly teachers preach themselves as the end; but this is not the object of faithful ministers. It is not that you may praise them; but Christ Jesus the Lord. Again, looking back upon our ministry, though I am not more free from fault than other men, I would not be a minister another day, if it were only for a name. But if we are Christ's, he will make us preach himself.

I sometimes feel, brethren, that I would willingly lie down beneath the sod in the churchyard, and be forgotten and trampled on, if only you were friends of Christ.

II. *Let us consider, secondly, that all faithful ministers preach from personal experience.* Verse 6: 'For God, who commanded the light to shine out of darkness, hath shined in our hearts, to give the light of the knowledge of the glory of God in the face of Jesus Christ.' There are many teachers, dear friends, and I believe them to be honest worldly men, who do not preach from personal experience; they have been brought up for the ministry, but they know not Christ; they speak like Balaam, of a star they have never seen. This was not the case with Paul. God had shone into his heart. Observe what he got — 'the light of the knowledge of the glory of God.' It was not a sight of Christ with the bodily eye. Many saw the face of Christ who will wail in hell. What was it then he got? God gave him a true, divine, spiritual knowledge of the power, love, and beauty of Christ, that he could not but preach him. O brethren, it was this that enabled him to preach among the Gentiles the 'unsearchable riches of Christ.' It was this that made him stand undaunted before Nero. Brethren, can you say God has shined into your hearts? Observe where conversion comes from. It comes from God, who commanded the light to shine out of darkness. There was a time when the world was all in confusion. What could bring light on such a world? There cam ̣ still small voice, saying, 'Let there be light,' and there was ligh ̣ ̣ nversion. 'God, who commanded the light to shine out of ̣ ̣ ̣ess, ha ̣h shined in your hearts, to give the light of the knowledge of the glory of God in the face of Jesus Christ.' Can you say this? If not, you are still in darkness.

O brethren, pray that ministers may preach from personal experience. It is only those that see Christ that can make him known. It is only when the living water is springing up that we can tell of the power that sanctifies. Pray, then, that we may have such ministers.

III. But I hasten to the third point, and that is, *the manner of a faithful minister.* Verse 1: 'Therefore, seeing we have this ministry, as we have received mercy, we faint not,' etc.

1. *We preach without fainting.* There are many things that are apt to make a minister faint; no natural man could bear what faithful ministers do. One thing that is apt to make us faint is the reproach of the world. You remember what they called our master; they called him a 'wine-bibber, a friend of publicans and sinners.' These words are very bitter. And then again, I do not know anything more difficult to bear than the reproach of rich worldly men; they look on all our endeavours to save them as hateful. Another thing is, when they leave our ministry; when they go away, and we have the sad thought concerning them that they went back and walked no more with Jesus. Another thing is seeing many of you staying, and yet living unconverted. Brethren, if there is anything that is like to make us faint,

it is these things. I have often felt as if I were standing on the sand, and hearing a ship strike on the rock, I have cried that there was a rope, but the wave washed it by. How many have I seen pass away in this way! Ah! brethren, that is enough to crush a man. Another thing is when we see some of you who are like the stony-ground hearers. But we faint not. I will tell you why we faint not. It is because it is so sweet to preach. I would say with Henry, 'I would beg six days, to be allowed to preach the seventh.' Christ will be glorified, though you are not saved: you will not wear the white robe, but many will.

2. *All faithful ministers preach holily.* Verse 2: 'But have renounced the hidden things of dishonesty,' etc. There are many ministers who are outwardly ceremonious, but inwardly they are not so. But this was not the case with Paul. I believe that we could not preach if we had not an evil heart; but we have gone to the fountain, and got it washed; we have renounced the hidden things of dishonesty. Pray for holy ministers.

3. *We preach not deceitfully.* 'Not handling the word of God deceitfully.' The Word of God is a dangerous thing; and I fear that many ministers handle the Word of God deceitfully, in not letting you see your state. How many times the very best do it! Ah! brethren, pray that we may lead you where Paul led those he preached to.

IV.   I come now to show you that *under all faithful ministers many will be lost.* Verse 3: 'But if our gospel be hid, it is hid to them that are lost; in whom the god of this world hath blinded the minds of them that believe not, lest the light of the glorious gospel of Christ, who is the image of God, should shine unto them.' Now, you will see from these words that Paul reckoned upon it that some of his hearers would be lost, and accordingly this was the case. When Paul came to Iconium the city was divided, and part held with the Jews, and part with the apostles. And what is our experience? Is not this thing true of this congregation? Some have believed, some have believed not. What is the reason of it? Satan has blinded your mind, lest the light of the glorious gospel of Christ, who is the image of God, should shine unto you. Your lusts have made a thick veil to hide the gospel from you. And what will be the end? You will be lost. Oh! dreadful word — a lost soul! Lost to your believing friends; they will look around the innumerable company in heaven; but you will not be there! Lost to Christ — Christ will not own you! Lost to God — God will say, This is not mine. O brethren, are there any of you who have sat for five years under my ministry and yet are lost! Ah! brethren, our gospel is hid to you, and you will be a lost soul to all eternity. All the angels could not tell you the misery of that — to be a lost soul!   Amen.

SERMON III

MINISTERS AMBASSADORS FOR CHRIST

2 Corinthians 5.20,21. *Now then we are ambassadors for Christ, as though God did beseech you by us: we pray you in Christ's stead, be ye reconciled to God. For he hath made him to be sin for us, who knew no sin; that we might be made the righteousness of God in him.*

There are three things in these words which we would consider.

1. The character of faithful ministers set forth in these words, 'We are ambassadors for Christ.' We do not come to you in our own name.

2. There is contained in these words the substance of our message, 'Be ye reconciled to God.' It is a message of mercy we have got to preach, not one of wrath.

3. There is contained in these words the grounds of our embassy, verse 21, 'For he hath made him to be sin for us,' etc. If there were no ground to go upon we would be mocking men when we entreated them to be reconciled to God; but ah! there is ground for the embassy.

I. Let us go over these three things, and let us take the last first. *The ground of the embassy which God hath sent his ministers on.* 'For he hath made him to be sin for us, who knew no sin; that we might be made the righteousness of God in him.' There are three things contained in this. 1. 'He knew no sin'; 2. 'He hath made him to be sin for us'; 3. The object he gained by this — 'That we might be made the righteousness of God in him.'

1. Observe *the description here given of Christ* — 'He knew no sin.' I believe it is the most remarkable description of Christ you will find in the Word of God. We are told that at his birth he was holy. The angel said to his mother, 'The Holy Ghost shall come upon thee, and the power of the Highest shall overshadow thee; therefore also that holy thing, which shall be born of thee, shall be called the Son of God.' And he was holy in his life; 'Such an high priest became us, who is holy, harmless, undefiled, and separated from sinners.' And we are told that he was perfectly holy in his death; 'Who, through the eternal Spirit, offered himself without spot to God,' Heb. 9.14. But observe, brethren, in this passage we are told it in a different manner — 'He knew no sin,' that is, he did not know what it was to have sin in his bosom.

Learn from this, dear friends, what a lovely person Christ is. You know it is said in Canticles, 'He is altogether lovely.' It is this that ravishes the hearts of seraphs when they sing, 'Who shall not fear thee, and glorify thy name, for thou only art holy.' This is the bloom of beauty on the Rose of Sharon — 'He knew no sin.' Do you love Christ because he knew no sin? There are many among you who detest the name of Christ. And why? just because he knew no sin.

Learn, again, from this, what a suitable Saviour Christ is — 'Such an high priest became us.' He was suitable because he was man. But ah! this is the main thing — 'He knew no sin.' This is the thing that makes him infinitely suitable — 'He knew no sin.' He was a high priest that knew no sin.

2. Observe *how God dealt with him* — 'He hath made him to be sin for us.' This is described in the Bible in a great many different ways. In the fifty-third chapter of Isaiah it is said, 'All we like sheep have gone astray, and the Lord hath laid on him the iniquity of us all'; and, verse 10, 'it pleased the Lord to bruise him,' etc. The same thing is described to us by Peter, 1 Peter 2.24, 'Who his own self bare our sins in his own body on the tree.' But in this passage you will observe it is described in a far more dreadful manner. He heaped upon his Son all our sins until there was nothing but sin to be seen. He appeared all sin; nothing of his own beauty appeared; God took him as if he were entirely made up of sin. You know that unconverted men are all sin. You say you have many good things about you; you are sometimes light in your walk, and take a glass occasionally; 'but I'm a good fellow after all.' Ah, you do not know that you are one mass of sin; your mind, your understanding, your affections, and your conscience. Brethren, look at the love of Christ, that he should be willing to be made sin for us, and this was his love.

3. Observe *what the object was that he gained by this.* 'That we might be made the righteousness of God in him.' They are remarkable words. You know, brethren, that the pardon and justification of sinners is spoken of in different ways in the Bible. In Romans 3.24, it is said, 'Being justified freely by his grace, through the redemption that is in Christ Jesus.' Again, in Romans 5.19, 'For as by one man's disobedience many were made sinners, so by the obedience of one shall many be made righteous.' But observe that these words express it more fully. I think it means that those of you who have come to the Lord Jesus, his righteousness shall cover you, that you will appear one mass of righteousness. And, brethren, observe what a provision is here for sinners — for the chief of sinners; for it matters not how great or how small a sinner you are; if you come to Christ, his righteousness will cover you so that none of your sin will be seen. O my friends, is not this a gospel worth preaching? May you now say as Luther used to do, 'Thou art made my sin, and I am made thy righteousness.'

II. *The message contained in these words, which we are sent on.* 'Now then we are ambassadors for Christ as though God did beseech you by us; we pray you in Christ's stead, be ye reconciled to God.' When Christ came into this world, he was an ambassador from God. He is the great messenger that came not to do his own will but the will of him that sent him. He came as the messenger of God to man; but when he was about to ascend up on high, he came to his disciples and said unto them, 'Go ye into all the world, and preach the gospel.' And so they were ambassadors for Christ.

Learn from this, how we should preach, and how you should hear. We do not come in our own name, but in Christ's. We are to do as the disciples did when they received the bread from Christ. We are to receive our message from him and give it unto you; so, in one sense, it is immaterial to us whether you receive the truth or not. Observe, we are to speak with authority. Many of you are not pleased at what we say; you say we might have spoken less severely; you quarrel at our words; but ah! if you look into your own heart, you would see, that it is not us you quarrel with, it is with Christ. Observe, still farther, that we are ambassadors; we must speak tenderly. God is love. Christ is love. I am afraid it is here we err, and show that the vessel is earthly. When Christ came into the world, it was a message of love he brought; what love is in these words, 'O that there were such an heart in them, that they would fear me, and keep all my commandments always, that it might be well with them, and with their children for ever,' Deut. 5.29. What words are these — 'O that thou hadst hearkened to my commandments, then had thy peace been as a river, and thy righteousness as the waves of the sea.' But how has our message been received?

III. I come now to the last thing to be considered, and that is *the message itself,* 'Be ye reconciled to God.' Observe what it is you are invited unto; you are invited into union with God. We are told, when we come to men, to call that they may be reconciled to God. O brethren, you are invited into reconciliation this day; you have been long in sin. Is it not time to be reconciled to God? Be reconciled, sinner. O come, come, old sinner! O come, young sinners! Remember you are beseeched to come. I beseech you, brethren, to come. If you had been at Mount Sinai when the law was delivered, would you not have listened? Brethren, it is God that beseeches you now. It is God beseeching; it is Christ beseeching you sinner. Had you heard his gracious words to the multitudes that came around him, or had you heard him at the last supper saying, 'Let not your hearts be troubled,' brethren, would you not have listened? Brethren, it is him still. Sinner! Sinner! if you do not listen, how will you meet a beseeching God? God beseeches you; Christ beseeches you; and the Holy Ghost beseeches you. Brethren, you will see him soon, and if you hearken not now to his voice, he shall say, 'Because I have called, and ye refused; I have stretched out my hand, and no man regarded; but ye have set at nought all my counsel, and would none of my reproof; I also will laugh at your calamity; I will mock when your fear cometh,' Prov. 1.24.   Amen.

SERMON IV

THE TRUE AND FALSE SHEPHERD

John 10. 1—6

We learn, dear brethren, from the sixth verse that this passage is one of considerable difficulty. How much need then have I of a fresh baptism that I may speak rightly from it; and how much need have you to have your heart opened, as was that of Lydia, that you may attend unto the things that are spoken, if you would understand them. 'This parable spake Jesus unto them; but they understood not what things they were which he spake unto them.'

Let us notice:

1.   The false shepherd. 'Verily, verily, I say unto you, he that entereth not by the door into the sheep-fold, but climbeth up some other way, the same is a thief and a robber.'

2.   The true shepherd. 'But he that entereth in by the door is the shepherd of the sheep.'

3.   The character of the sheep, which I fear I will not have time to enter upon.

I.   First of all let us meditate for a little on what is said of the *false shepherd*. And we shall consider: 1. Who the false shepherd is. 2. What is the mark of the false shepherd. 3. What is the object of the false shepherd.

1.   Who the false shepherd is. It seems evident that this chapter is a continuation of the last. Christ had been speaking of the Pharisees — those false shepherds, and in this chapter he shows that all false shepherds that will ever be in the world enter not in by the door, but climb up some other way. It is evident that he speaks of one great false shepherd, and I have no doubt that it means the great false shepherd, the god of this world, who is continually trying to climb over the wall into the sheep-fold.

Now, Satan has got three ways in which he attacks the sheep-fold.

The first of these is by Antichrist. We know quite well that it is Satan who gives Antichrist all his power. You will see this in 2 Thessalonians 2.8: 'And then shall that Wicked be revealed, whom the Lord shall consume with the spirit of his mouth, and shall destroy with the brightness of his coming; even him whose coming is after the working of Satan, with all power, and signs, and lying wonders.' Compare this with the thirteenth chapter of Revelation, verses 1 and 2: 'And I stood upon the sand of the sea, and saw a beast rise up out of the sea, having seven heads and ten horns, and upon his horns ten crowns, and upon his heads the name of blasphemy. And the beast which I saw was like unto a leopard, and his feet were as the feet of a bear, and his mouth as the mouth of a lion; and the dragon gave him his power, and his seat, and great authority.' Now, we know quite well that the beast is the Church of Rome; we are told that the beast sits on seven hills; and we are told at the end of the 2nd verse that the dragon gave him his power, and his seat, and great authority. So that there is no doubt, dear brethren, but that the great enemy of the sheep — the false shepherd, who comes like a lamb, but who has the paw of a bear — is Antichrist. Now, there can be no doubt but that he gets his power from Satan.

But there is another way in which Satan attacks the sheep-fold, and this is by the world. All you who are the children of disobedience, are the children of the devil. Satan has two ways in which he attacks the sheep-fold by the world. 1. He makes the world to frown. 2. He makes it to smile upon you. Another way is through false teachers. It is said that Satan entered into Judas; and it is said that Satan filled the hearts of Ananias and Sapphira. So no doubt he fills the hearts of many who are false ministers. You will see this in 2 Corinthians 11.13-15: 'For such are false apostles, deceitful workers, transforming themselves into the apostles of Christ. And no marvel; for Satan himself is transformed into an angel of light. Therefore it is no great thing if his ministers also be transformed as the ministers of righteousness; whose end shall be according to their works.' So you see, brethren, that there are many who are the ministers of righteousness, who are the ministers of Satan. It is he that helps them over the wall.

2. *The marks of the false shepherd.* Verse 1: 'Verily, verily, I say unto you, he that entereth not by the door into the sheep-fold, but climbeth up some other way, the same is a thief and a robber.' The great mark of false shepherds is that they enter not by the door. Verse 9: 'I am the door; by me, if any man enter in, he shall be saved, and shall go in and out, and find pasture.' Christ is the door into the sheep-fold. The mark of every false shepherd is, he is not saved himself. This is the mark of the devil; he is lost! lost! lost! Those of you who follow Satan as a master are following one who is lost himself. And this is the mark of the Antichrist, just that he enters not in by the

door. They make another way into the sheep-fold; they have other mediators than the one Mediator between God and man. This is the mark of the world, they enter not in by the door. Is it a lost world? Oh, dear sheep, why do you fear the world? It will soon perish. The same is the mark of all false ministers. Ah, brethren, remember that you live in a dangerous time.

3.   But farther, let us observe *the object of the false shepherd*. Verse 10, 'The thief cometh not but for to steal, and to kill, and to destroy.' You know, dear brethren, this is Satan's great object in the world; it is to steal, and to kill, and to destroy. This is the object of Antichrist. This is the object of the world. This is the object of all false ministers. This is the object of your enemies, little flock, for whom it is the Father's good pleasure to give you the kingdom. Satan comes to rob God of your souls; Antichrist comes to rob God of his throne — to rob God of his laws; and the world comes to rob God of his Sabbath. So with worldly ministers in like manner, they come to rob you of your soul, of peace, of joy, of holiness. Antichrist robs you of the true way to the Father. And the world comes to rob you — that pleasant world which says, 'Stolen waters are sweet, and bread eaten in secret is pleasant.' And so with worldly ministers — this is their object, to rob, to steal, and to destroy. O my brethren, be warned to flee; be warned to flee from Antichrist; be warned to flee from an ungodly world! 'Make no friendship with an angry man; and with a furious man thou shalt not go,' Prov. 22.24; or with a covetous man thou shalt not go. And beware of worldly ministers; if your minister should be taken from you, beware of them, for they will come to destroy.

II.   *The true shepherd,* verses 2, 5. The shepherd of the sheep is Christ himself. He says, verse 11, 'I am the good shepherd: the good shepherd giveth his life for the sheep'; verse 14, 'I am the good shepherd, and know my sheep, and am known of mine.' And why is he called the shepherd of the sheep? Just because he died for them. The sheep were once condemned to die; he came in the character of a man and died for them. Is he not worthy, then, to be called the shepherd of the sheep? He did not flee when he saw the wolf come. He sees the sheep that is lost, and goes after it. 'What man of you, having an hundred sheep, if he lose one of them, doth not leave the ninety and nine in the wilderness, and go after that which is lost, until he find it?'

Then, let us consider what are *the marks of the shepherd of the sheep:*

1.   He that entereth in by the door is the shepherd of the sheep,' verse 2. We see that the door is Christ himself. Some of you will ask, then, Why could Christ enter in by the door, when he is the door himself? But this is just the very thing he did. Hebrews 9.11, 12: 'But Christ being come an high priest of good things to come, by a greater

and more perfect tabernacle, not made with hands, that is to say, not of this building; neither by the blood of goats and calves, but by his own blood, he entered in once into the holy place, having obtained eternal redemption for us.' He showed himself the good shepherd by his entering in by the door, that is, 'by his own blood, he entered in once into the holy place, having obtained eternal redemption for us.' True, if he had remained without our taking our sins upon him, he would not need to have entered in, but he took our sins upon him. Ah, brethren, this is the mark of every true shepherd whom Christ sends — he comes in by the door, that is, the blood of Christ. He speaks of sin, because he has seen its greatness; he speaks of pardon, because he has been forgiven; of blood, because he has felt its power. 'He that entereth in by the door is the shepherd of the sheep.' No other qualification will do. All the learning at colleges will never make a minister. All the eloquence in the world will never make a minister. Pray that Scotland may have such ministers.

2.   There is another mark here given of the true shepherd — verse 3, *'He calleth his own sheep by name.'* This, first of all, shows the complete knowledge he has of the sheep. You remember Zaccheus, when he was a stray sheep, Christ said to him when he was in the tree, 'Come down; for today I must abide at thine house.' You remember Nathaniel, when a stray sheep under the fig-tree, 'he saw him.' You remember, after his resurrection, he saw Mary, and said to her, 'Mary'; and she turned herself, and said unto him, 'Rabboni: which is to say master.' So it is still. Ministers do not know you; elders do not know you; but Christ knows you, and he calls his own sheep by name, and they follow him. And this implies, also, the love of Christ. You know when you love one, you love their name. Christ does not only know you, but he calls you by his name. He called Bethany, 'the town of Mary and her sister Martha.' Christ loves the names of those for whom he died. Your names are graven on his heart, and on the palms of his hands; and this shows he changes their names. He said to Abraham, 'Thy name shall no more be called Abram, but Abraham shall thy name be.' And you remember he said of Peter, 'Thy name shall be called Peter,' which means a stone. And it is said of the Jews, 'I have called thee by my name, thou art mine.' So it implies that they get a new name, that is, a new nature. And, when we come to the temple above, he says, 'Him that overcometh will I make a pillar in the temple of my God, and he shall go no more out; and I will write upon him the name of my God, and the name of the city of my God, which is new Jerusalem, which cometh down out of heaven from my God; and I will write upon him my new name.' And you that are of the world, if you will come, you will get a new name.

3. Last of all, there is another character of the true shepherd here mentioned, and that is, *'He goes before them,'* verse 4. In the countries of the east, brethren, you know that the shepherd goes before the sheep, and they follow him. When he says, 'Let us go to the well,' they follow him. When he says, 'Let us go down into that dark valley,' they go after him. So it is with Christ. Christ never asked a sheep to go where he never went himself. He has borne all that he calls his sheep to bear. Christ went in a lower level of sorrow than you will be called to bear. Do not be alarmed then when you are called to suffer, you will not be called to go where he has not gone. Do not be afraid to put down your tender feet where he put down his. And it is still true that he goes before you. 'When thou passest through the waters, I will be with thee, and through the rivers, they shall not overflow thee; when thou walkest through the fire, thou shalt not be burned, neither shall the flame kindle upon thee.' Do not be afraid then when Christ is before you.

Brethren, let me ask you, in conclusion, Are you following him, or are you following a stranger? I do not ask you, Are you following a godly minister? but, Are you following Christ? Do you hear his voice in the Word? Do you hear his voice in the preaching of the gospel? And do you follow him? Happy flock, follow on to know the Lord: soon shall we be where no tempting devil — where no deceiving world — where no false ministers are. There 'they shall hunger no more, neither thirst any more; neither shall the sun light on them, nor any heat. For the Lamb, which is in the midst of the throne, shall feed them, and shall lead them unto living fountains of water; and God shall wipe away all tears from their eyes.' Amen.

Sabbath Forenoon,
4th September 1842.

SERMON V

CHRIST THE DOOR INTO THE CHURCH

John 10. 6 - 10

Christ is the kindest of all teachers. He was speaking to a crowd of ignorant and prejudiced Jews, and yet how kindly he deals with them. He told them one parable, but they understood not. 'This parable spake Jesus unto them; but they understood not what things they were he spake unto them.' And yet, we are told, Christ spake unto them again. He hath given them a description of the true and false shepherd, and of the door into the sheepfold; but they seem to have been at a loss to know what the door meant; therefore he says, 'Verily, verily, I say unto you, I am the door of the sheep.' You see how kindly he tries to instruct them. My brethren, Christ is the same kind teacher still. Are there not many stupid and prejudiced persons here? And yet has he not given you 'precept upon precept, precept upon precept; line upon line, line upon line; here a little, and there a little,' Isaiah 13.28. He has broken down the bread for you.

Let us now examine this explanatory parable:

1. Christ is the door into the Church.
2. The invitation here given to enter in.
3. The promise to those that enter in.

I. *Christ is the door into the Church.* 'I am the door.' The only way into the Church of God, either for ministers or members, is by Christ, and through faith in him. Many enter in by learning; learning is not to be despised, but yet it is not the door. There are many that have entered into the ministry, by having eminent gifts, but these are not the door. And those who enter in such a way are thieves and robbers, for they enter not in by the door. Again, many enter in by the door of worldly favour, some by the favour of the rich, some by the favour of the common people, some by the favour of the patron; but still they are thieves and robbers, for they enter not in by the door. Remember then, and never forget it, that the right way into the ministry is through Christ. None can tell of sin, but those who have felt its burden. None can tell of pardon, but those who have tasted of it. None can tell of Christ's power to sanctify, but those who have holiness in their hearts. Brethren, hold such in reverence; flee from all others; they may have learning, they may have gifts, they may have the flattery of the common people, but they are thieves and robbers.

But further, there are many members who enter into the fold another way; they also are thieves and robbers. There are many who enter in by the door of knowledge — they have got acquainted with Bible knowledge, they can tell of the way of a sinner's acceptance with God; but if you have not come into the fold by being washed in the blood of Christ, you are a thief and a robber.

Some enter into the fold by a good life. As touching the law they are like Paul, blameless. You are not a thief, you are not a swearer, you are not a drunkard, and you think you have a right to enter in — a right to sit at the Lord's table; but Christ says it over and over again, you are a thief and a robber. Ah, brethren, remember if you are admitted into the fold on account of your morality — your outward decency — your good life, you are a thief and a robber. Brethren, there is a day coming when those who have entered into the sheepfold, not by the door, but some other way, will look back and see their guilt when they shall enter an undone eternity.

Observe, brethren, before I leave this part of the subject, that Christ is a present entrance. Brethren, there is a time in each of your lives — or rather I should say, history — that the door of the sheepfold is open to you. 'I am the door; by me if any man enter in, he shall be saved'; but that time will pass away. It is but a moment compared to eternity. This is a solemn truth. Brethren, if I could promise you that the door will stand open for a hundred years, yet it would still be your wisdom to enter in now; but I cannot answer for a year, I cannot answer for a month, I cannot answer for a day, I cannot answer for an hour; all that I can answer for is, it is open now — tomorrow it may be shut for ever.

II.   I come now to the second thing proposed, and that is, *to shew you Christ's invitation.* 'I am the door; by me if any man enter in he shall be saved.' There are many sweet invitations to sinners in the Bible; I have often felt these words to be the sweetest. There are some invitations addressed to those who are thirsty. It is said in Isaiah, 'Ho, every one that thirsteth, come ye to the waters,' etc. Christ said on the last day, that great day of the feast, 'If any man thirst, let him come unto me and drink.' And he says, near the end of Revelation, 'I will give to him that is athirst of the fountain of the water of life freely.' Again, there are some invitations that are addressed to those that have a burden; 'Come unto me all ye that labour and are heavy laden, and I will give you rest.' Again, there are some that are addressed to those who are prisoners; 'Turn you to the stronghold ye prisoners of hope.' But this appears to me the sweetest of all, for it is said, 'If any man.' It is not said, if any thirsty man, if any weary man, if any burdened man, but if any man enter in he shall be saved. I have seen some rich men's doors, where none could enter but the rich; and where the beggar must lie at the gate. But Christ's door is open to any man, whatever your life, whatever your character may be. Christ is not like the door of some churches, where none can enter in but the rich; Christ's door is open to the poor; 'To the poor the gospel is preached.' Some, perhaps, can say, 'I am the most vile one in this congregation,' yet Christ says, 'Enter in.' Some, perhaps, can say, 'I have sinned more than all; I have sinned against a father, I have sinned against a mother, I have sinned against mercies, and against judgments, against the invitations of the gospel, and against light,' yet Christ says, 'Enter in.'

Observe still farther that the invitation is not to look at the door, but to enter in. There are many that hear about the door, but that is not enough; it is to enter in at it. And there are many that like to hear about the door, but yet they do not enter in. Ah, my brethren, that's a great cheat of the devil. I am persuaded many of you will go away this day well pleased because you heard about the door, but you do not enter in. There are many that go a step farther, they look in at the door, but yet they do not enter in. I believe that many of you are often brought there; but when it comes to the point, that you must leave your idols, that you must leave your sins, you do not enter in. 'By me, if any man enter in, he shall be saved.'

Again, there are some who see other people enter in, but they do not enter in themselves. You, perhaps, have seen a father, or a mother, or a neighbour enter in; you have seen a change come over them, and a peace possess their minds, and you say, 'I wish I were them'; but you do not enter in. Ah! if you would be saved, you must enter in at the door; convictions will not do, tears will not do, etc. And this is the reason why so many of you are not happy; you do not enter in.

III. I now come to the third and last point, and that is, *the promise;* 'If any man enter in, he shall be saved, and shall go in and out, and find pasture.' 'I am come that they might have life, and that they might have it more abundantly.' The *first* part of the promise is, 'They shall be saved.' Christ pledges his word for it, that those who enter in shall be saved. Those who do not enter in shall be damned. If you are not Christ's, you are without, and without are dogs, and sorcerers, and whoremongers, and murderers, and idolators, and whosoever loveth and maketh a lie. But those who enter in *shall* be saved. It is immediate pardon. There will be even now no condemnation to them that are in Christ Jesus. O my brethren, it is immediate pardon we offer you from the Father, 'If any man enter in, he shall be saved.' And then, 'He shall go in and out, and find pasture.' That is to say, you will have all the privileges of a sheep; it goes out to the well; it goes out to the pasture. So, if you are his, you can go in and out to find pasture. My dear brethren, there may come a time in Scotland, when there will be little pasture, when there will be no under-shepherd, when the witnesses will be slain. Yet the Lord will be your shepherd, he will feed you. You shall 'go in and out, and find pasture.'   Amen.

Sabbath Forenoon,
11th September 1842.

SERMON VI

THE HIRELING AND THE TRUE SHEPHERD

John 10. 11 - 15

In our first lecture we saw that the people did not understand Christ. There were two things that they did not understand. The first thing that they did not seem to understand was the door of the sheepfold; the second, who the shepherd was. And we saw last Sabbath that he explained to them what the sheepfold was. And now he begins to show who the shepherd is: 'I am the good shepherd: the good shepherd giveth his life for the sheep.' It is exceedingly interesting to know the many names by which Christ calls himself in the Bible. These are above a hundred, I think a hundred and seven. He calls himself a rose, 'I am the rose of Sharon,' and a lily, 'I am the lily of the valley.' The reason why he has so many names is that one name would not describe him; he has so many offices that one name would not explain them; nay, all of them put together do not, for Paul said, 'Unto me who am less than the least of all saints is this grace given, that I might preach among the Gentiles *the unsearchable riches of Christ.'* Of all the names given, that of a shepherd is the sweetest. We understand things best by figures; so, at the beginning of this chapter, he contrasted himself with a stranger, and in these words he contrasts himself with a hireling, whose own the sheep are not.

We shall consider these two things, the hireling and the true shepherd.

I.   *The hireling,* verses 12, 13. There can be little doubt, I believe, that the hireling represents unfaithful ministers. Let us then go over the features, here laid down, of an unfaithful minister:

1.   *He is a hireling;* that is to say, the end he seeks is the hire. You know, dear friends, that a minister should be maintained. It is written in the law, 'Thou shalt not muzzle the ox when he treadeth out the corn.' 'They that preach the gospel should live of the gospel,' 1 Cor. 9.14. But then, dear brethren, observe that this should not be the end of the ministry. The hireling here mentioned, is one who seeks the hire and not the flock. This was often complained of by the prophets. Isaiah complained of it in his day. 'His watchmen are blind: they are all ignorant, they are all dumb dogs; they cannot bark; sleeping, lying down, loving to slumber. Yea, they are greedy dogs which can never have enough, and they are shepherds that cannot understand: they all look to their own way, every one for his gain, from his quarter.' Isaiah 56.10, 11. Now, this is just the hireling. Jeremiah complained of them in his day: 'For, from the least of them even unto the greatest of them, every one is given to covetousness; and from the prophet, even unto

the priest, every one dealeth falsely,' Jer. 6, 13. This is the hireling again. Ezekiel complained of them in his day. 'Woe be to the shepherds of Israel that do feed themselves! should not the shepherds feed the flocks?' Ezek. 34.2. Paul complained of them in his day: 'For I have no man like-minded, who will naturally care for your state. For all seek their own, not the things which are Jesus Christ's,' Phil. 2.20, 21. Ah! brethren, this is the black mark of the hireling: verse 12, 'He that is a hireling, and not the shepherd, whose own the sheep are not, seeth the wolf coming, and leaveth the sheep and fleeth,' etc. But, brethren, it is not merely the seeking money that marks the hireling, but seeking our own ease — our own honour — our own fame. Pray for ministers — pray that they may not be given to covetousness.

2. *'Whose own the sheep are not.'* You know, dear brethren, that faithful ministers stand in a peculiar relation to the sheep. They are called fathers — watchmen that stand on the watch tower, etc. It is a relation that outlasts death. You know, dear friends, that Paul often calls himself a father; see 1 Cor. 4.15; Gal. 4.19; 1 Tim. 1.2; Philemon, 10th verse. Ah, friends, this shews you the union between the minister and the flock. He is a father — he begets them through the gospel. It is not so with a hireling — his own the sheep are not. God does not own him as a father. God does not own him in the conversion of souls. He cannot say as Paul said, 'My dearly beloved and longed for, my joy and crown.' He will not meet a crown of saved souls in the judgment. Ah! this is the mark of a hireling — a withered branch. Pray that ours may not be so.

3. *'The hireling fleeth because he is a hireling, and careth not for the sheep.'* You know that the ministers who are sent of God, take care of the sheep. Observe the apostle Paul — what labours did he not undergo; what sufferings did he not endure! 2 Cor. 11.23. Hear how he prayed for them — 'God is my witness, whom I serve with my spirit in the gospel of his Son, that without ceasing I make mention of you always in my prayers,' Rom. 1.9. 'For I would that ye knew what great conflict I have for you, and for them at Laodicea, and for as many as have not seen my face in the flesh,' Col. 2.1. How he cared for the sheep! And hear how he speaks to the elders at Ephesus — 'Remember that by the space of three years I ceased not to warn every one night and day with tears,' Acts 20.31. And observe, brethren, what tears he used to shed for them — 'For out of much affliction and anguish of heart, I wrote unto you with many tears,' 2 Cor. 2.4. 'I fear lest when I come, my God will humble me among you, and that I shall bewail many which have sinned,' 2 Cor. 12.21. And then what thanksgiving he used to offer up to God — 'I thank my God upon every remembrance of you, always in every prayer of mine for you all, making request with joy,' Phil. 1.3. 'For what thanks

can we render to God again for you, for all the joy wherewith we joy for your sakes before God,' 1 Thess. 3.9. 'I cease not to give thanks for you, making mention of you in my prayers,' Eph. 1.16. This is the mark of a true shepherd. But a hireling cares not for the sheep, he does not and cannot weep for the sheep, he has no anguish of heart for them. Pray that we may so love Christ that we may care for the sheep.

4. *He flees away when the wolf comes;* verse 12, 'But he that is an hireling, and not the shepherd, whose own the sheep are not, seeth the wolf coming, and leaveth the sheep and fleeth.' The wolf is taken in Scripture to represent two things, either false ministers or heresy. See Acts 20.29. 'For I know this, that after my departing shall grievous wolves enter in among you, not sparing flock.' The grievous wolves are evidently those false teachers who bring in another gospel which is not another. See also Matt. 10.16, 'Behold I send you forth as sheep in the midst of wolves,' etc. There you see the wolves are evidently those men who bring them before the councils. The time when the wolf comes is the time to mark who the true shepherd is. He stands between them when heresy comes in, or when a persecuting world stretches out its hand towards them; that is the time for the true shepherd to stand between the fold and it; but ah! the hireling flees. The time when he can get no more his own ease — his own comfort — is the time he flees. Pray that Scotland may have true shepherds; not those who care not for the sheep; not those whom God has never owned in the conversion of souls; not those who will flee in a time of heresy or persecution. Pray that the true shepherds may be known in a time of heresy or persecution, and that the day may never dawn on Scotland when it will be given over to hireling ministers.

II.   I come now, secondly, to consider *the true shepherd.* Oh! it is sweet to turn from looking at the hireling to the true shepherd: "I am the good shepherd, the good shepherd giveth his life for the sheep,' etc. Christ here gives us three marks of the true shepherd.

1. *The true shepherd gives his life for the sheep.* Jacob was a good shepherd to Laban. You remember his care of the sheep; he says, 'That which was torn of beasts I brought not unto thee; I bare the loss of it; of my hand didst thou require it, whether stolen by day or stolen by night,' etc., Gen. 31.39,40. But he did not give his life for the sheep. David was a good shepherd. You remember when a lion and a bear came and took away the sheep, that he went after it and rescued it, and slew both the lion and the bear; 1 Sam. 17.35. But David did not give his life for the sheep; but Christ gave his life. The sentence was written against the sheep, 'Thou shalt die;' — Christ came between and died for them. Observe, brethren, that it was not

merely temporal death that he died; but it was equal to eternal death. It was death under uniquity — 'He was wounded for our transgressions, he was bruised for our iniquities,' Isa. 53.5. It was a death under sin — 'The wages of sin is death.' Rom. 6.23. And observe, it was freely; he did it out of free love; therefore it is always said, 'He gave himself for us'. Love one another, even as Christ loved the church, 'and *gave himself* for it.' There is one Mediator 'who *gave himself* a ransom for all.' Brethren, observe that Christ so loved the sheep that he gave his life 'What are these wounds in thy hands? These are the wounds I have received in the house of my friends.' Brethren, if ever you and I get to heaven, this is what we will see, 'A Lamb as it had been slain.' Are you attracted by the sight? What are you made of, that you do not see this love? O brethren, to whom will you go if not to him? Observe what he offers — himself. 'I am the good shepherd, the good shepherd giveth his life for the sheep;' that is, I am willing to give myself to you.

2. *'I know my sheep, as the Father knoweth me.'* You know, brethren, how completely the Father knows his Son. He knew him from all eternity: 'Then I was by him as one brought up with him, I was daily his delight, rejoicing always before him.' Brethren, so Christ knows his sheep. 'He hath chosen us in him before the foundation of the world.' You know, brethren, that the Father knows him with a love of delight. So Christ knows his sheep with the same love; 'Thou art all fair, my love, there is no spot in thee.' 'As the lily among thorns, so is my beloved among the daughters!' 'My love, my undefiled is but one, she is the only one of her mother.' Christ delights in every one of his sheep. And you know the Father knew Christ during all the time of his sufferings on earth. So Christ knows his sheep in all their temptations. And you know the Father will know Christ to all eternity. So Christ says, 'I know my sheep.' Christ knows his sheep to all eternity. 'They shall never perish, neither shall any pluck them out of my Father's hand.' Ah, brethren, is there any shepherd like this shepherd?

3. *'I am known of mine.'* The sheep know Christ, and Christ knows the Father. Christ has a perfect acquaintance of the Father: 'O righteous Father, the world hath not known thee, but I have known thee,' so the sheep know Christ: he manifests himself unto them. Ah, brethren, has Christ made himself known unto you? Has he given you an understanding to know him that is true, and are you in him that is true? This is the mark of all his sheep. 'I am known of mine.' And this is one of the excellencies of Christ to his own. He lets fragrance forth when he passeth by, and we follow him. Brethren, has he let out his fragrance to you, and do you follow him? Are you known of him even as he is known of the Father? Amen.

SERMON VII

THE FREE OBEDIENCE OF CHRIST

John 10. 17,18. *Therefore doth my Father love me, because I lay down my life, that I might take it again. No man taketh it from me, but I lay it down of myself. I have power to lay it down, and I have power to take it again. This commandment have I received of my Father.*

The death of Christ is, my friends, the most wonderful event past, present, or future in the whole universe. It is so in the eye of God — 'Therefore doth my Father love me, because I lay down my life.' There is nothing in the whole world so lovely as his Son. It is not only for his Godhead, but on account of his manhood, through which he laid down his life — 'Therefore doth my Father love me, because I laid down my life.' These words of Christ, 'I lay down my life,' are dearer to God than a thousand worlds. It is the same in the eyes of the redeemed. All the redeemed love Christ, because he laid down his life. John says, 'I beheld, and lo, in the midst of the throne, and of the four beasts, and in the midst of the elders, stood a lamb as it had been slain . . . And when he had taken the book, the four beasts, and four and twenty elders fell down before the Lamb, having every one of them harps, and golden vials full of odours, which are the prayers of saints. And they sang a new song, saying, Thou art worthy to take the book, and to open the seals thereof; for thou was slain, and hast redeemed us to God by thy blood.' And again they sing, 'Worthy is the Lamb that was slain, to receive power, and riches, and wisdom, and strength, and honour, and glory, and blessing.' Still, brethren, you see that it is the death of Christ that is the joy of the new Jerusalem. And, still further, the death of Christ is the greatest wonder in hell. This was one thing which Satan did not know the meaning of — the death of Christ. Ah! Satan thought when he got Judas to betray him, and the Jews to crucify him, that he had prevailed against him — that he had gained the victory; but ah! Satan hath found it out now, that Christ has triumphed over him in his cross. Ah! then, brethren, Calvary is a wonder in hell. Tell me then, brethren, who is it in all the universe that thinks little of Christ's laying down his life. Shall we find them in heaven? No. Shall we find them in hell? No; 'they believe and tremble.' Where, then, shall we find the man that thinks little of Christ? O Christless sinner! it is you. 'We preach Christ, to the Jews a stumbling block, and to the Greeks foolishness.' 'For the preaching of the cross is, to them that perish, foolishness.' O Christless man! you little think of the death of Christ; even the devils do not think it foolishness. Sinner, do not you think there must be something wrong about the state of your mind, that sees no beauty in the death of Christ?

From these words I would notice:

1. The awful command here spoken of: 'This commandment have I received of my Father.'

2. The free obedience of Christ: 'I lay down my life.'

3. The father's love to Christ: 'Therefore doth my Father love me, because I lay down my life.'

I. *The awful command here spoken of,* verse 18, at the end, 'This commandment have I received of my Father.' This passage shows us plainly that the death of Christ was arranged beforehand by the Father and the Son. The Father laid it upon him that he should come into the world and lay down his life. Some may say, When did God lay this command upon him? I answer, it was before the world was. 'But we speak the wisdom of God in a mystery, even the hidden wisdom, which God ordained before the world unto our glory,' 1 Cor. 2.7. And then his purpose in grace, before the world began, was to send his Son; so that there can be no doubt that this command was given to Christ at the beginning, when there was no sea or land, when there was neither sun nor moon. It was before the world was that the Father said, Go into the world and lay down your life. 'This commandment have I received of my Father.' Brethren, this command was not given by sinners; there was no cry, Come over and help us. The world was steeped in sin. There was a cry for vengeance rising up from earth to heaven; but there was no cry for mercy. 'This commandment have I received of my Father.' The world did not desire that Christ should die. It was altogether become unprofitable, there was none that did good, no not one. All were lying under wrath. You will notice that this is the very command we find spoken of in Psalm 40, verse 7, 'Then said I, Lo, I come: in the volume of the book it is written of me. I delight to do thy will, O my God.' Compare this with Hebrews 10. 7, 10. You will notice that the 'will' here spoken of in the 40th Psalm, and the command spoken of in Hebrews is the very same that is spoken of in the 10th of John. My dear brethren, this lays open to you the great and amazing truth that the Father loves sinners. You know we often speak of the love of Christ; but here is a new object of love. It was the Father that sent the Son — it was the Father that provided the sacrifice.

Learn this solemn truth that the Father loves you, the Father wants you to be saved, the Father wants you to believe on the Son; the very Father who commanded Christ to lay down his life for sinners. You will notice from this that the Father is clear from the blood of all men. He does not want you to perish. 'Turn ye, turn ye, why will ye die?' He is not willing that any should perish. 'He willeth all men to be saved, and to come to the knowledge of the truth.' He does not want you to perish. He commands Christ to go into the world, and lay down his life for sinners. Oh! it is true: the Father does not want you to perish. 'God so loved the world, that he gave his only begotten Son.' 'God sent not his Son into the world to condemn the world; but that the world through him might be saved.' God the Father is as earnest in your salvation as Christ is. It was God's part to send the Son, and the Son's part to come and die. And as God the Son has done his part, so God the Father has done his. So that, sinners, if you perish, it is because you will not come to him, that you may have life.

II. *The free obedience of Christ.* 'I lay down my life. No man taketh it from me, but I lay it down of myself.' Brethren, there is nothing more certain than that no man can lay down his life for another. But you will observe, there were two things that made it right in Christ to lay down his life. 1. He is the Lord of all. 2. The Father gave him a commandment to lay it down. 'I have power to lay it down, and I have power to take it again. This commandment have I received of my Father.' And you will notice from this that in laying down his life, he was not forced to do it. This is brought out in the example of Isaac. You remember that God commanded Abraham to take Isaac his son, and to go into the land of Moriah, and offer him there for a burnt-offering; but you will notice that he was a young man, and his father an old man, so that, had he wanted, he could have resisted his being bound. Now, brethren, this was intended to be a type of Christ. It is true that men bound him, but it is also true that he laid down his life himself. Observe, first, that no man forced it from him. If you read the life of Christ, you will observe that he often escaped out of their hands. You remember, at Nazareth, they tried to cast him over the hill on which the city was built, but he passed through the midst of them and escaped. And so, brethren, he could have done this to the very end. He could have escaped that very night. When he saw them at a distance, coming down the hill with their torches, he could have fled; but he would not. 'The cup that my Father hath given me, shall I not drink it?' And you will notice that when they came to the garden he said, 'Whom seek ye?' and they said, 'Jesus'; he said, 'I am he,' and they fell backward. He could have escaped then, but he would not. 'He, through the eternal Spirit, offered himself without spot to God.' And even when he was nailed to the tree, when they said to him, 'Let him come down from the cross and we will believe him,' he could have come down, but Jesus wanted to die; this is the reason. And, brethren, this statement is true in regard to the Father, 'no man taketh it from me.' Not even the Father took it from him. The Father said, 'Go into the world, and lay down your life for sinners.' And we are told in Isaiah, 'He shall divide him a portion with the great, and he shall divide the spoil with the strong, because he hath poured out his soul unto death.' And it is said in Luke, 'Father, into thy hands I commit my spirit'; he did it freely to God. So he said, 'Lo I come freely to do thy will.' It is true, it pleased the Lord to bruise him, but he put himself into the hands of divine justice.

Dear brethren, from this let us learn two things:

1. *The justice of this act.* There are many persons say that, it is not just for an innocent person to die for the wicked, but this is an extraordinary case. The Father was willing to take Christ as the substitute, so that it is in perfect accordance with law and justice.

2. *The love of Christ to sinners.* Here is his love: 'I lay down my life, no man taketh it from me,' and yet he laid it down. Christ put himself into the hands of justice. He said, 'Lo I come to do thy will.' O brethren! this is the free love of Christ. That command was written upon his heart, 'Die for sinners.' 'I lay down my life.' Ah! sinner, 'scarcely for a righteous man will one die; yet peradventure for a good man some would even dare to die; but God commendeth his love toward us, in that, while we were yet sinners. Christ died for us.' Sinner, this is the love of Christ that he came for such as you and me.

III. *The Father's love to Christ:* 'Therefore doth my Father love me because I lay down my life.' I do not know any word in the Bible that is more sweet to meditate on than the love of the Father to the Son. There are many things that induce the Father to love the Son. He loved him for his Godhead. But here is another reason why the Father loves the Son — he loves him for his holy manhood. 'He was holy, harmless, undefiled, and separate from sinners.' God never saw anything so like himself. When God made Adam, he said, 'It is very good'; but oh! when he saw Jesus, he saw a loveliness in him such as he never saw in any created thing. But here is another reason why the Father loves him — 'Therefore doth my Father love me, because I lay down my life.' We are told that he grew in favour both with God and man. He was every day fulfilling a part of his holy obedience, until he came to the last, and then the Father saw obedience as he had never seen before. Oh, brethren! it was love that was never seen before, that he should die for the lowest — for the vilest. And that appears to be another reason why Jesus died: it is, that the Father got a vent for his love to flow out to sinners — 'Therefore doth my father love me, because I lay down my life.'

From all this, dear brethren, learn:

1. *Though a child of God carries the cross, he may be under the*

love of God. Never did God love Christ so much as when he was heaping wrath upon him — 'Therefore doth my Father love me, because I lay down my life.' And, oh, brethren! so it often is with a saint. Often God puts a cross upon a child of God, and then takes it off, and lets us sing — 'I will yet praise him who is the health of my countenance and my God.'

2. *Learn how sinners are to come into the love of God.* Dear friends, I have often pleaded with you to come into the love and peace of God; but you may say, I do not know how to come; then, listen — the Father loves you because Jesus has finished the work. Come! O believe on him, and you will be brought into the love of God! Amen.

SERMON VIII

THE MARKS AND BLESSINGS OF CHRIST'S SHEEP

John 10. 26-30

There is nothing more surprising to an attentive reader of the gospel than to notice the little success Christ had in the conversion of sinners. Although he speaks with love such as never man spake with, yet for all that, Christ had to complain, just as we have, 'Ye believe not.' O brethren! is it to be wondered at, then, that there are so few believers among us, when there were so few converted under Christ? We are always to expect this, then. Observe still further that the more that Christ opened out his mind to them, they seemed to hate him the more. They said, 'He hath a devil, and is mad; why hear ye him?' They were pulling one another away from hearing him. Brethren, it is the same now; the more that ministers have Christ in their sermons — the more faithfully they preach — the more you will say they are mad, and have a devil. Is the servant greater than his master, or the disciple than his Lord? Still farther, observe, when Christ pressed the truth hard upon them, they could not bear it; verse 31, They were not content with disbelieving what he said, but they stoned him; and he asked this question, 'Many good works have I shewed you from my Father; for which of these works do you stone me?' Brethren, the same is true still; the nearer we come to your conscience — the nearer we bring the Word home to you, if you are not converted by it, no doubt you hate us. If it is not the savour of life unto life, it will be the savour of death unto death. 'Am I become your enemy, because, I tell you the truth?' And yet, brethren, it is sweet to notice that Christ had his sheep for all that. 'My sheep hear my voice and they follow me.' Although it is a world of adversaries, yet there is a sheepfold.

Let us notice two things today:
1. The marks of Christ's sheep.
2. The blessings of Christ's sheep.
I. *The marks of Christ's sheep.* 1. 'My sheep hear my voice'; and, 2. 'They follow me.'
1.   *They know my voice.* You know, brethren, this is the characteristic of the sheep of the east, they know the shepherd's voice. There was once a traveller in the east who denied that they knew the voice of the shepherd, and contended that it was the voice they knew; and to prove it, they changed clothes. The person called the sheep, and they moved not; but when the shepherd called them, they instantly followed him. Now, this is just the way with Christ and his sheep. Christ may be disguised, but faith hears his voice. The first time they hear his voice is the time of conversion. You remember Zaccheus, he was up in the sycamore tree, and he might think, 'Christ's word will not reach me'; but Christ said to him, 'Come down, Zaccheus, for today I must abide at thy house.' The voice of the shepherd reached him. This was the first day that Zaccheus heard the shepherd's voice. You remember Lydia, she sat among the Grecian matrons by the river side, and heard Paul preach. Someone opened her heart, and said, 'Come away'; it was the voice of the shepherd. 'The Lord opened the heart of Lydia to attend unto the things that were spoken.' It was the outward voice of Paul, but it was the inward voice of Christ.

Again, all that are Christ's hear his voice in the time of duty. They hear a voice behind them saying, 'This is the way, walk ye in it, when ye turn to the left.' They hear the voice of Christ directing them how to go. 'The Lord is my shepherd, I shall not want. He maketh me to lie down in green pastures, he leadeth me beside the still waters.' When the world are in perplexity and know not what to do, the sheep of Christ hear his voice and follow him. And they hear his voice in the time of secret prayer. Mary sat at Jesus' feet and heard his word. And when they open the Bible in secret they hear the voice of the beloved saying, 'Come unto me, and I will give you rest'; — 'My grace is sufficient for you'; — 'Fear not, for I am with thee; be not dismayed, for I am thy God, I will strengthen thee, yea I will uphold thee with the right hand of my righteousness.'

There is another hour in which they hear his voice — it is that of affliction. They hear the voice of the shepherd — they hear the voice of the rod, and say, 'It is the Lord, let him do what seemeth him good.'

Again, in the hour of death, when the Christless hear nothing but coming wrath, the sheep hear his voice. They hear it when they pass through the valley. 'When thou passest through the waters, I will be with thee, and through the rivers they shall not overflow thee,' etc. 'Fear not, I will strengthen thee, yea, I will uphold thee with the right hand of my righteousness.' 'O'death, I will be thy plagues, O grave, I will be thy destruction; repentance shall be hid from mine eyes.'

Ah, brethren, do you hear the voice of Christ? Those of you who are Christless hear the voice of business or of pleasure. You hear the call of the strange woman, 'Stolen waters are sweet, and bread eaten in secret is pleasant'; but ye do not hear the voice of Christ, when he says, 'Come to me, and I will give you rest.' You shut your ears, you believe not, because you are not of his sheep. Those of you that are Christ's are as in a solitude, and there is one voice that you hear so shrill and loud; it is the voice of Christ — he says, 'Be of good cheer, I have overcome the world.' You that hear the voice of Christ, love him, and not another.

2. *'They follow me.'* You know this is the case in eastern countries; the sheep follow the shepherd. There are two ways the sheep follow the shepherd — when they are looking at his person, and when they hear his voice. So it is with those that are Christ's. The wounds in his side, in his hands, and in his feet, are attracting things in a believer's eye. Why do they follow him? They follow him that they may get pardon; they follow him that they may get living water. Just as the sheep follow the shepherd to the well, or down into the valley, or beneath some shady rock, so those that are Christ's follow him. They follow him every day; they follow him in all parts of the world. In whatever they do, they follow Christ. They follow him in bearing his cross; they follow him in reproach. 'Reproach hath broken my heart.' Christ could say, 'I am the song of the drunkard.' So the sheep can say the same. They follow him in his love. 'Christ loved us and gave himself for us.' So Christ's sheep have the same love in their hearts. If you are Christ's, you will have the same love he had. Christ died for his enemies; so you will be willing to do the same if you are Christ's. They follow him in prayerfulness. Christ was a man of prayer. He often went out and continued all night in prayer; he could say, 'I give myself to prayer.' So it is with all the sheep of Christ — they follow him. As he had communion with the Father, so have they. They follow him in holiness. Christ was separate from sinners, he was of a different nature from them. So will we, if we are his; we will not be of the world, even as he was not of the world. Whom do you follow? Do you follow the world? then ye are not of his sheep. Do you follow Christ? are you following him? then you are one of his sheep, and if you follow him now, you will follow him to all eternity.

II. *The blessings of Christ's sheep.*

1. 'I know them.' 2. 'I give them eternal life.' 3. 'They shall never perish.'

1. *'I know them.'* The shepherd in the east knows his sheep — he knows them by appearance: 'I know my sheep.' Christ knew his sheep from all eternity. We spoke of this last Sabbath. Just as he said, 'Before Abraham was, I am,' so does he know us. Ah, the eternal love of Christ passeth knowledge! To think that there never was a time that he did not know them. But 'I know them' in time. The world does not know them; the world thinks that they are wolves in sheep's clothing. They give no credit to your new birth; they say, wait a while, and we will see what it will come to. The church does not know them. You remember Paul, when he came to Jerusalem, the disciples did not believe that he was a disciple. And Ananias said, 'Lord, I have heard by many of this man, how much evil he hath done to thy saints at Jerusalem.' So it may be with you. Perhaps they will not let you into their society; but, 'I know you.' And then he knows your wants: 'I know them.'

2. *'I give unto them eternal life.'* You know that the shepherd leads the sheep to a living well or to some gushing stream that flows between two rocks. So is it with Christ. Observe, it is said, 'I give unto them eternal life.' If you are one of Christ's flock you will never want. 'I give unto them eternal life.' What does this imply. It implies *daily pardon.* You know when the Queen sends a pardon to any condemned criminal, she is said to give the man his life. If you are Christ's you need daily pardon. If there is any sin separating between you and a loving God, you need it pardoned. It implies *spiritual life.* The life that Christ gives flows through the heart. If the Holy Spirit were to leave the heart, you would lose spiritual life. Thus David says, 'Take not thy Holy Spirit away from me. Restore unto me the joy of thy salvation, and uphold me with thy free Spirit.' Brethren, are you daily drinking of this living water? Does it spring up within you? Ah! remember it is Christ's gift; 'I give unto them eternal life.'

3. *'They shall never perish.'* You know, brethren, that the shepherd often loses his sheep. Thus Jacob did, he sometimes lost the sheep. And you remember David sometimes lost the sheep. A lion and a bear came once and carried away one of the sheep. But there is one shepherd that never loses any. 'These are they which thou has given me, and I have kept them, and none of them is lost,' 'They shall never perish, neither shall any pluck them out of my hand.' Those that are Christ's sheep have got many adversaries; there is the devil, like a roaring lion, going about seeking whom he may devour; there is the world, gaping like strong bulls of Bashan; and then there is the old heart striving to get back to its pleasures; but you shall never perish. It is true that you have got many tossings.

Oftentimes God's people cry to the Rock, but it hears not. Often they cry, 'My way is hid from the Lord, and my judgment is passed over from my God.' But that word will stand, 'I know them — they shall never perish.' Never did one sheep of Christ's perish yet. Ah, it is true that there are many falls — that there are many backslidings; but they shall never perish. There have many perished out of this place — many that seemed to be his; but Christ's sheep shall never perish. Why can they not perish? There are three reasons: 1. They are in 'my hand.' 2. They are in 'my Father's hand.' 3. 'I and my Father are one.'

1.   They are in *my hand.'* You know what is in his hand is safe. Whose hand is stronger than his? 'He is able to save them to the uttermost that come unto God by him.' 'They shall never perish, neither shall any pluck them out of my hand.'

2.   They are in *'my Father's hand.'* 'My Father gave them to me'; he said, 'I commit these sheep into thy hand.' Christ accepted them, and the Father draws them to him. So that there are two hands upholding the sheep, one below the other, so that if you were to fall out of one hand, you would just fall into the other.

3.   *'I and my Father are one'* — one in essence, one in power, one in purpose, one in love. If one hand was pulling the one way, and the other the other, then we do not know what might be the case; but they are both pulling the same way. Are you Christ's? then you will never perish. But I believe there are some here that will perish. You know I have sometimes said, if there was but one sitting in the middle of the church that should perish, then you might all gather around him, and weep over his awful state; but I believe that there are many sitting in all parts of the church that will yet perish. But if you are in Christ's hand; you are in his Father's hand, and he and his Father are one.   Amen.

Sabbath Forenoon,
25th September 1842.

SERMON IX

THE SALVATION OF GOD

Isaiah 55. 6 - 9

This is one of the sweetest portions of the Word of God, and yet it strikes me that it is seldom understood. I observe that it is very frequently one of the devil's plans to prevent a proper understanding of these passages of the Word of God that are the sweetest and plainest, and thus to turn the honey into gall. Now, this passage is often understood in this way, Let the wicked forsake his way, and the unrighteous man his thoughts, and then God will have mercy on him. But you will notice, first of all, that this puts sanctification before justification; now we are justified and then sanctified. Those that are justified are then brought into the image of God's Son, and then those who are sanctified are glorified — this is the Scripture plan. Now, if we were to change our lives, and God on that account to have mercy, and abundantly pardon us, then there is no need of Christ. If righteousness come by the law, then Christ is dead in vain.

I desire, by the help of the Holy Spirit, to show you the right meaning of this passage. I will have only time to open it up without dwelling upon it; but you can do so yourselves.

Let us notice:

1. What is to be forsaken.
2. What you are to return to.
3. What you will get by returning.
4. The time when you are to return.

I. Let us see *what is to be forsaken,* verse 7: 'Let the wicked forsake his way, and the unrighteous man his thoughts.' Compare this with the eighth verse: 'For my thoughts are not your thoughts, neither are your ways my ways, saith the Lord.' Observe then, dear brethren, what it is that all unregenerate men are called upon to forsake. You are called upon to forsake your way — your way of pardon — your way of peace with God, and the reason given is that God's way is not as your way, neither his thoughts as yours. Now, observe first that every carnal man has got some plan by which he thinks to get to heaven. This is what God thinks of here. The wickedest man here has got some kind of a way of pardon of his own. You will not find a man on the earth but hopes that at death, or at the judgment day, he will get free. Ah, brethren, if it were not for this, you could not rest as you do. If you had no thoughts of pardon, you could not laugh as you do. And, therefore, you may lay it down as an axiom that every natural man has a way by which he hopes to be saved. 'Let the wicked forsake his way, and the unrighteous man his thoughts; and let him return unto the Lord, and he will have mercy upon him; and to our God, for he will abundantly pardon.'

The plans of all worldly men may be resolved into this one — self-righteousness. There is one man who says he hopes to be saved, for God is merciful. God will not destroy the souls that he has made. Another man thinks God will save him for his sincere endeavours. He is a kind God, and he will save me for my best endeavours. I dare say, the hearts of many agree to that. This is the answer I get in most houses I go to, when I ask, Are you willing to be saved? You say, I am trying to do the best I can. Another man not so ignorant of the Bible, hopes to be saved by faith as a work. He reads, 'Abraham was justified by faith.' Now, he says, If I could get this faith I would be saved. You think that God would save you if you had faith. No such thing, God will not save you for your faith. I believe this is one of the commonest ways by which many deceive themselves.

These are some of the ways that men look to for salvation. You will see that their aim is self-righteousness. This is the way you are commanded to forsake this day. O brethren, what is your way? Sinner, you are commanded to forsake your way.

Observe, farther, that *this way is different from God's way* — 'For my ways are not as your ways, neither my thoughts as your thoughts.' God's way of justifying a sinner is by the death and obedience of his Son. It is not by washing away your sins yourself, but it is by casting yourself under the doing and dying of his Son. I say, then, it is not your way; I say farther, it is higher than your way. You are groping in the dark, but God's way is in the light. And then it is a more glorious way; just as there is a greater glory spread over the bespangled heaven than there is over this poor earth, so is there over God's way. God's is high up — a perfect, righteous way. Your sins may be covered by this way as completely as the waters of the flood covered the earth.

Now, brethren, your way must be forsaken. This is a hard saying. Self-righteousness is engraved in your nature. Every natural man here is determined to be saved by his own righteousness. 'Let the wicked forsake his way, and the unrighteous man his thoughts: and let him return unto the Lord, and he will have mercy upon him; and to our God, for he will abundantly pardon.' I often observe that when you drive a man out of one way, he goes to another; when you drive him out of his past life, he flies to his future life. But, brethren, if you would be saved, you must forsake your own way. You must forsake the tops of the houses. You must not be like the spider who, as soon as it is driven from the web it was weaving, begins to weave another. You must put self away as a corrupt thing. An unconverted man is like one in a burning ship; he will cling to the ship till it is burned to the water's edge, and sinks. Now, if a lifeboat comes, he must let go his hold of the burning ship, and drop into it, if he would be saved. Now, observe, the first thing is, to let go, and then drop into the lifeboat. Now, you must let go your own way, if you would be saved.

II. I come now to the second thing — *What must you return to?* 'Return unto the Lord, and he will have mercy upon you; and to our God, for he will abundantly pardon.' The 'Lord' here spoken of is the Lord Jesus Christ, the same that is spoken of in the fourth verse; 'I have given him (that is, Christ), for a witness to the people, a leader and commander to the people.' This is the Lord you must seek; this is the Lord you must return to. You will observe he is called 'our God'; this expression is the same as Emmanuel — God with us — God in our nature. This is the being you are to seek. You will observe, dear friends, first of all, it is not enough to forsake your own thoughts — your own way. Just as in the case of the burning ship, it was not enough for the man to let go his hold, but he must drop into the boat, so you must not only leave your own way, but you must return to God. And notice, farther, it is not getting some new view, some new opinion — it is not such things; conversion is something real. Ah, that is no true conversion that does not come from God! There are many that get new views; but if you would be saved, you must come to God.

Oh! I would here plead with those of you who seem to have forsaken your own mercies. Once you thought you could stand in the judgment; now you have found out the reverse; you say, 'Enter not into judgment with me, for in thy sight shall no flesh living be justified,' You have forsaken you own way; well now, sinner, return unto the Lord, return unto God manifest in flesh. 'Let us join ourselves to the Lord in a perpetual covenant that shall not be forgotten.' Why will you stay back? Are you thinking God will not receive you, but does he not promise that if you come he will in no wise cast out; but ah! you say, perhaps, I must wait till I am somewhat better, and then I will come. Ah! then, you have not forsaken your own way. I thought you had forsaken your own way. He is the Lord our righteousness. Oh! then, return unto him.

III. I come now, thirdly, to show you *what you will get.* 'He will abundantly pardon,' or, as the meaning is, he will multiply pardon. Verse 3: 'Incline your ear, and come unto me; hear, and your soul shall live.' etc. So he here says, 'Return unto the Lord, and he will have mercy upon you, and to our God, for he will abundantly pardon.' There is a stress to be laid on the word 'will,' he *will* abundantly pardon. My dear friends, the mercy that is laid up in Christ is sure mercy, none yet have been disappointed that came. The greatest sinner that comes finds his mercy the sweeter. Mary Magdalene came, the woman that was a sinner came, Manasseh came, a persecuting

Saul came, and they all found mercy — they all forsook their own way. He has mercy, and it is sure mercy. All that ever came found mercy. And then, 'He will abundantly pardon,' or he will multiply pardon. The meaning is twofold — it is either, he will pardon great sinners or he will pardon pardoned ones. Those of you who are unregenerate men, he will pardon you. Then the other meaning is, he will pardon upon pardon. When you go away and sin and come back again, he will pardon you, if only you will give over your own way and follow God's way of righteousness. If only you will give over that way and return to Christ, then God swears by himself that he will receive you, and will multiply pardon unto you.

I would here plead with those of you who have sinned against much light, and for that reason keep away from Christ. Dear fellow-backslider, why do you stay away? You say, he has pardoned me before, will he pardon again? Ah, he will multiply pardon. Sin is a darkening thing; when we have sinned and been pardoned we often go back to our sin and dread to return; but ah! if we would be pardoned we must return to him.

IV.   Now, there is just a fourth thing remaining, and that is *the time*. Verse 6: 'Seek ye the Lord while he may be found, call upon him while he is near.' My dear brethren, you will observe that this controversy is not between you and me, but between God and you. You will not always hear about this way, it is only for a time. Ordinarily, I believe that the whole period of life is given to man to seek Christ. I believe your lifetime is the boundary God has set for you to find Christ. O seek him, sinner, while he may be found! Some of you may say, If my lifetime is the period, then I will wait till death. But observe it is said, 'while he is near.' There are times when Christ is nearer than others. A faithful ministry is a time when Christ is near. When the Spirit is poured out, that also is a time when he is near. You know when a man is breathing on you, you say, he is near. So when the Spirit is breathing on you, then he is near. O seek him now while he may be found, call upon him while he is near! My dear brethren, if you will not call upon Christ when he is near, the time will come when you will call but he will not hear. I think I have seen some calling, and he did not hear. If you will not call on him while he is near, perhaps, brethren, there may come a time when you may knock at Christ's door, and he will not hear. If you have as many silent Sabbaths as you have had preaching ones, will it not be righteously done?' 'Seek ye the Lord while he may be found, call upon him while he is near: let the wicked forsake his way, and the unrighteous man his thoughts: and let him return unto the Lord, and he will have mercy upon him, and to our God, for he will abundantly pardon.'   Amen.

SERMON X

THE IMPROVEMENT OF AFFLICTION

Job 34. 31, 32. Surely it is meet to be said unto God, I have borne chastisement. I will not offend any more: that which I see not, teach thou me; if I have done iniquity, I will do no more.

This world is a world of trouble: 'Man that is born of woman, is of few days, and full of trouble.' 'We dwell in cottages of clay, our foundation is in the dust, we are crushed before the moth,' Job 4.19. This world has sometimes been called 'a vale of tears.' Trials come into all your dwellings; the children of God are not excepted; there is a need be that you be in many temptations. 'Count it not strange when you fall into divers temptations, as though some strange thing happened unto you.' If this be so, of how great importance is it, that you and I be prepared to meet it. The darkest thunder cloud only covers the heavens for a time. 'Surely it is meet to be said unto God, I have borne chastisement. I will not offend any more: that which I see not, teach thou me; if I have done iniquity, I will do no more.'

From these words, I would desire to show you the right improvement we should make of affliction and the meetness of inquiring into God's reasons of affliction.

I. *The threefold improvement of affliction.*

1. Verse 31, 'Surely it is meet to be said unto God, I have borne chastisement. I will not offend any more.' The first improvement of affliction is *submission*. It is the temper of one who justifies God: 'I have borne chastisement.' This was the feeling of Daniel in the midst of the affliction which God brought on Israel. This is shown in Daniel 9. 7, 8, 'O Lord, righteousness belongeth unto thee, but unto us confusion of faces,' etc.; verse 14, 'Therefore hath the Lord watched upon the evil, and brought it upon us: for the Lord our God is righteous in all his works which he doeth; for we obeyed not his voice.'

You will notice, in the 9th chapter of Nehemiah, and the 33rd verse: 'Howbeit thou art just in all that is brought upon us; for thou hast done right but we have done wickedly.' The same thing you will notice in the 26th of Leviticus, 40th verse: 'If they shall confess their iniquity, and the iniquity of their fathers, with their trespass which they have trespassed against me, and that also they have walked contrary unto me.' And then the middle of the 41st verse: 'If then their uncircumcised hearts be humbled, and they then accept of the punishment of their iniquity,' etc.; to the end of the chapter. God here says, if they accept of the punishment of their iniquities, he will remember them. Now, this is the first improvement you should make of the affliction. How different is this from many of you; you do not accept of the punishment of your iniquities; your heart rises against God. 1. In your thoughts. 2. In hard words. The man begins to blaspheme God; he says God is a tyrant — Could God not have spared my child? This is what is spoken of at the pouring out of the fifth and sixth vials. These are their words in hell; when God pours out his wrath, they will blaspheme him. There is still a third way, and that is in your actions. Your words are not only against God, but your actions are against him. If I could lay bare your hearts, you would see such complaining, such anger against God, that you would see the truth of what I am saying. Remember, it is right to learn contentment. What right have you to complain? What right have you to challenge God's dealings with you? If little children were to take upon them to decide upon the proceedings of both houses of Parliament, what would you think of it? And what right have you to challenge God's government? We should say, with Job, 'The Lord gave, and the Lord hath taken away; blessed be the name of the Lord.'

2.   The second improvement of affliction is *humble inquiry into God's meaning:* 'What I know not teach thou me.' This is the proper improvement of affliction. This is the way in which Job himself received his trial. Job 10.2: 'I will say unto God, Do not condemn me: show me wherefore thou contendest with me.' The same you will notice in the 23rd chapter, 3rd verse: 'O that I knew where I might find him! that I might come even to his seat! I would order my cause before him, and fill my mouth with arguments. I would know the words which he would answer me, and understand what he would say unto me. Will he plead against me with his great power? No; but he will put strength in me. There the righteous might dispute with him; so should I be delivered for ever from my judge.' You will notice that Job was to be made acquainted why God dealt thus with him. The same was the case with Joshua, 7th chapter, 6th verse: 'And Joshua rent his clothes, and fell to the earth upon his face before the ark of the Lord until the even-tide, he and the elders of Israel, and put dust upon their heads. And Joshua said, Alas, O Lord God, wherefore hast thou at all brought this people over Jordan, to deliver us into the hands of the Amorites, to destroy us? would to God we had been content and dwelt on the other side Jordan! O Lord, what shall I say when Israel turneth their backs before their enemies? For the Canaanites, and all the inhabitants of the land, shall hear of it, and shall environ us round, and cut off our name from the earth: and what wilt thou do unto thy great name?' When affliction came, Joshua waited for an explanation. This also seems to have been the case with the apostle Paul when he

said, 'Lord, what wilt thou have me to do?' Brethren, the opposite of this is very common among you. When God sends affliction into an ungodly family; when God takes away a child, or lays a father on a bed of affliction; do they inquire at God why he did it? Ah, you despise the chastening of the Lord. Brethren, it is a fearful thing not to ask God's meaning in affliction. It is his loudest knock, and often his last. The same thing happens with God's children. You have been loving some idol — some secret sin — some secret lust, and God afflicts you. Do you ask an explanation? The same thing takes place in a church. The members are unholy, etc. Then, perhaps, he afflicts it as he did Laodicea. Do we seek an explanation? Ah, no! This is what this town should do in its poverty.

3. There is a third improvement of affliction, that is, *the forsaking of sin*, 'I will not offend any more.' 'If I have done iniquity, I will do no more.' God's great design in affliction is to make you forsake your sin: 'He that covereth his sins shall not prosper; but whoso confesseth and forsaketh them shall have mercy,' Prov. 28.13. This was God's way with Manasseh: so it should be in all affliction. God afflicts you that you may cast away your sin; you will not hear his voice of mercy; you will not hear his voice of love; but he brings you under the rod, in order to bring you into the covenant. How often does it to the contrary? I have seen a drunkard afflicted, and he went deeper into sin — farther away from God. 'Ephraim is a cake not turned.' There are some among you that remind me of an aged tree that has been struck with lightning, and now stands stript of its leaves, a monument in the earth. So are many of your families. I tell you, brethren, if mercies and judgments do not convert you, God has no other arrows in his quiver.

II. *The meetness of inquiring into God's reasons of affliction.*

1. It is meet, because *it is God that is dealing with you*. This affliction in your family, this affliction with yourself, is from God. 'Who hath hardened himself against him, and hath prospered?'

2. It is meet, because *this is God's meaning in your affliction*. God's meaning is, to save the unconverted, and to sanctify his own. I believe that every time the sun shines into your dwelling, it is meant to make you turn unto God; and it is the same with affliction. It is meant to make you turn to him; or if you be a child of God, every affliction is meant to make you cast your idols to the moles and to the bats, and to turn to God.

3. It is meet, because God *can destroy*. You know, brethren, that the same hand that afflicts can destroy. The same hand that kindled the burning fever in your breast, can kindle up the flames of hell for you. Amen.

SERMON XI

ADOPTION

1 John 3.1. Behold, what manner of love the Father hath bestowed upon us, that we should be called the sons of God.

I desire, my friends, to open up to you shortly the subject of adoption. By nature you are the children of Satan; I would here show you how you may be made sons of God: 'Behold what manner of love the Father hath bestowed upon us, that we should be called the sons of God.'

I. *What is the fountain of adoption?* In answer to that, I say, it flows from the love of the Father: 'Having predestinated us unto the adoption of children by Jesus Christ to himself, according to the good pleasure of his will,' Eph. 1.5. Observe that the only reason why God adopts any one is the good pleasure of his will: 'So then it is not of him that willeth, nor of him that runneth, but of God that showeth mercy.' I suppose that this congregation may be divided into two parts: the one are the children of Satan; the other, the children of God. Who can tell why it is so? Who can tell why you were chosen and not another? It was the good pleasure of his will: 'Behold what manner of love the Father hath bestowed upon us, that we should be called the sons of God.' Ah, my friends, this is a humbling doctrine. There is no difference between us and the children of wrath; some of us were more wicked than they, yet God set his love on us. We were like the prodigal, yet he put on us the best robe. This should humble us in the dust. If there are any here that think they have been chosen because they were better than others; ah! if you think that, you are grossly mistaken.

II. I would show you a second point, and that is, *the power by which God brings the children of the wicked one, and makes us children of God.* Can we do it ourselves? No; the answer you will find in Matt. 3.9: 'And think not to say within yourselves, We have Abraham to our father; for I say unto you, that God is able of these stones to raise up children to Abraham.' See also the 4th chapter of Romans, 17th verse: 'God, who quickeneth the dead, and calleth those things which be not as though they were.' See also Rom. 11.23: 'And they also, if they abide not still in unbelief, shall be graffed in; for God is able to graff them in again.' So you see, dear brethren, that the only power that can bring a child of Satan and make him a child of God, is God himself. God is able to graff them in again. Ah! dear friends, the power is not in creatures. It is not in the power of man — it is not in the power given to ministers; they cannot make you children of God. O my unconverted friends, observe what the power is that can take you out of the family of nature, and put you among the children: 'How shall I put you among the children, and give thee a pleasant land, a godly heritage of the host of nations? and I said, Thou shalt call me, My father; and shalt not turn away from me.' Jer. 3.19. It is God that must put you among the children. You that have been brought up in an ungodly family, God alone can bring you into his family. It is God alone that can do it. There is no power in earth, in heaven, or in hell, that can do it. Adoption is God's bestowment. Look then to him for it.

> *Upon the Lord my waiting eyes*
> *Continually are set,*
> *And he it is that shall bring forth*
> *My feet out of the net.*

Set your eyes on God, then wait upon him.

III.   Let me inquire into *the steps by which God brings a child of the devil, to make him a child of God:* 'Behold what manner of love the Father hath bestowed upon us, that we should be called the sons of God.' There are two steps, regeneration and faith — if indeed, they can be separated, because the first breath of the new soul is faith; but in speaking of them we may consider one, and then the other. You will see it very beautifully brought out in the first chapter of the Gospel of John, 12th and 13th verses: 'But as many as received him, to them gave he power to become the sons of God, even to them that believe on his name; which were born, not of blood, nor of the will of the flesh, nor of the will of man, but of God.' Now, here you require just to take this passage backward, in order to understand it. The first thing is, 'They were born, not of blood, nor of the will of the flesh, nor of the will of man, but of God.' The first thing towards faith, is regeneration. The next step is, he 'believes on his name,' and then he is adopted into his family: 'As many as received him, to them gave he power,' or, as in the margin, the right, or privilege, 'to become the sons of God.' Here you see the exact process. First of all, he is born of God; the soul that was dead in trespasses and sins is born, 'not of blood, nor of the will of flesh, nor of the will of man, but of God.' God drops the life of grace into his soul. And then comes the next step — he receives faith; that is, he believes on his name. And then comes the next step — 'As many as received him, to them gave he power to become the sons of God': that is, he gives them the privilege to become the sons of God. O my brethren! this is the way in which he is made a child of God. Tell me, are you a child of God?

Again, are there any of you that think you are sons of God, though ye have not believed on his name? It is a lie; for it is only those that receive him that get power to believe on his name. Ah! my brethren, will you not be driven from this time to cry, 'My Father, thou art the guide of my youth'; will you not cry to him?

IV.   *The blessedness of being a son of God:* 'Behold what manner of love the Father hath bestowed upon us, that we should be called the sons of God!' Ah! there are many things to make it a blessedness beyond compare.

1.   The *first* thing that makes it a blessedness is that *we get the love of the Father.* The moment you become a child, the Father loves you. This is shown in what Christ said to Mary: 'I ascend unto my Father and to your Father, to my God and your God.' Christ here intimated, that we have the same love that he had. We have not got so much of the love of the Father as Christ, because he has got an infinite capacity; but it is the same love. The sun shines as much upon the daisy as it does upon the sunflower, though the sunflower is able to contain more. Christ plainly shows you that in the 17th chapter of John, where he prays that the same love may be in us that was in him. O how much better is it, then, to be under the love of God, than under the wrath of God!

2.   Let me mention to you a *second* part of the blessedness we get. *The Spirit of the Son dwells in us.* You will see this in Galatians 4.6, 'Because ye are sons, God hath sent forth the Spirit of his Son into your hearts, crying, Abba, Father.' Brethren, when Christ comes, the first thing he does is to redeem you from under the curse of the law, and then he makes you a son. O it is sweet to have the smile of Christ! it is sweet to get the love of Christ; but I will tell you what is equally as sweet — that is to receive the Spirit of Christ. Has he given you the Spirit? He will do it if you are a son, that you may be made to cry, 'Abba, Father.'

3.   Let me mention to you another part of the blessedness of being a son of God. *You get the likeness of the Father.* You know this is the case in an adopted family; an adopted child in the course of time gets the very features of the family. So you get the image of the Father, and you get the love of the Father. You are taught that in Matthew 5, where Christ says, in his Sermon on the Mount, 'Love your enemies, bless them that curse you, do good to them that hate you, and pray for them which despitefully use you, and persecute you; that ye may be the children of your Father which is in heaven,' that ye may bear the image of the Father. Have you that mark of adoption? Are you turning like God?

4.   Let us mention another part of the blessedness. Some of you may be surprised at it. *We get the chastisement of the Father.* If we have no chastisement, then we are bastards, and not sons, for what son is he whom the Father chasteneth not. The world are allowed to

get fat; but it is not so with those that follow God; if they wander, he puts up a hedge, and if they fall into it, he puts up a wall.

5. Let me mention the last part of the blessedness. *We receive the inheritance as heirs.* Paul says, 'If sons, then heirs.' Every child in a rich family gets something when the father dies; often he shares his fortune equally among them, and the adopted child is not forgot. If we are Christ's we get all things with him. If we are Christ's, we share the government of the world with him. If we are his, we shall share the crown with him. It is called the inheritance of the saints in light. I cannot tell the blessings of being an heir of God; but I know that it is better than being an heir of hell: 'He that overcometh shall inherit all things,' and that for eternity — it cannot fade away. O my brethren! will you still remain heirs of hell? If you come to Christ you will be made heirs of God. Whether is it better to get the pleasure of the world, and hell at the end, or to be made a child of God, and an heir of Christ? 'They shall hunger no more, neither thirst any more; neither shall the sun light on them, nor any heat. For the Lamb which is in the midst of the throne shall feed them, and shall lead them unto living fountains of water: and God shall wipe away all tears from their eyes,' Rev. 7. 16, 17. O that God would make you like Mary, to choose that good part that shall never be taken away from you! O that God would put life into the dead stones, and from these stones raise up children to Abraham!   Amen.

Thursday Evening,
9th September 1842.

SERMON XII

ELECTING LOVE

John 15.16. *Ye have not chosen me, but I have chosen you, and ordained you, that ye should go and bring forth fruit, and that your fruit should remain.*

This is a very humbling, and at the same time, a very blessed word to the true disciple. It was very humbling to the disciples to be told that they had not chosen Christ. Your wants were so many, your hearts were so hard, that ye have not chosen me. And yet it was exceedingly comforting to the disciples to be told that he had chosen them: 'Ye have not chosen me, but I have chosen you.' This showed them that his love was first with them — that he had a love for them when they were dead. And then he showed them that it was love that would make them holy: 'Ye have not chosen me, but I have chosen you, and ordained you, that ye should go and bring forth fruit, and that your fruit should remain.'

Let us take up the truths in this verse as they occur:

I. *Men naturally do not choose Christ,* 'Ye have not chosen me.' This was true of the apostles; this is true of all that will ever believe to the end of the world. 'Ye have not chosen me.' The natural ear is so deaf that it cannot hear; the natural eye is so blind that it cannot see Christ. It is true in one sense that every disciple chooses Christ; but it is when God opens the eye to see him — it is when God gives strength to the withered arm to embrace him. But Christ's meaning is, You would never have chosen me, if I had not chosen you. It is quite true that when God opens a sinner's heart, he chooses Christ and none but Christ. It is quite true that a heart that is quickened by the Spirit, ever chooses Christ and none but Christ, and will forego all the world for Christ. But, brethren, the truth here taught us is this that every awakened sinner is willing to embrace Christ, but not till made willing. Those of you who have been awakened, you did not choose Christ. If a physician were to come into your house, and say he had come to cure you of your disease, if you felt that you were not diseased, you would say, I have no need of you, go to my neighbour. This is the way you do with Christ; he offers to cure you, but you say you are not diseased; he offers to cover your naked soul with his obedience, you say I have no need of that covering.

Another reason why you do not choose Christ is, *you see no beauty in him.* He is a root out of a dry ground, in which there is no beauty nor comeliness. You see no beauty in his person, no beauty in his obedience, no glory in his cross. You see him not, and, therefore, you do not choose him.

Another reason why you do not choose Christ is, *you do not want to be made holy by him:* 'He shall be called Jesus, for he shall save his people from their sins.' But you love your sin, you love your pleasure, therefore when the Son of God comes and says, he will save you from your sin, you say, I love my sin, I love my pleasure. So you can never come to terms with Christ: 'ye have not chosen me'; although I died, yet you have not chosen me. I have spoken to you many years, and yet you have not chosen me. I have sent you my Bible to instruct you, and yet you have not chosen me. Brethren, this accusation will meet you in the judgment — I would have covered you with my obedience, but ye would not have me.

II. *Christ chooses his own disciples:* 'I have chosen you.' Christ looked upon them with a look of divine benignity, and said, 'I have chosen you.' Every one whom he brings to glory, he chooses.

1. *The time when he chooses them.* I observe that it was *before they believed:* 'Ye have not chosen me, but I have chosen you,' as much as to say, I began with you, you did not begin with me. You will notice this in Acts 18.9, 10, 'Then spake the Lord to Paul in the night by a vision, Be not afraid, but speak, and hold not thy peace: for I am with thee, and no man shall set on thee to hurt thee; for I have much people in this city.' Paul was at this time at Corinth, the most lascivious and wicked city in the ancient world; they were given over to banqueting and grievous idolatry, and yet Christ said to Paul, 'I have much people in this city.' They had not chosen Christ, but he had chosen them; they had not repented, yet Christ fixed his eye on them. This plainly shows you that Christ chooses his own before they seek him.

2. But further, Christ chooses his own *from the beginning;* 2 Thess. 2.13: 'But we are bound to give thanks alway to God for you, brethren, beloved of the Lord, because God hath from the beginning chosen you to salvation through sanctification of the Spirit, and belief of the truth,' Eph. 1.4, 'According as he had chosen us in him before the foundation of the world, that we should be holy and without blame before him in love.' So, brethren, it was before the foundation of the world that Christ chose his own; when there was neither sun nor moon; when there was neither sea nor land — it was from the beginning. Ah, he might well say, you have not chosen me. It was before man loved man, or angel loved angel, that Christ chose his own. Now, I know the meaning of Paul when he says, That you may be able to know the length and breadth, the height and the depth of the love of Christ, which passeth knowledge. Now, I am not surprised at the death of Christ! It was a love so great that it broke over the banks that held it in; a love that broke over a Calvary and a Gethsemane. O brethren! do you know this love?

But I come now to *the reason of his love* — 'Ye have not chosen me, but I have chosen you.' Now, it is a very natural question, Why did he choose me? I answer, that the reason why he choose you was, the good pleasure of his will. You will see this illustrated in Mark 3.13: 'And he goeth up into a mountain, and calleth unto him whom he would: and they came unto him.' There was a great crowd round about him; he called some, he did not call all. The reason here given why he did it is, 'He called whom he would.' There is no reason in the creature; the reason is in him who chooses. You will see this in Malachi 1.2: 'I have loved you, saith the Lord; yet ye say, Wherein hast thou loved us? Was not Esau Jacob's brother? saith the Lord: yet I loved Jacob, and I hated Esau.' Were they not of the same mother? yet I loved Jacob, and I hated Esau. The only reason given, you see, is, 'I will have mercy on whom I will have mercy.' You will see this also in Rom. 9.15, 16. The only reason given in the Bible why Christ loved us — and if you study till you die you will not find another — is, 'I will have mercy on whom I will have mercy.' This is evident from all those that Christ chooses. We read of two great apostacies — one on earth, the other in heaven. First of all, one in heaven; Lucifer, the son of the morning, through pride, sinned, and God cast him, and those that sinned with him, into hell. The second was on earth; Adam sinned, and was driven out of paradise. They were both deserving of punishment. God had a purpose of love; which is it for? Perhaps angels pleaded for their fellow-angels; yet Christ passed them by, and died for man. Why did he die for man? The answer is, 'I will have mercy on whom I will have mercy.' The same thing is evident in the individuals Christ chooses. You would think Christ would choose the rich, and yet what says James? 'Hath not God chosen the poor of this world, rich in faith, and heirs of the kingdom, which he hath promised to them that love him?'

Again, you would think Christ would choose the noble; they have not the prejudices that the poor have; but what says the Scripture, 'Not many rich, not many noble are called.'

Again, you would think he would choose those that are learned. The Bible is written in difficult language; its doctrines are hard to be understood; yet what says Christ? 'I thank thee, O Father, that thou hast hid these things from the wise and prudent, and hast revealed them unto babes.'

Again, you would think he would have chosen the virtuous. Though there are none righteous, yet there are some more virtuous than others; yet what says Christ? The publicans and the harlots enter the kingdom of heaven while the Pharisee is shut out. 'O the depth both of the riches and knowledge of God! how unsearchable are his judgments, and his ways past finding out!' Why did he take the most vile? Here is the only reason I have been able to find ever since I read my Bible — 'I will have mercy on whom I will have mercy, and I will have compassion on whom I will have compassion.'

Christ chooses some that seek him, and not others. There was a young ruler came to Christ, and said, 'Good Master, what good thing shall I do that I may inherit eternal life?' He was in earnest, yet something came in the way, and he went back. A woman that was a sinner came behind Christ weeping, she also was in earnest, Christ said unto her, 'Thy sins which are many are forgiven thee.' What made the difference? — 'I will have mercy on whom I will have mercy.' 'He called unto him whom he would.' O my brethren, be humbled under the sovereignty of God! If he will have compassion, then he will have compassion.

III.   But I hasten to the third and last point: *'I have ordained you that ye should go and bring forth fruit, and that your fruit should remain.'* Christ not only chooses who are to be saved, but he chooses the way; and he not only chooses the beginning and the end, he chooses the middle also. 'God hath from the beginning chosen you to salvation, through sanctification of the Spirit and belief of the truth.' 'According as he hath chosen us in him before the foundation of the world, that we should be holy and without blame before him in love,' Eph. 1.4. And in the eighth chapter of Romans it is said, 'Whom he did predestinate, them he also called; and whom he called them he also justified: and whom he justified, them he glorified.' Salvation is like a golden chain let down from heaven to earth; two links are in the hand of God — election and final salvation; but some of the links are on earth — conversion, adoption, etc. Brethren, Christ never chooses a man to believe, and then leap into glory. Ah, my brethren, how this takes away the feet from all objections raised against this holy doctrine of election. Some here perhaps say, If I am elected, I will be saved, live as I like. No; if you live an unholy life, you will not be saved. Some may say, If I am not elected, I will not be saved, do as I like. Whether you are elected or not, I know not, but this I know — if you believe on Christ you will be saved.

Let me ask you, Have you believed on Christ? Let me ask you another question, Do you bear his whole image? Then you are elected, and will be saved. But if there are any here who have not believed on Christ, and who do not live a holy life, then, whatever you think now, you will find it true that you were among those who were passed by.

Ah! my brethren, those who deny election, deny that God can have mercy. O it is a sweet truth that God can have mercy! There is nothing in the hardness of your hearts that will keep God from having mercy on you. Go away home with this truth, that God can have mercy. 'Ye have not chosen me, but I have chosen you,' etc.   Amen.

SERMON XIII

THE TRANSFIGURATION OF CHRIST

Luke 9.28-36. *And it came to pass about an eight days after these sayings, he took Peter, and John, and James, and went up into a mountain to pray, etc.*

The transfiguration of Christ seems ordinarily to be but little understood. It is like Gethsemane, darkness hangs around it. Gethsemane showed the deepness of his sorrow; mount Tabor showed the height of his glory, which passeth knowledge.

Let us go over the different things mentioned in these words.

I.   Let us observe the *favourite three.* Verse 28, 'And it came to pass, about an eight days after these sayings, he took Peter, and John, and James, and went up into a mountain to pray.' It is interesting to notice that these three disciples were often peculiarly favoured of the Lord. Christ seems to have exercised peculiar sovereignty to the three. The first time that he distinguished them was when he raised the ruler's daughter. Mark 5.35: 'While he yet spake, there came from the ruler of the synagogue's house certain which said, Thy daughter is dead: why troublest thou the Master any farther?' etc. Verse 37: 'And he suffered no man to follow him, save Peter, and James, and John the brother of James.' You will notice that these three were the same three. He took them into the ruler's house and showed them his power to raise the dead. The second time that he distinguished them is in the passage before us. A little before he said (verse 27), 'But I tell you of a truth, there be some standing here, which shall not taste of death till they see the kingdom of God.' And eight days after he took them up to the mount, and gave them a glimpse of the coming glory. The next time was when in the garden of Gethsemane. When he wanted some to be witnesses of his agony, he took with him Peter, James, and John. O brethren! it was a great honour to be permitted to see his glory; but oh! it was more glorious to see his agony.

There have always been men in the Church greatly honoured by God. Some are not only of the twelve, but of the three. There was a Noah, and there was a Daniel. You remember, God says, 'O Daniel, a man greatly beloved.' And there was Abraham, who was called 'the friend of God.' There have been many in the Church who have been eminent believers. Ah! brethren, covet earnestly the best gifts. It is good to be among the twelve, but it is far better to be among the three. And this is quite different from worldly covetousness — it is quite different from mere worldly ambition. It is not like the wish of Zebedee for her children; she wanted them to have more worldly honour and glory than the rest. But oh! to covet Christ, to be like Christ — this is to be happy. Mr Edwards says, 'Suppose there never were to be but one in the world at a time, who is properly a complete Christian, in all respects of a right stamp, having Christianity shining in its true lustre, appearing amiable from whatever part, and under what character soever viewed. Resolved to act just as I would do, as if I strove with all my might to be that one.' Ah, brethren, resolve to be an eminent Christian. There are not many Christians now-a-days that see far into Gethsemane's gloom — they are not many who have glimpses of Tabor's glory. One star of the first magnitude gives more glory to God than a dozen lesser stars do. One eminent minister given more honour to Christ than a dozen other ministers do. One eminent Christian gives more honour to God than a dozen others. Covet earnestly, brethren, to reflect all Christ's image.

II. The next point to consider is *the prayer meeting on the hill.* Matthew says, 'He went up into a mountain apart.' Luke says, it was 'to pray.' Christ loved to pray alone. We are told by Mark that he arose a great while before day and went out to pray. We are told by Matthew that after feeding the five thousand, he went up into a mountain apart to pray; and we are told by Luke at another time, when he was beset by his enemies, he went into the wilderness to pray; and we are told at another time by Luke, when he was to ordain elders, he went out, and continued all night in prayer. This shows that Christ loved secret prayer. Ah, you are no Christian, if you do not love secret prayer. O brethren! a prayerless man is an unconverted man. Disguise it as you may; defend it as you can; explain it as you like; but a prayerless man is a Christless man. Christ loved the prayer meeting. We are told in the 18th chapter of Luke, 1st verse, of Christ praying with his disciples. Another example is where we have been reading — the 17th of John. O how wonderful to have heard Christ pray! It must have been wonderful to hear Abraham pray — if you take the 11th of Genesis as an example; it must have been wonderful to hear Paul pray — if you take his prayer for the Ephesians as an example — the man who could pray that he might be filled with all the fullness of God. It was wonderful to hear Luther pray; one friend says, 'It was awful to hear him pray, there was such a reverence, and yet such a holy familiarity in his approaches to God.' But that was nothing like hearing Christ pray. It must have been wonderful among the trees of Tabor, to hear him confessing all the sins that had been put upon him. 'Innumerable evils have compassed me about, and mine iniquities have taken such hold upon me that I cannot look up.' It must have been wonderful to hear Christ's strong cries and tears for deliverance — to hear him say, 'Save me from the lion's mouth. Save me, O God; for the waters are come in unto my soul. I sink in deep mire where there is no standing; I am come into deep waters where the floods overflow me.' Or to hear him pray for his believing disciples. 'I pray for them; I pray not for the world, but for them which thou hast given me out of the world. I pray not that thou shouldst take them out of the world, but that thou shouldst keep them from the evil. Father, I will that they also, which thou hast given me, be with me where I am; that they may behold my glory.' Such, no doubt, was the prayer that was listened to on Tabor's mount that night. Brethren, such are the prayers that are offered up yet on Zion! Brethren, if you had been behind some of the trees on Tabor's mount, and heard him mention your name in prayer, saying, I do not pray for Peter only, or for James, or John, but for this soul. Father, sanctify this soul through thy truth. Father, I will that this soul be with me where I am, that it may behold my glory. Say, doubting sinner, if you had heard Christ mentioning thy name, would it not have given you peace? Does distance make any difference? Suppose you heard a friend praying for you in the next room, or suppose you were told that a friend residing in a foreign land prayed for you, would it make any difference? Now, suppose you are told Christ prays for you — for he prays for all his believing people — will you not take the comfort of it?

III. Let us look at *the answer to prayer*. The first answer to prayer was the transfiguration, verse 29: 'And, as he prayed, the fashion of his countenance was altered, and his raiment was white and glistening.' You will observe this was an answer to prayer, for it is said, 'As he prayed the fashion of his countenance was altered.' Matthew says, 'It did shine as the sun.' Luke says, 'his raiment was white and glistening.' Matthew says, 'it was white as the light.' I believe that the answer to prayer came for two reasons. 1st. For his own sake. 2nd. For his disciples' sake.

1. *For his own sake.* He prayed, 'Glorify thou me,' and here was the answer. Brethren, this was sweet proof to Christ that he would go through with his work. I believe that this was often his prayer — that he might finish his work; so here is a glimpse of the coming glory, as a proof that he would finish it.

2. *For the disciples' sakes* that they might believe in the coming glory. Peter, when an old man, often looked back to this scene. 'He received from God the Father honour and glory, when there came such a voice to him from the excellent glory, This is my beloved Son, in whom I am well pleased. And this voice which came from heaven we heard, when we were with him in the holy mount,' 2 Pet. 1.17, 18. You will notice, brethren, that Peter was now an old man, yet he looked back to the scene he witnessed on Tabor's mount that night. It was a sweet assurance to the disciples that Christ would yet finish the work and be glorified, and they glorified in him. Ah! brethren, it is a sweet assurance to you and me that Christ is now glorified. His raiment is now white as the light, and that raiment is what he offers

to you and me. 'I counsel thee to buy of me white raiment that thou mayest be clothed.' And that answer to prayer was given for our sakes.

There was another answer to prayer, verse 30, 31: 'And, behold, there talked with him two men, which were Moses and Elias: who appeared in glory, and spake of his decease which he should accomplish at Jerusalem.' Compare this with Luke 13.43: 'And there appeared an angel unto him from heaven, strengthening him.' In Gethsemane, you will notice it was an angel that came down from heaven to strengthen him. On Tabor's top, it was two redeemed sinners. I believe that this answer to prayer was also for his own and disciples' sake. I believe it was an answer to that prayer, 'Father, I will that they also which thou hast given me be with me, where I am, that they may behold my glory.' What an assurance was this that he would finish the work! The Father had received them into heaven on the ground of the work which Christ should finish. And it was a sweet assurance to the disciples; they learned that Christ can save sinners; and they learned also, that saints in glory love to talk about the decease which he accomplished at Jerusalem.

Brethren, let us take one of these lessons. Learn that the redeemed love to talk about the decease which he accomplished at Jerusalem. They love to sing about it: 'Worthy is the Lamb that was slain,' etc. Ah! there are some that would take this world as their portion; they love not to talk about the decease which he accomplished at Jerusalem. Ah, brethren, this shows you you are not saved. Brethren, think whether you would like to sing the song the redeemed sing in the New Jerusalem, or be back on earth again. Ah! filthy dreamers, how could you walk on the golden streets of the New Jerusalem who love earth better? — it cannot be: 'For there shall enter into it nothing that defileth, neither whatsoever loveth abomination, or maketh a lie.'

IV. I come now to the fourth thing, and that is to notice *the three disciples,* verses 32, 33: 'But Peter and they that were with him were heavy with sleep,' etc. Observe their sin — they were weary, and had fallen asleep. What! asleep, when there was such a glory around Christ. Asleep, when redeemed men had come down from heaven and were talking with him. O Lord, what is man? Man is but dust. Ah! brethren, does not this show that ordinances in themselves will not do? If anything could have kept them from sleep it was surely this; but just as they slept at Gethsemane, so they slept at Tabor; they slept both in his sufferings and in his glory. Often you say, If I had but these privileges — If I but sat under a faithful ministry, I would be holy. It is not all the ordinances in the world that will do; grace, and grace alone will do. Observe Peter's joy, 'Master, it is good for us to be here,' etc. There are many that could not have endured to be there. Many of you cannot bear the conversation of the redeemed on earth, how could you relish their conversation when they came down from heaven? This shows the old man, and this also shows the new man. The old man is, 'Let us make three tabernacles,' etc. The new man is, 'Lord it is good for us to be here.' So that you can say, it is good to be here.

V. Last of all, notice *the Father's answer*, verses 34, 35: 'While he thus spake, there came a cloud and overshadowed them; and they feared as they entered into the cloud. And there came a voice out of the cloud, saying, This is my beloved Son: hear him.' This was the third answer to prayer, 'This is my beloved Son.' He received from the Father honour and glory, when there came such a voice to him from the excellent glory, 'This is my beloved Son, in whom I am well pleased.' When the disciples came down from the mount, they would hear Christ in another manner, they would hear him as one whom they had seen in heaven. And so, brethren, in like manner, if you can get a sight of the glory to which the Father had exalted him, you will hear in a different manner; 'My sheep hear my voice, and they follow me.' Once we heard Christ's voice, and now we follow him, and soon we shall hear his voice again, and be where he is, and to all eternity we shall follow him.   Amen.

Sabbath Forenoon,
4th December 1842.

SERMON XIV

THE HEAVENLY BRIDEGROOM AND BRIDE

Ephesians 5. 25-27.   *Husbands, love your wives, even as Christ also loved the church, and gave himself for it; that he might sanctify and cleanse it with the washing of water by the word; that he might present it to himself a glorious church, not having spot or wrinkle, or any such thing; but that it should be holy, and without blemish.*

In this passage, the apostle, by the Spirit, directs husbands and wives in their duties to one another; and for a pattern, he points them to the heavenly bridegroom and bride — Christ and his Church. Now, we are to observe three things today.
   1.   Christ's love for his Church.
   2.   Christ's purpose with the Church in time.

3. Christ's purpose with the Church in eternity.

I. *Christ's love for his Church.* The object of his love is the Church. It is true, he willeth that all men be saved. You remember how he shed tears over perishing sinners; you remember how he sent apostles to teach them his willingness to save them; from this you see how he loved them. Yet the peculiar object of his love is the Church; and that is all that are chosen or given to him of the Father — all who are washed in the fountain opened for sin and uncleanness — all who are clothed in the wedding garment — all who shall stand upon Mount Zion with golden harps. Jesus loved them in a past eternity. He loved to look into futurity, and see their names written in the book of life; he would say, 'They shall walk with me in white, for they *shall* be worthy.' Oh, I have no doubt but Jesus looks upon this town and says, 'I have much people in this city, though they know me not.' He loved the Church. When they come to him he lets out all the love of his heart to them. Oh, yes, when a soul comes to Jesus it feels there is an eye that looks tenderly upon it. Jesus loves Scotland better than other lands; for his Church is in Scotland. He loves some towns and streets better than others; for more of his people are there. He loves some houses better than others. He loves some rooms in a house better than others; for his name is often called upon there. Sometimes he shows himself through the lattice. Sometimes they are asleep, but he says, 'Open unto me, my love, my dove, my undefiled.' Ah, you see how he loved the Church. Observe, farther, what was the state of the Church when he found her:

1. *It was lying under the curse of God.* He loved it and then gave himself for it, even when God was frowning on it. Ah, many a one marries an uncomely bride for the sake of her dowry; but Jesus got an ill dowry with his bride — he got nothing but the wrath of God with the Church.

2. *It was impure and unholy.* Observe the order — he loved it, and then gave himself for it. I could understand him making it holy and then loving it — but he first loved it. Ah! brethren, Jesus loved me in the pit of corruption; his love looked into the pit, and then took us from the fearful pit. Ah, there is nothing to draw the love of Jesus to us. We love for something fair or attractive, but such is not the love of Jesus; he loved his Father, for all was glory in him, but in the Church all was impure. Oh, then, learn the free love of Jesus. He did not love pain or suffering more than you or I; yet he gave himself for the Church. He loves us before we love him: 'Thou wast cast out into the open field in thy blood, and I passed by and said, Live; yea, I said unto thee, Live.' He looked upon us, 'and the time was a time of love.' Oh, then, look back, dear believer, to the time when Jesus first

loved you; look to your heart at that time; what a black soul thou wast when Jesus loved you! Oh, learn the love of Jesus! I have chosen thee, but thou has not chosen me. 'I have chosen thee, and refined thee, but not with silver.' Now, if ye do not understand that Jesus justifies the ungodly, ye are yet in your sins.

3. *The greatness of his love.* We can measure man's love by the sacrifices he will make. Some will not lay down a sixpence for Christ, nor give up a friend for Christ, nor give up a party for Christ; but Jesus gave himself. What can a man give more than himself? 'Greater love hath no man than this.' O think today of the greatness of the love of Christ! If he had created ten thousand angels and given them for the Church, this would have been condescending love; but, ah! Jesus gave himself, even while we were enemies. Oh, brethren, he bore guilt for us! I would rather bear sorrow, or suffering, or affliction, than guilt for you, but Jesus gave his holy soul an offering for sin. Oh, yes, he said, 'Mine iniquities' — he called them his own — 'have taken such a hold of me, I cannot lift up my head.' Oh! if you knew how he hated sin, ye would know what he felt. 'I gave my back to the smiters.' And then he gave himself to bear wrath. Oh! the holy soul of Jesus did not love wrath; but he bare the wrath of God. If you would ask an angel to leave his seat in bliss, and to bear the wrath of God, it would be hell to leave for a moment the love of God; yet Jesus gave himself up freely to death. Now, he knew more infinite love than the angels; yet he lost the love, and took the wrath. O never was love like this! 'Behold what manner of love!' So, you see, he loved the Church, and gave himself for it.

II. Let us consider, *Christ's purpose with the Church in time.* When the soul is brought to Jesus, and washed in his blood, its sanctification is just begun — it is the first dawn of an eternal day. Jesus is the author of sanctification; but there are many looking to the wrong airt for it. Now, all comes from the same hand that was nailed to the cross; look to him for sanctification — his name is Jesus, for he saves from sin. Oh, do any feel faint and weary? Lean on him, the Beloved; all comes from Jesus. You may as well try to hold up the sun in its course, as to hold up your own goings. Go, then, to Jesus for all you need; learn the means of sanctification — the Word. No holiness without the Bible! I believe God could sanctify without the Word. He made the angels holy without it, and he made Adam holy without it; but he will not do it. 'Sanctify them through thy truth, thy word is truth.' Just like a mother nourishing a child, Jesus takes a soul and nourishes it with the milk of the Word. No life without a Bible! It is just the breathings of God's heart — of his affectionate bosom. Oh, yes, if you would walk much with Jesus, you would become like him. Oh, you would get the heart and

likeness of Jesus. There are some believers, and you may know them
by their breath that they have been with Emmanuel, the lovely Rose
of Sharon.

Learn, then, that there is no other means of sanctification, and
without holiness no man shall see the Lord. Unless you love your
Bibles, and feed upon them, you will never stand with the Lamb
upon Mount Zion, with the golden harps.

Learn the certainty of sanctification. Rutherford said, 'Blessed be
God, Christ is a whole Saviour — he not only justifies, but he
sanctifies too.' Oh, no, he will not lose the end for which he died —
to make you not of this world, while you are in the world. He came to
this miserable world, and took stones to polish for his Father's
palace. Do you think he will leave you unholy? This is the will of the
Father, even your sanctification. Jesus died, and the Spirit is sent as
the sanctifier. There is much sin between you and God — many
temptations — yet you shall be made holy.

III. Let us consider *Christ's purpose with the Church in eternity*.
This is the day when the Lord Jesus is sanctifying his Church; but a
day is coming when it shall be a holy Church. Dear believer, the day
is coming when you and I shall be holy. Here nothing is perfect but
Christ's righteousness. Often have we to mourn over a body of sin
and death. This is a world of imperfection. We are here as in the
furnace; but we shall come out pure. Ah, yes, there is a glorious
bridal day coming, when the king's daughter shall be all glorious
within. Oh, our Church this day is spotted — many have not got the
wedding garment, and many who are God's people have got a sinful,
unholy heart. But the day is coming, when we shall be all glorious,
with his righteousness on us, and his holiness in us. Learn the
certainty of your sanctification.

But there are some who, after all, fear they may be cast away.
When you feel the power of temptation — when you feel the old
heart within you — oh, do not fear; God is the sanctifier: 'Whom he
called, them he also justified; and whom he justified, them he also
glorified.' Rom. 8.30. Ah, that is a golden chain that all the devils in
hell cannot break. It is a golden chain. Oh, if you have one of those
links, you are sure of them all — you are one of the glorious Church.

Learn what he will do in *that* day. He will present it to *himself*. Ah,
yes! it is too dear to him to give it to another. Oh, do you know what
this intimates? It is that you and he shall never be parted again.
Here you are often saying, 'Saw ye him whom my soul loveth?' Oh,
then, there will be no more mountains of Bether. You shall see the
King in his beauty. Like the disciples, you shall talk with him, and
lean on his bosom. There shall be no veil between you then. You
shall see eye to eye. He shall talk with you of the decease he

accomplished at Jerusalem. What can you have more? Ye shall be his eternally holy ones. May this be the portion of you all, and may God bless his own word, and to him be the glory.   Amen.

Action Sermon,
3rd January 1841.

SERMON XV

BELIEVERS NOT ASHAMED OF THE CROSS OF CHRIST

Romans 1. 15-18. *As much as in me is, I am ready to preach the gospel to you that are at Rome also, etc.*

The first thing I desire you to notice, brethren, is *the place where Paul was desirous to preach the gospel.* Verse 15: 'As much as in me is, I am ready to preach the gospel to you that are at Rome also.' We find Paul mentioning the same thing in the verses before: verse 11: 'For I long to see you, that I may impart unto you some spiritual gift, to the end ye may be established.' And then the 13th verse, 'Now I would not have you ignorant, brethren, that oftentimes I purposed to come unto you, that I might have fruit among you also, even as among other Gentiles.' Rome was the mightiest city in the world at that time. Daniel compares it to a great beast which devoured, and brake in pieces, and stamped the residue with the feet of it. We know that Rome was at this time called the 'mistress of the world.' It was at this time the most learned city in the world. It had its buildings and baths, its painters and orators, and philosophers; and it was for this reason that Paul desired so earnestly to preach the gospel to them. But, more than that, it was one of the most wicked cities in the world. One historian calls it 'the place where common sewers meet'; and he that sat on the throne was the wickedest of all, yet Paul desired to preach the gospel there.

The second thing I want you to notice is *what Paul wanted to do at Rome.* 'I am ready to preach the gospel to you that are at Rome also.' When Paul wanted to go to Rome it was not to see it; many went to Rome to see it, to see its marble baths, its theatres, its palaces, etc., but Paul did not want to see Rome. And it was not to show himself off; all learned men went to Rome to show off their learning, and to publish their works. It was not so with Paul; all that he wanted to do was this — 'I am ready to preach the gospel to you that are at Rome also.' 'I determined not to know anything among you save Jesus Christ and him crucified.'

I want you to notice, in the third place, *what Paul's feelings were in the prospect of going to Rome.* 'I am not ashamed of the gospel of Christ,' etc. These words are very remarkable; there is more meant in them than at first appears. They are like these words, 'He will not break the bruised reed, nor quench the smoking flax'; which means, that instead of breaking the bruised reed, he will bear it up; and that, instead of quenching the smoking flax, he will fan it into a flame. So, in these words, when Paul says, 'I am not ashamed of the gospel of Christ,' it means, I glory in the cross of Christ. This passage is the same in meaning with that in Galatians 6.14, 'But God forbid that I should glory, save in the cross of our Lord Jesus Christ,' etc. The meaning of both passages is just this, that the way of righteousness through Christ was what Paul gloried in. There are two things implied in it. First, he was not ashamed of the gospel before God. Paul rested his eternal salvation on the righteousness of Christ. Like David, he said, 'This is all my salvation and all my desire.' He had no other way of access to God but that; if that failed, all failed. He had no other way of going to God in secret but that, therefore he says, 'I am not ashamed of the gospel of Christ.' But again, there is implied in it that he was not ashamed of the gospel before men. Many men are ashamed of the gospel, but Paul was not ashamed of it. Paul wished that he had a voice that could reach throughout the world, that he might proclaim the gospel. Many men would have smiled at him entering Rome with only a few words in his mouth, but Paul was not ashamed of the gospel of Christ. Ah, brethren, many men would have thought he was a blabber, who told them to be righteous without works, but Paul did not care for that; 'I am not ashamed of the gospel of Christ.' And many would have smiled at Paul coming to such a wicked place as Rome with nothing to tell them of but another's righteousness; but ah! he saw that Christ's righteousness was able to cover them. Pray that we may get such a sight of Christ this day.

Let me show you, from these words: 1. Some of the reasons why men are ashamed of the gospel of Christ. 2. Some of the reasons why Paul and all like him are not ashamed of the gospel of Christ.

I. *Some of the reasons why men are ashamed of the gospel of Christ.*

1. *Unregenerate men are ashamed of the gospel of Christ because it seems a foolish way to them.* Look at the 1st chapter of 1st

Corinthians, 18th verse, 'For the preaching of the cross is to them
that perish foolishness,' etc.; 2nd chapter and 14th verse, 'But the
natural man receiveth not the things of the Spirit of God; for they
are foolishness unto him,' etc. This is the first great reason why
unregenerate men are ashamed of the gospel; it appears so foolish
that one man should be accounted righteous for the obedience of
another. 'The cross of Christ is to them that perish foolishness,' and
it will be so to the end of time. Do not think you are different from
your fathers; you are just the same. To those of you in this
congregation who will perish, the cross of Christ is foolishness. Oh,
brethren, if the gospel were by works you could understand it. If you
could get into heaven by your works, you would say, That is a good
gospel, that is good preaching; but righteousness by another, that is
foolishness. Or suppose salvation was in this way — by God being
lenient to the law, that you could understand; or suppose salvation
was by your repentance, tears, etc., then you could know its
meaning; but that salvation is by the righteousness of another, that
is utter foolishness: 'To them that perish, the preaching of the cross
is foolishness.' Ah, brethren, did you never notice that you are
ashamed of hearing of the righteousness of another. Many worldly
men would not come in at the door of this church, and why? Just
because they would hear of the righteousness of another. Are there
not many of you who do not like to hear about the righteousness of
Christ, that say, when you hear it, O that is one of his rash
expressions? And you are ashamed to go to God in this way; to them
that perish, this way is foolishness. And you are ashamed to speak
about it; you do not tell your children about the white robe — the
white linen, clean and white, which is the righteousness of saints and
why? Because you do not like it. 'The preaching of the cross is to
them that perish foolishness.'

  2.   *Then you are ashamed of its teachers.* You are told by the
evangelist Mark that Christ's audience said to him, 'Is not this the
carpenter, the son of Mary, the brother of James and Joses, and of
Jude and Simon? and are not his sisters here with us? And they were
offended at him.' And we are told about the apostles, in the Acts,
that the chief priest took notice that they were ignorant and
unlearned men. And we are told that when Paul went to Corinth,
they said his speech was weak and his appearance contemptible.
Now, Christ has not sent angels, neither has he sent infallible men to
preach the gospel; 'We have this treasure in earthen vessels that the
excellency of the power may be of God and not of us.' I do not know
a faithful minister in Scotland that has not some defect either in his
appearance, or his speech, or his manner; and will you not say, 'Is
not this the carpenter?' 'We have this treasure in earthen vessels.'

Will you not say, 'That minister is often angry; that one is rude in his manner'? Ah! you are like flies that fasten on the sore on the horse's back. O foolish men! you stick at the faults, and do not take the blessing.

3. Another reason why you are ashamed of the gospel is, *you hate its holiness.* This is the main reason; if it were not for this, the other reasons would not stand. If it was a gospel that would let you live in your sins, you would say, 'All hail'; but God gave his Son to bless us, in turning each of us away from our iniquities. The Lord Jesus, when he finds a sinner, clothes him with his righteousness, and then he makes him all glorious within. Christ will not leave a sinner till he sees his Father's image within him. He will not leave a sinner till he has left his own image there—his own lamb-like image. That is the reason why you despise the gospel. Those of you who are drunkards, say, He would take me from my glass; those of you who are card-players, say, He would take me from my play. Ah, it is a holy gospel. 'From all your filthiness, and from all your idols, will I cleanse you, a new heart also will I give you,' etc. Ah, brethren, I would say for one, if it were not for the holiness of the gospel, it would not be worth the having; and yet this is the reason why you hate the gospel, and reject the counsel of God against yourselves. O brethren, it will be to your condemnation that light came into the world, and that you loved the darkness rather than the light, because your deeds were evil.

II. *I come now to the reasons why Paul and all like him are not ashamed of the gospel of Christ.*

1. *Because of the power there is in it,* verse 16. To unregenerate men the gospel appears the most foolish thing in the world. The scheme of salvation, by the obedience of another, is to them foolishness. And then men think there is nothing in it — there is no power in it. But to us who are saved, it is the power of God, and the wisdom of God; to those who have seen the power of it on others — to them that believe its power, it is the power of God unto salvation. My brethren, there is a divine power sleeping in the gospel, if I may be allowed so to speak, which is able to break the hardest heart. That gospel that you despise — the dogma that you hate, is all powerful. Brethren, it is more powerful than the thunder or lightning, for it converts the soul. Paul once felt its power; once he hated the gospel, and made havoc of the Church, entering into every house, and hailing men and women, committing them to prison. Brethren, what could turn such a heart? You might as well think of turning back a river, as changing such a heart; but God revealed his Son to him, and from that day the river was turned back, and he became a new creature in Christ Jesus. And, brethren, Paul had seen

its power on others; he had seen its power on the hearts of multitudes, and, therefore, Paul was not ashamed of the gospel. Brethren, it is the power of God unto salvation, not to destruction. Paul had seen so much of the power of the gospel when wielded by God — he had seen that, when it was wielded by God, there was not so much as one Jew or Gentile, bond or free, that could resist; it was this that nerved the arm of Paul when he went to Rome to preach the gospel — he felt he had that which was the power of God unto salvation to every one that believeth. And oh! brethren, it is this that gives us strength. I am sure, since I came among you, I have felt the hardness of your hearts; but, ah! I know that if God will make use of the gospel, it will bring down the proudest of you all. Awakened sinner! there is a power in the gospel to pardon you, though your sins reach up to heaven.

2. I come now to a second reason why we are not ashamed of the gospel, that is, *that the righteousness of God is revealed in it,* verse 17. This is a reason that grows out of the other reason: it is the righteousness of God that gives it all its power. The righteousness of God here spoken of is just the doing and dying of the Lord Jesus. It is called the righteousness of God, because it is that of God himself. You remember when Christ was a child, it is said he was 'the mighty God': and then it is said that it is the blood of God. See Acts 20.28, 'Take heed, therefore, unto yourselves, and to all the flock over which the Holy Ghost hath made you overseers, to feed the Church of God, which he hath purchased with his own blood.' The blood that was shed on Calvary was the blood of one who was called God. And then all the sufferings of Christ have got a divine value in them that satisfies the demands of the law in a way which no other can do. And, in the same manner, the obedience of Christ was the obedience of one who was God; and when he obeyed his parents, it was the obedience of one who was God; and when he obeyed the law, it was the obedience of one who was God. Then the obedience and suffering of Christ when he stood in the room of many, is called the righteousness of God, and it is offered to you as such in the gospel. Ah! my brethren, this was the reason why Paul was not ashamed of the gospel. Paul knew that, suppose he came to Rome, and met in with the chief of sinners, he could tell him a way to be forgiven. I know that those of you who hate the gospel despise this way, but that will never make me hate the gospel. Brethren, in the gospel there is the righteousness of one who is God offered to the chief of sinners — yet you despise it; yet this does not, so to speak, prick a hole in it. Those of you who are awakened sinners, here is a righteousness that can cover you; behold, for each of your crimson sins, here is a stripe on one who is God. And, brethren, more than that, here are acts of

holy obedience to cover your naked soul—here are holy words to cover your unholy words — here are holy deeds to cover your unholy deeds. O brethren! here is a lifetime of obedience to cover your soul. You know, brethren, at the time of the deluge, it covered the highest mountains to the height of fifteen cubits. Now, suppose you had been above the world and looked down, you would not have seen one mountain. So it is with you; if you have on this righteousness you will be covered, and when God looks down, he will see nothing but the glassy sea of his Son's obedience. O brethren! this is the only way of being saved; if there were another way, I would let you alone to choose your own way; but there is not another way, 'There is none other name under heaven given among men whereby we must be saved,' but the name of Jesus Christ. God give you to choose this day the righteousness of Christ.

In conclusion, I would just mention *a reason why you should now choose Christ:* verse 18. When Paul approached the gates of Rome — when he looked at its marble baths — when he saw the multitudes flocking to the theatre — and when he saw the crowds bowing down to the statue of Jupiter or Minerva, the heart of Paul was touched, and why? Because the wrath of God was revealed from heaven against them, and he knew that he had in his hand that which could cover every sinner. O, said Paul, if I could get them to put on this righteousness: 'For the wrath of God is revealed from heaven against all ungodliness and unrighteousness of men.' O my brethren! it is this that saves you! — it is this that nerves me to preach! for I know if you do accept it you will be saved, but if not, you will be lost. Brethren, I tell you that you must either put on this righteousness, or the wrath of God will be revealed against you. Oh! my brethren, learn the folly of those of you who reject the gospel of Christ; you think that you have all the wisdom in the world, and that it will perish with you; you think that we are mad, but we will see when we stand *that day,* when the wrath of God will be revealed from heaven against all ungodliness and unrighteousness of men. O happy are those of you who are clothed in this righteousness! 'I will blot out your iniquity for mine own name's sake, and will not remember thy sins.' It is like casting a stone into the deep; it sinks, and it is not seen. It is like the water at the deluge, which covered the loftiest mountains. 'Thou hast cast all my sins behind thy back.' Amen.

ADDRESS AT FENCING THE TABLES

I would now, as was the custom of our fathers, put a fence around the Lord's table; and in doing so, permit me to read to you Luke 14.33. My dear friends, you are this day about to perform one of the

most solemn acts in your life. Those of you who are coming for the
first time to the Lord's table are professing before men, and angels,
and devils, that you do choose Christ to be your righteousness and
strength. Those of you who have often sat down at the Lord's table
are coming to renew your engagement to be the Lord's; and you say:
So surely as I take this bread and wine, so surely do I take Christ as
my righteousness. When you take the bread and wine you say, I do
feed on Christ. And those of you who are coming for the last time,
make the declaration of Mary, that you have chosen that good part
that shall never be taken away from you. All I ask of you at this
moment is that you count the cost. 'Whosoever he be of you that
forsaketh not all that he hath, he cannot be my disciple.'

1. First of all, in the name of my Master, I ask you, *Have you
forsaken all your own righteousness?* You have heard that salvation
is not of works. Have you forsaken your own righteousness? It is
written, 'Let the wicked forsake his way, and the unrighteous man
his thoughts, and let him return unto the Lord, and he will have
mercy upon him, and to our God, for he will abundantly pardon.'
Tell me, brethren, have you forsaken your own way of righteousness?
Have you put away yourself for righteousness? Do you look upon
yourself as a condemned sinner? Do you say, looking fully at your
life from the cradle to the grave, 'Enter not into judgment with me,
for in thy sight shall no flesh living be justified?' Are you completely
divorced from you own righteousness? and have you laid hold on
gospel righteousness? Then welcome to the Lord's table, welcome to
the bread and wine; and when you take it, look up to heaven, and
say, Father, I forsake all for Christ.

Brethren, is there a man here who is a legalist, who is looking for
righteousness from his life? — you are not welcome to the Lord's
table, for in laying hold of the bread and wine you say you have
renounced yourself for righteousness.

2. *Have you forsaken the esteem of all the world for Christ?* If
you will be justified by the word of Christ, the world will despise you.
Have you determined to forsake the esteem of the world for Christ,
even though it should be a dear world — though a wife or a
husband? Do you count their favour all dung compared with Christ
shining into your soul? Then you are welcome to the table; you have
made Moses' choice, you esteem the reproach of Christ greater
riches than the treasures of Egypt. You are welcome to the Lord's
table. We are a poor and afflicted people, but we have got the favour
of the Lord — cast in your lot among us. Welcome are you, brother,
welcome are you, sister. Christ welcomes you; the Father welcomes
you. In the name of my Master, I say, All welcome. Brethren, I
believe the most of you are not willing to leave the world for Christ —

you are not willing to be hated of all men for the name of Christ. Ah! then, you cannot be his; you may put your hand on the table, but remember, it is a Judas' hand — it is the hand of a betrayer.

3. *Have you forsaken all your sins for Christ?* I have no doubt many of you will say, Yes, yes, to the first two questions, that will shrink from this one. Have you forsaken your idols? Have you forsaken the pleasure of the flesh for the mind of the Lord Jesus? 'Whosoever he be of you that forsaketh not all that he hath, he cannot be my disciple.' 'If any man be in Christ Jesus, he is a new creature; old things are passed away, behold, all things are becoming new.' Remember, do not mistake me, I do not say that all who are come to Christ are perfectly holy; you need not stumble at that stone except you like; but they hate all sin, they have forsaken heart and life sin. Oh! brethren, 'Whatsoever is born of God doth not commit sin.' If we are born of God all that is divine in us will be against all sin. I tell you, brethren, if there is a man or woman here who is coming to the Lord's table, who is not seeking deliverance from all sin, then you have no right to come to this table; you are like Judas, who was a thief and kept the bag, and kept what was put in it. 'Whosoever he be of you that forsaketh not all that he hath, he cannot be my disciple.' But oh! brethren, if there be any one here who is seeking a warrant to come to the table, I would just mention what is my own warrant. If there is any one who feels that they are all sin, and if you are willing to be righteous in the righteousness of another, then you are welcome. Again, if you feel that your old heart is all for sin, and that your new heart is all for righteousness — if you feel that it will be your present heaven to be holy, then you are welcome to the Lord's table. I seek no other warrant for myself to come. Fellow-sinner, come, come cleaving to Christ; come pleading that the Holy Ghost may change us, that we may serve him as we have never done before, that the world may take notice of us what we have been with Jesus. Amen.

TABLE SERVICE BEFORE COMMUNICATING

My dear brethren, this table is spread for those of you who are followers of the Lamb. These are they that follow the Lamb withersoever he goeth. If you are rightly seated at the Lord's table, you are following the Lamb for justification. If you are rightly coming to the Lord's table you will look to none other righteousness to cover your naked soul, but that of the Lamb. You will follow the Lamb whithersoever he goeth. And then you will follow the Lamb in his sufferings: 'If we suffer we shall also reign with him.' Remember we will be like Christ in his sufferings, if we would be like him in his glory. And, brethren, if you are really followers of the Lamb, you will follow him for sanctification; he will follow you as the water of the rock followed the Israelites in the wilderness. Brethren, why do you follow the Lamb? Is it because he has washed you? Another reason why you follow the Lamb is, you love the Lamb: 'If any man love not the Lord Jesus Christ, let him be anathema maran-atha.' And, brethren, if you follow the Lamb, you will have the peace of the Lamb: 'Peace I leave with you, my peace I give unto you.' It is not the peace of an angel, but that of the Lamb. And, brethren, another advantage is, you will be made like the Lamb: 'Beholding as in a glass the glory of the Lord, we are changed into the same image, from glory to glory.' And, brethren, another advantage of following the Lamb is, we will follow the Lamb to all eternity. 'And God shall wipe away all tears from your eyes.' My dear brethren, I hope you are rightly come to the Lord's table, for it is the place where his blessing is; 'In all places where I record my name, I will come and bless you.' Where does Christ record his name but at the table. Those of you who are not Christ's, are betrayers at the table. But if you are Christ's you may bless the day that ever you were born, and you may bless the day of your death, for it will be your third birth-day — your birth-day into glory.

AFTER COMMUNICATING

'I will come and heal him.' 'I will, be thou clean.' 'Be of good cheer, thy faith hath made thee whole.' 'O woman, great is thy faith, be it unto thee even as thou wilt.' 'I am the way, the truth, and the life.' 'These things have I spoken unto you that in me ye might have peace: in the world ye shall have tribulation; but be of good cheer, I have overcome the world.' Remember that one Scripture, beloved, 'Be not conformed to this world, but be transformed to it.' Brethren, you are not of this world, why should you be like the world? 'You are born, not of blood, nor of the will of the flesh, nor of the will of man, but of God.' Why, then, should you be like the world? Christ said of you and me, 'They are not of the world, even as I am not of the world.' Could there have been a more unearthly being than Christ was? Now he says we are no more of the world than he. Why then should you be like the world? The world are not going to the same place — the world are going to hell, we to the many mansion house.

Why then should we be like the world? Brethren, let me speak to you plainly. Be not like the world in secret. The world in secret plot mischief on their bed. Let there be the most complete friendship between you and God. And then, be not like the world in your family. You know the worldly do not govern their house right. O brethren! if there is one thing I long for more in this place than another it is to see you governing your own house well, bringing up your family for heaven, and not for the world. And, brethren, do not be like the world in not praying. Remember it is written in Jeremiah, 'Pour out thy fury upon the heathen, and upon the families that call not upon thy name.' Be not conformed to this world in the company you keep. Publicans seek publicans; sinners, sinners; 'Be not comformed to this world, but be transformed to it.' If you are Christ's, you will not invite worldly company to your house. It is not possible for you to keep your house as the temple of God if you invite worldly company. Be not like the world in your joy. The world have their joy in a newspaper or in a novel. Remember you have got the cup of the Lord, and you should not drink the cup of devils — make your company those that love Christ — you broke bread with them just now. Be not like the world in their sorrow, they have got angry sorrow. Be not like them. Remember, though ye be poor ye are known by Christ. And do not be like the world in their troubles. Remember you must have a holy carefulness — 'Seek ye first the kingdom of God and his righteousness, and all other things shall be added unto you.' Dear brethren, some of you will say, How is it possible? do not I live in an ungodly family? do I not live in Sodom? But, dear brethren, here is the secret. If you will not be like the world, be transformed to it. God is able to keep you from falling and to present you faultless before the presence of his glory with exceeding joy. God is able to enlarge your heart so that you will run and not weary in God's ways. Then be of good courage, for there is enough in Christ to satisfy you. Do you want to be holy? Then God wishes to make you holy. Then God's will and yours are one. Say, then, 'Make me holy, I want to be holy.' Holiness is the brightest attribute of Jehovah. Ah! I fear we are not living up to what is in Christ, or we would not live as we do. How much useless talk and conversation is there? Oh! the time of our life is more than sufficient to have wrought the will of the flesh. Let us now live to him. Let us give ourselves away to Christ — solemnly to him; give your wills and affections to him for time and for eternity. The grace of the Lord Jesus be with your spirit.   Amen.

ADDRESS AFTER THE DAY'S SERVICE

Suffer me now, brethren, to send you away with a few words of exhortation from Revelation 3.4. There is a voice comes to us this night, saying, 'Thou hast a few names even in Sardis which have not defiled their garments,' etc. *'Thou hast,'* these words are addressed to the angel — the minister, the star which God set over the Church. Now, to the angel, God says, 'Thou hast a few names even in Sardis that have not defiled their garments.' There is a strange connection between a minister and each saved soul — the connection is not between all the people, but with a few. I never feel as I do on a communion Sabbath. Those of you, of whose conversion I have been the means, are my children. And the union between a pastor and the souls he has gotten is eternal. The union of a father and his children is not eternal, but this union is eternal. The union between a pastor and each saved soul is spoken of in many parts of Scripture. Paul, in writing to Timothy, says, 'Unto Timothy my own son in the faith.' And again, 'I beseech thee for my son Onesimus whom I have begotten in my bonds.' And, brethren, those of you who have been really converted under my ministry, we are united for ever. You will be my joy, 'My dearly beloved and longed for, my joy and crown, stand fast, my dearly beloved.' For what is our hope or joy or crown of rejoicing but this? And, brethren, let the same link that has united us today be acknowledged with thankfulness to God. 'Not unto us, Lord, not unto us, but to thy name give glory.' Ah, remember when Herod refused to give God the glory, he was eaten up of worms, and if we do not give him the glory, such will be our condemnation.

But notice, further, *'thou hast a few names'* — not all. There have been many names in this place today, but then only a few that have not defiled their garments. So it was with Enoch. So it was with Noah; he had only eight names. So it was with Abraham; he had but few names. So it was with Lot; he had his own name and none other. And so when our Lord came into the world, he said, 'Fear not, little flock.' And so it is now, we have a few names; but oh, let us not be discouraged, for one soul is worth all the material universe; for when the sun grows dim with age, that soul will still live; oh! brethren, it is worth the universe. And had this church been built, and I sent, and no more saved than what have been saved, it would have been worth it all. When our Lord went across the lake in a storm, it was to save one soul. Christ loves single souls, Christ died for single souls. Ah! brethren, one single soul is precious to Christ, therefore precious to me.

'Thou hast a few names *even in Sardis.'* Brethren, Sardis had a fair outside, but no more. It is the same with our town, but what is the life? It is nothing. 'But thou hast a few names even in Sardis.' Even in Sardis, Christ could keep a few names alive. Dear brethren, I believe that open formality is a greater snare than open wickedness. I believe there is less difficulty in walking in Sodom than in Sardis. I remember of one person who, I have no doubt, was a child of God; she said, 'Ah, sir, I went to a town, and went into a family where family worship was kept without the power of godliness — they were not saved'; this was the reason why she had backsliden. These seem to be the days that are coming; 'Men shall be lovers of themselves, having a form of godliness, but denying the power thereof.' Many of you live in Sardis; but ah, my brethren, remember that God can keep you in Sardis, even in the midst of lifeless professors — even he can keep your soul alive.

But further, 'Thou hast a few names, even in Sardis, *that have not defiled their garments.*' My dear brethren, I would have you to go away from the Lord's Table with this prayer: 'Lord keep me from defiling my garments.' It does not mean that they have never defiled their garments, neither does it mean that they had no inward corruption. The meaning is that their garments were washed. But some may ask, How will I keep my garments?

1. *Never forget that you had defiled your garment* — never forget that. 'Then you shall remember and be confounded, and never open thy mouth any more when I am pacified toward thee, for all that thou hast done against me.' My brethren, if you would keep your garments clean, walk softly, and you should never forget what an enemy to God you have been.

2. *Get a deep acquaintance with your own heart.* It is fearful to think how little young believers know of their own heart. Pray to get a deep sight of the desperate wickedness of your heart. I believe that it is ignorance that is the cause of many of your falls. Ignorance is at the bottom of them.

3. *Be constantly washing in the fountain open for sin.* Remember pardon is not one act, and then over — it must be continually repeated. Remember to go to the fountain, this is the only way to walk with clean garments.

4. *Pray for the Holy Spirit to uphold you.* My dear brethren, if sensible of your weakness, then lean upon this proved Comforter. Pray much for the Comforter that he may enlighten your mind, that he may fill your hearts. O pray for the Spirit of God! for there is no other way of walking to heaven but by the Spirit. Let him lead you. 'Thy Spirit is good: lead me to the land of uprightness.' My dear brethren, in this way, and in this way alone, will you not defile your garments.

Last of all, remember the promise: 'They shall walk with me in white, for they are worthy.' I believe that there are many who have sat with us who are walking with Christ in white, and many who have sat this day will be with him before another Communion Sabbath: 'I will that they also may be with me where I am; that they may behold my glory.' Christ wants you to be with him, and were it not that he has purposes to serve with us, he would pluck us from the table to glory. Never forget, dear brethren, that you are to walk with Christ. This walk expresses the most near intimacy with him. You know it is a mark of near intimacy to admit one to walk with us in our solitary rambles. So will Christ: 'Ye shall walk with me.' And remember, brethren, you are to walk with Christ 'in white' — clothed with Christ's robe. Brethren, it is heaven's wear. I believe that the very angels will know us by our robe; for it is written, 'He is coming to be glorified in his saints, and admired in all them that believe.' Dear brethren, remember, since you are to walk with Christ, not to walk with his enemies. 'Be not unequally yoked together with unbelievers,' etc. Why should we walk with the world, when we are to walk with Christ amid the bowers of Paradise? When the world tempts you to join its dance and its pleasures, you should remember that you are to walk with Christ: 'They shall walk with me.' Brethren, it may be next week — it may be in a few hours. O walk with him now! Walk here with him, and you shall soon put your head where John put his.

Last of all, prize the white robe; it is what they will wear in heaven; it is the robe that Christ giveth to him that overcometh. 'I will not blot his name out of the book of life,' etc. Oh! brethren, remember it is white as the light — broad as the law; wear it, and we shall soon walk with him in heaven, being found worthy. The Lord bless you, and bring the few names in Dundee to walk with him in white.   Amen.

It was customary with the author, at the end of each day's service, to leave a text of Scripture with each of the classes of individuals that might be present. On this occasion, they were the following — 'To those of you who are God's people — 1 John 5.21. For those of you who are labouring and heavy laden — Jer. 13.27 (last clause). For those of you who are unconverted — 1 Pet. 4.18.'

SERMON XVI

THE ARK

Hebrews 11.7. *By faith Noah, being warned of God of things not seen as yet, moved with fear, prepared an ark to the saving of his house; by the which he condemned the world, and became heir of the righteousness which is by faith.*

It is a wonderful fact of human nature that we learn far more easily from example than we do in any other way. Now, you have in this passage an example of a sinner saved by faith. It shews you how a sinner is saved. And as Noah fled into the ark which he had prepared, so should you. You too, have an ark provided; and just as Noah thereby condemned the world — that is, shewed that the world was righteously condemned — so will you; if you enter in, you will shew by your faith that its condemnation is just.

Let us go over these things and see:

I. *Noah's warning:* 'By faith Noah, being warned of God of things not seen as yet, moved with fear, prepared an ark to the saving of his house.' We have an account given us of the warning of Noah in the 6th chapter of Genesis, 1st, 2nd, and 3rd verses, 'And it came to pass, when men began to multiply on the face of the earth, that the sons of God saw the daughters of men that they were fair; and they took them wives of all which they chose. And the Lord said, My spirit shall not always strive with man, for that he also is flesh; yet his days shall be an hundred and twenty years.' That was the first warning. Verse 7, 'And the Lord said, I will destroy man, whom I have created, from the face of the earth; both man and beast, and the creeping thing, and the fowls of the air: for it repenteth me that I have made them.' This is the second warning. That was the warning which God gave to Noah; he told him that the Holy Spirit would not always strive with man, and then he told him that he would destroy man whom he had created. Now, if Noah had been like some of you, he might have said, God is a merciful God — he will not destroy the souls that he has made. Or, like some of you, he might have said, O! it is a long time yet; it will be time enough to turn to God a year before the flood comes. But, no; 'Noah, being warned of God of things not seen as yet, moved with fear, prepared an ark to the saving of his house.'

Now, brethren, if you would be like Noah, you should be moved with fear. God has warned you, not once, nor twice, but a hundred times. God warns you in the Bible that 'his wrath is revealed from heaven against all ungodliness and unrighteousness of men.' It says,

'If you are not converted, you will not see the kingdom of God'; it says, that 'if you commit such things you shall die'; it says that 'if you do not believe you shall be damned'; it says that 'if you are not converted and become as little children, you shall never see the kingdom of God.' Ah, then, man, have you ever trembled at the warning of God? No; then you are not like Noah; you are not like him, for he believed God. I tell you, you could not live on as you do, if you believe God's Word; it is because you are infidel at heart — that is the reason why you do not tremble at his Word: 'By faith Noah, being warned of God of things not seen as yet, moved with fear, prepared an ark to the saving of his house.'

Again, you are warned by ministers. We are to receive the word at God's mouth, and warn the people; and if we do not warn you, God says he will require it at the watchman's hands. This is one of the chief parts of a minister's duty — to warn the unconverted. This is what I have done, both in public and private. I have warned you, and how have you received it? O, you say, do you think I would be afraid of the word of a man? Well, if so, I tell you that it is not our word, it is the Word of God; and, oh! if you do not take the Word of God, spoken through the minister, you are not like Noah.

Again, you are warned by providence. Some of you have seen souls cut down, and yet you are left. Some of you have seen those whom you led into sin taken away, and yet you are left. Ah, brethren, can you say that you have not been warned? and how have you taken it? Some of you have gone deeper into sin. Ah! you are not like Noah. But some of you will make this objection. I do not like to be moved with fear; I like it to be all love. It is quite true that none were ever brought to Christ by fear. We must be brought to Christ by a sight of his love. But then, it is quite as true that you will never be brought out of your security but by fear: you must be drawn *out* by fear, and drawn *in* by love. Ah, brethren, do not you despise fear. How was the jailor brought to Christ? 'He called for a light, and sprang in, and came trembling, and fell down before Paul and Silas, and brought them out, and said, Sirs, what must I do to be saved?' What was it that made him ask the question? It was fear. What was it that made the three thousand on the streets of Jerusalem cry, 'Men and brethren, what shall we do?' It was fear. What was it that made Saul cry, when he lay on the ground, 'Lord what wilt thou have me to do?' It was fear. And so must it be with you, if ever you are brought to Christ. Awake, 'What meanest thou, O sleeper; arise, call upon thy God.' Ah! do not despise fear. I tell you, as long as you remain in that carnal lifeless state, like wine settled on its lees, you will never come to Christ. The Holy Spirit is like a dove, but the first thing he does is to convince of sin.

II.   I come now, in the second place, to consider *the ark*. 'By faith Noah, being warned of God of things not seen as yet, moved with fear, prepared an ark to the saving of his house.' We are told about the preparation of the ark in the 6th chapter of Genesis, 14th verse: 'Make thee an ark of gopher-wood: rooms shalt thou make in the ark, and shall pitch it within and without with pitch'; then, verse 16: 'A window shalt thou make to the ark, and in a cubit shalt thou finish it above: and the door of the ark shalt thou set in the side thereof, with lower, second, and third stories shalt thou make it'; verse 21: 'And take thou unto thee of all food that is eaten, and thou shalt gather it to thee; and it shall be for food to thee, and for them. Thus did Noah; according to all that God commanded him, so did he.' Observe, brethren, how completely the ark represents Christ. It was of God's planning; and so it is with Christ and the gospel salvation. All the men that lived could not have devised an ark to hold so many: so, in like manner, neither man nor angel could find out a way whereby the sinner could be saved. 'God so loved the world that he gave his only begotten Son.' It is said, the angels desire to look into the plan of redemption. It is said, 'it is unsearchable.' It is a plan that saves the sinner, and that gives glory to God. It is a plan laid so as to bring the sinner to God — a plan that gives glory to God in the highest, peace on earth, and good will to man. Observe still further, the strength of the ark. God knew what the billows were it would have to contend with. So it is with Christ; God made him strong enough to bear all that came against him, so that he is able to save to the utmost all that come unto God by him. And it was a roomy ark. So it is with Christ; the commission given to ministers is, 'Yet there is room.' And you will notice there was a door made in the side of it. So it was with Christ; there was a spear thrust into his side; so it is said, 'I am the door.' 'We both have access by one Spirit unto the Father.' 'He that cometh unto me I will in no wise cast out.' There are no steps up to it, so we have nothing to do but to believe. Again, there was a window on the top of it, that looked up to heaven. So, in Christ, we can look up to a reconciled God. Again, there was provision in the ark. So is there in Christ; 'My God shall supply all your need.' You need gold? Christ has it to bestow. You are polluted, and need a fountain? There is a fountain opened for sin and uncleanness. You are hungry, and need bread? Christ says, 'I am the bread of life.' There is everything you need in the ark. Brethren, how will you escape, if you neglect so great salvation? If you despise an ark so strong, so filled with provision, how will you escape?

III.   This leads me to the third point, and that is to inquire, *how Noah saved his house*. 'By faith Noah, being warned of God of things not seen as yet, moved with fear, prepared an ark to the saving of his house.' Noah saved his house by fleeing from all other refuges. Genesis 7.1: 'And the Lord said unto Noah, Come, thou and all thy house into the ark.' Verse 7: 'And Noah went in, and his sons, and his wife, and his sons' wives with him, into the ark, because of the waters of the flood. Of clean beasts, and of beasts that are not clean, and of fowls, and of every thing that creepeth upon the earth, there went in two and two unto Noah in the ark, the male and the female, as God had commanded Noah.' Observe, dear brethren, that the way in which Noah saved his house was by entering in. First of all, he entered in. Carnal men would have said, Better go to the top of the mountains; but Noah believed God, and fled from all other refuges; and not only did he go to the threshold, but he entered in, and his wife and his sons, and their wives with him, into the ark, and the Lord shut him in. So must it be with you if you would enter in. First of all, you must forsake all other arks. Carnal men will say, There are arks as good as it. Some rest in the ark of God's general mercy, but that is a false ark. Some rest in the ark of their decent moral character. Some rest in their knowledge of the ark, but these are all false arks; all that proceeds from man is false. Brethren, we must flee from all refuges of lies, and remember you must not stop on the threshold; there are many that look in, but do not enter in. There are many that know what is in the ark, but they do not enter in. But come thou into the ark, thou and thy wife, and thy sons' wives with thee, and the Lord will shut you in. You must not only hear about the ark, but you must enter in. You are not safe because you have wept and prayed. You are only safe when you enter in. 'If any man be in Christ he is a new creature: old things are passed away; behold, all things are become new.'

All the beasts entered in. There came a lion and a lioness — they, too, entered in. And then there came in the tall cattle; there came a camel-lopard, with its long majestic neck bent down — it, too, entered in. And then came the birds; the eagle that loves to soar aloft in the sky, and feed upon its prey — it, too, entered in. And then the creeping things; there came a serpent, and perhaps, Noah might say when he saw them creeping along the ground, 'These will bite us' — but they, too, entered in. So, brethren, it is true that all kinds of sinners may enter in. And it is sweet to see what a change came over them when they entered in. The lion lay down beside the lamb, and the leopard beside the kid. So it is with those that came to Christ. The lion-like nature is changed into the gentle nature of the lamb — the proud man is made humble. 'If any man be in Christ Jesus he is a new creature: old things are passed away; behold, all things are become new.' Some of you think you are Christ's, and yet your old nature is not taken away.

IV. *What came of the world.* It is said he condemned the world.
When Noah entered into the ark he condemned the world; not that
he judged them, for it is said he was a preacher of righteousness —
but he entered in, and thereby condemned the world. So is it yet;
when a child in an ungodly family is saved, he enters into the ark,
and thereby condemns those that do not. Brethren, the most of the
world did not know when Noah entered into the ark. Matthew 24.37:
'As the days of Noah were, so shall also the coming of the Son of man
be. For as in the days that were before the flood they were eating and
drinking, marrying and giving in marriage, until the day that Noah
entered into the ark, and knew not until the flood came, and took
them all away,' etc. Brethren, they were eating and drinking,
marrying and giving in marriage. The bride was standing up putting
her hand into the bridegroom's hand, and promising herself many
happy days — that day the flood came. Some said, Come, let us see a
man making a ship on the dry land. They mocked Noah until the day
that the flood came. So it is still. Though we tell you of a better ark,
yet you go on with your ways, 'Eating and drinking, marrying and
giving in marriage.' Brethren, I believe that the most of you, who
ever will be, are gathered already, you are becoming gospel proof,
and so you will live on, eating and drinking, marrying and giving in
marriage, until the flood of wrath come and sweep you away. Ah,
brethren, you mock at the man building the ark; you do this by not
entering in. Ah, my brethren, many of you say, when you see persons
striving to enter in, they are mad, and this is what they said to Noah.
O brethren! it is a happy madness to enter into the ark. But,
brethren, I believe that there are many that did not mock Noah, and,
perhaps, they helped to build the ark; they, perhaps, went and cut
down wood to build it, but they did not enter in. Ah! so it is with you;
there are many who say that we are good people, but we carry things
too far. Ah, there are many ministers who help to build the ark, that
do not enter in themselves; there are many Sabbath school teachers
help to build the ark, but do not enter in themselves. It is very
probable that some came down to the ark that morning when Noah
entered in; but it was too late; God had shut him in. I believe that
most of you will come when it is too late. I know that many of you
have your convictions, but do not enter in; you will come to the door
when it is shut, like the foolish virgins, saying, 'Lord, Lord, open to
us,' but he shall say, 'I know you not.' You will seek to enter in when
you hear the rumbling of the chariot of Emmanuel, but it will then
be too late. Brethren, it is the devil that is shutting your eyes from
seeing these things.

Last of all, it was an awful deluge that came. It came on them
before they were aware — when they were 'eating and drinking,

marrying and giving in marriage.' The taverns were all full — the bride was happy — all were full of mirth. And so it will be when the Son of man comes. It will be a sudden flood.

And it was a deep flood. It lifted the ark to the top of Ararat. It is calculated that the water rose four hundred feet the first day. Ah, brethren, it was a deep and awful flood, none were able to stand against it — it covered the proudest. Ah, brethren, it is the same word that reserves the world for a flood of fire. And it is said, 'In that day who shall be able to stand?' O be warned, by a sinful worm like yourselves, to flee! 'Can thine heart endure, or can thine hands be strong in the days that I shall deal with thee.' The flood came upon Christ, and oh, how fearful was his agony! But if you are his, it will not come upon you — if you are in this ark, you will be saved; but, if not, you will be lost. God pity you, dear friends, I cannot. God grant that he may do it, before the flood come and sweep you all away. Amen.

Sabbath Afternoon,
5th December 1842.

SERMON XVII

A GOSPEL MINISTRY THE GIFT OF CHRIST

Ephesians 4. 11-13. *And he gave some, apostles; and some prophets; and some, evangelists; and some, pastors and teachers, etc.*

It is six years today since I first preached to you as your minister, and it is three years today since I preached to you on my return home![1] These words lead you and me to inquire into the end of the ministry. It is for this reason that I have chosen this passage, that we may look into it, as into a mirror, and see ourselves.

I. Let us notice first, that *the gospel ministry is a gift from Christ,* verse 11; 'And he gave some, apostles; and some, prophets; and some, evangelists; and some, pastors and teachers.' It is Christ who sends them. 'He gave some, apostles; and some, prophets; and some, evangelists; and some, pastors and teachers; for the perfecting of the saints, for the work of the ministry, for the edifying of the body

---

1 Referring to his mission to the Jews.

of Christ.' It is quite true that he gave some of them before he ascended on high. He gave some before he left, as we are told by Mark — 3.13, 14, 'And he goeth up into a mountain, and calleth unto him whom he would: and they came unto him. And he ordained twelve, that they should be with him, and that he might send them forth to preach.' And yet, brethren, it is as true, that it was not till he ascended up on high, leading captivity captive — not till he shed forth the Spirit on the Church — it was not till *then* that he gave them; *before* they had little or no strength. We will just take the example of Peter; he trembled at the voice of a woman, but after Christ had ascended on high, and shed forth his Spirit, he stood before kings and rulers, and testified of Christ. So that it is quite true, when he ascended up on high, 'He gave some, apostles,' etc. It is quite true that pastors and teachers are chosen, not in an audible manner now; and yet it is true that every faithful pastor is raised up by Christ, and is his gift to the Church — 'I will give you pastors according to mine heart, who shall feed you with knowledge and understanding.' He often calls *weak* men to be ministers of Christ. And it is quite true that he chooses them before they are born. He said to Jeremiah — 1.5, 'Before I formed thee in the belly I knew thee; and before thou camest forth out of the womb I sanctified thee; and I ordained thee a prophet of the nation.' And what was true of Jeremiah, is also true of Paul; for he says, Gal. 1.15, 16, 'But when it pleased God, who separated me from my mother's womb, and called me by his grace, to reveal his Son in me, that I might preach him among the heathen: immediately I conferred not with flesh and blood.' And just as it is Christ that calls them before they are born, so he converts them for this very end. And it is also Christ that furnishes his ministers. He walks in the midst of the seven golden candlesticks, supplying all the branches with oil. And he places them. It is the same hand that guides the stars above, that guides the stars below.

From this let us learn, first of all, *to esteem ministers, as ministers of Christ.* I believe you will come one day to know that the ministry is one of Christ's best gifts. You know a gift is not valued on account of its intrinsic value, yet they are to be valued as being the gifts of Christ. I do not know, but I think that the ministry is not esteemed among you as it ought to be; I may be wrong, but I think it. You are like the horses that have got so much hay that they pull it down among their feet and trample on it.

Another lesson to be learned is, *if these are Christ's gifts, then you ought to ask for them.* Just as an affectionate father loves to be asked by his child for these things that he is willing to give, so ought you to ask Christ. 'Pray ye the Lord of the harvest that he would send forth labourers into his harvest.' Brethren, it is a great blessing that the calling of the ministry is put on a scriptural footing in this place; but remember, you must ask it, and just as it should be asked from Christ, so Christ should be thanked for it. 'Were not ten cleansed, but where are the nine?' Ah! this shows that unthankfulness is in our nature.

Another lesson we should learn from this is that, as *Christ gave pastors, so he may take them away:* 'The Lord gave,' Job says, 'and the Lord hath taken away, blessed be the name of the Lord.' He that gives children can take them away, and, in like manner, he that gives pastors and teachers, can withdraw them. If it is true that Christ is to withdraw his ministers in Scotland — if it is true that three hundred and forty pastors in Scotland are to be withdrawn, ah! then, you will see that he can take them away.[1]Ah brethren, though I feel that I have been unfaithful, far more than I can bear, yet you have been so too. Scotland has abused the ministry for a long time; many come to hear, and go away displeased — many come to hear and criticise. Ah! think if God take away your candlestick, it will be righteously done.

II. I come now to the second thing, and that is, *the use of the gospel ministry,* verse 12. I observe from these words, that the use of the gospel ministry is twofold: it is for perfecting those that are saints, and then for the edifying of the body of Christ.

1. *To perfect the saints.* This is one great half of the work of the ministry. It is the same that Christ spoke of to Peter, 'Lovest thou me?' then 'Feed my lambs, feed my sheep.' It is the same as what Peter wrote, 'The elders which are among you I exhort. Feed the flock of God which is among you.' It is the same which Paul spoke of to the Ephesian elders, 'Take heed to the flock over the which the Holy Ghost hath made you overseers, to feed the church of God which he hath purchased with his own blood.' Now, this is one great half of the gospel ministry, to feed the lambs and the sheep. I feel, brethren, that I have greatly omitted this part of my ministry among you because of the cry of the wicked, they are so many. Often in my secret retirement, when poring over my Bible, I have been driven past those texts which are for the perfecting of the saints, to be made a son of thunder. Observe, brethren, that the pastoral work is twofold: we are to perfect you in knowledge, and we are to make you perfect in practice.

We are to perfect you in knowledge. When Paul wrote to the Corinthians, he told them that they came behind in no

---

1 Referring to the impending Disruption of 1843.

gift. Ah! I feel that this does not apply to us. I fear that the words of Paul to the Hebrews are more applicable: 'For when for the time ye ought to be teachers, ye have need that one teach you again which be the first principles of the oracles of God.' How little knowledge believers as yet have of their own hearts — how little knowledge you have of Christ — how little knowledge of the wiles of the devil — how much need have we to become *more fully acquainted* with the Word of God. The other half of the pastoral work is to make you perfect in practice. Many among you think that it is not desirable to be complete Christians. Now, this is a great mistake; the great object of the gospel ministry is to get you entirely like Christ — is to get you entire Christians — Christians in public and Christians in private.

2. Let me speak now of the other half of the work of the ministry, that is, *the edifying of the body of Christ.* Now, the word 'edify' is used in two ways in the New Testament. First, it refers to the work of a mason; he polishes and prepares stones, and then puts them on a building, so that it grows higher and higher. This is exactly the work of the ministry. See 1 Peter 2.5: 'Ye also as lively stones are built up a spiritual house.' Then 'edify' also means 'to sanctify.' See Acts 9.31: 'Then had the churches rest throughout Judea and Galilee and Samaria, and were edified; and walking in the fear of the Lord and in the comfort of the Holy Ghost, were multiplied.' In our text, the word seems to have the first of these meanings — that is, of bringing stones to a building. But perhaps both ideas are intended. The use of the ministry is not only to bring stones to the building, but also to raise it; this has been where I have failed, and yet I think I can say, I have never risen a morning without thinking how I could bring more souls to Christ. It is not the work of a minister to wear a peculiar garb, or to baptize; nor is it the work of a minister to marry. This is not the work of the ministry. The great use of the ministry — engrave it on your hearts, tell it to your children — that the use of the ministry is to convert your soul. Ah! brethren, if we part, and you are not saved, then you will wish that we had never met — that you had been born in Africa, whose woods never resounded with the glad tidings of salvation. I am deeply persuaded that you do not believe this, that unless you are saved, our ministry is of no use to you. You may think you have got some good, but, if you are not converted to Christ, our ministry has been in vain for you. 'I beseech you, brethren, that you receive not the grace of God in vain.'

III.   I now come to the third and last point and that is, *the great end and consummation:* verse 13. This verse is difficult, and I therefore request you will give your attention to it. There is a glorious time coming, and it is described in three ways. First, it is described as being one — one in faith, etc. Then it is described as the time when the man will be perfect. And lastly, it is described as reaching unto the measure of the stature of the fulness of Christ. It is described as a time when all believers will be one, one in unity, one in faith, one in knowledge. At present we are different; we do not all believe the same thing, but the time is coming when we will be all one; we will not be all one in experience — that will never be; but there is one thing in which we will be the same, that is, faith; every man and woman will see a oneness in Christ.

And then it is called the time of a perfect man. You know, brethren, a man is not a perfect man if he wants anything, if he wants a hand, or an arm, or a finger. But when the last sinner is saved, then the man will be perfect; and this is explained fuller in what follows. We are told in the same epistle that it is the fulness of his body, the Church; so that Christ is not fully complete until all are brought in. Now, this will be seen when we will be brought to the measure of the stature of the fulness of Christ.

Learn from this:

1. *That the ministry is an ordinance of the Lord Jesus Christ, till he come.*

2. *That when Christ s body is completed, then there will be room for no more.* At present ministers are sent to say, 'Yet there is room.' But there is a day when Christ mystical shall be complete, and Christ will never want another added — Christ's body will be saved. Ah, brethren, what a thought it will be if you perish, that it is Christ's glory that you should perish, and that his body should be complete without you.

3. *To pray for oneness, till the day come when Christ will reach to perfection,* when all shall see eye to eye. I am assured that there are times coming when there will be rents in the Church, when the question will be, Who have a right to sit at the Lord's table? And therefore, as long as I have a voice to speak, I will plead still that there be oneness of the body of Christ.   Amen.

Sabbath Forenoon,
27th November 1842.

SERMON XVIII

THE CALL OF ABRAHAM

Genesis 12.1-3. *Now the Lord had said unto Abram, Get thee out of thy country, and from thy kindred, and from thy father's house, into a land that I will show thee: And I will make of thee a great nation, and I will bless thee and make thy name great; and thou shalt be a blessing: And I will bless them that bless thee, and curse him that curseth thee: and in thee shall all the families of the earth be blessed.*
Compare this with Acts 7.2, 3; Heb. 11.8.

In these words, dear brethren, we have an account of the conversion of Abraham. This is the record given us of the second birth of Abraham. My dear friends, it is the second birth that will be remembered in heaven, and not the first. You know it is common for men to keep their birth-days. Now, the second birth-day is what we will remember in heaven — it is what we will tell the angels in glory: 'Come, hear, all ye that fear God — I'll tell what he did for my soul.'
Let us notice from these words:
1. Abraham's conversion.
2. Abraham's trial.
3. Abraham's promise.
I. *Abraham's conversion.* 'Now the Lord had said unto Abraham'; or as Stephen says, 'The God of glory appeared unto our father Abraham.' Let us observe first, *the great sovereignty of God in the conversion of this man.* We are told by Stephen that he was in Mesopotamia at the time. It is a beautiful country — an immense plain lying between the Tigris and the Euphrates. We learn from the previous chapter that it was a place of great wickedness. It was the place where Nimrod, the great robber, dwelt — or, as he is called, 'The great hunter.' And it was the country where they built the tower of Babel. It was also the land, as we are told by Jeremiah, of graven images. It is believed by divines that it was the place where they first bowed down to graven images. Jer. 50. 38, 'For it is the land of graven images, and they are mad upon their idols.' Another remarkable fact connected with this land was, that the very family out of which Abraham was chosen worshipped graven images. Josh. 24. 2: 'And Joshua said unto all the people, Thus saith the Lord God of Israel, Your fathers dwelt on the other side of the flood in old time (that is, on the other side of the Euphrates), even Terah, the father of Abraham, and the father of Nahor; and they served other gods.' Such was the country, and such the family out of which God raised

Abraham. You would have thought that God would not have come into such a place; and, O brethren! you would have thought, least of all, that he would have come to the house of Terah, who served other gods! Again, you wonder why he came to Abraham. You would have thought he would have come to Terah. Why, then, did he take Abraham — a man seventy years old — spent in sin? — 'Even so, Father, for so it seemeth good in thy sight.' When he looked down upon that great plain, why did he come to the house of Terah, and say to Abraham, 'Get thee out of thy country, and from thy kindred, and from thy father's house, unto a land that I will show thee?' Ah, brethren, God is a God of grace. None of you can say, 'He came to me because I sought him.' How often has God come into this place and gone into the most wicked family, and drawn out those that were deepest down in the pit, just to show how deep his hand could reach?

But notice who it was that converted him: 'The *Lord* had said unto Abraham.' Stephen tells it more fully: 'The God of glory appeared unto our father Abraham.' I have no doubt that it was the same glorious person that appeared to Jacob at the top of the ladder, and blessed him. I have no doubt that it was the same that met with Jacob when it is said, 'There wrestled a man with him until the breaking of the day: and he said, Let me go, for the day breaketh; but he said, I will not let thee go, except thou bless me.' I have no doubt but that it was the same that appeared to Saul when on his way to Damascus. So, in like manner, it was the same God of glory that appeared unto Abraham, and said, 'Get thee out of thy country, and from thy kindred, and from thy father's house, unto the land that I will show thee.' Brethren, all conversion comes from God. You might rather expect the icebergs of the Atlantic to melt without the sun than expect a sinner's heart to change without God. Brethren, it was not Abraham that sought him, but the God of glory that came to him, and said, 'Behold, I stand at the door and knock. If Abraham hear my voice, and open the door, I will come in to him, and sup with him, and he with me.' It is not you that seek his face, but he that seeks you. Brethren, it is not a minister's coming to you that will save you. Who sat under a godlier minister than Judas? Yet he got no grace by it.

But, further, it is said 'the God of glory appeared unto him.' This is what Christ says — 'Abraham rejoiced to see my day, and he saw it and was glad.' I do not pretend to say how much was revealed to him. It is curious to remark how much Christ reveals himself to some. 'The first time,' said one, 'that I remember of ever tasting of the sweetness and blessedness of the gospel was in reading these words — "Now, unto the King eternal, immortal, invisible, the only wise God, be honour and glory for ever and ever. Amen." Never words of scripture appeared to me like these words; they came into my soul with such power and tenderness, and I longed to possess such a being as my God.' Such was the experience of one of the most eminent saints that ever lived. It perhaps was such that Abraham got, and that made him leave his father's house. And, brethren, it is the same truth that will convert a soul now. You *may* be moved with fear, as Noah was, but you *must* be drawn by love. I believe that never a soul was converted without a sight of the God of glory.

I have just one observation more on this part of the subject, and that is *the almighty power by which it was done*. You will see this very evidently shown in Isaiah 41.2, 'Who raised up the righteous man from the east, called him to his foot, gave the nations before him, and made him rule over kings?' etc. Notice also what is said in the fifty-first chapter, 1st and 2nd verses — 'Hearken unto me, ye that follow after righteousness, ye that seek the Lord; look unto the rock whence ye are hewn, and to the hole of the pit whence ye are digged. Look unto Abraham your father, and unto Sarah that bare you; for I called him alone, and blessed him, and increased him.' Now, in these two passages you will notice that God says it was he himself that called Abraham. And observe the words used are very remarkable — I found him like a rock, yet I melted the rock. God found him fallen down to graven images, and he called him to his foot. My dear friends, this is the way God does with every soul whom he converts. God finds you like a rock; yet of these stones he raises up children to Abraham. This is my only hope of those of you who are unconverted. I have no hope of the words of man; but I would trust in God — my hope is in his Word. He that raised up the righteous man is able to call you, and make you willing in the day of his power.

II. *Abraham's trial.* 'Get thee out of thy country, and from thy kindred, and from thy father's house, unto the land that I will show thee.' The trial of Abraham was two-fold: First, he was tried in what he was to leave: Second, in that he did not know where he was to go.

1. *In what he was to leave.* 'Get thee out of thy country.' One's country is dear to him. The Greenlander loves his icy region, and the Arab loves his sterile sand, and we love our own brown hills. But God said to Abraham, 'Get thee out of thy country.' And every man loves his kindred. We do not like to bid those we love farewell. Will strangers care for them? — will strangers be kind to them? — are thoughts that occur to our mind. Yet this was God's command to Abraham — 'Get thee out of thy country, and from thy kindred.' But the worst was yet to come — 'Out of thy father's house.' We love our father's house. Our father's house is dear to us. I do not envy the man that does not love his father's house. Yet God said, 'Get thee out

of thy father's house.'

2.   But there was a second trial. *He did not know where he was to go.* 'Unto a land that I will show thee.' What kind of a land is it, Lord? — 'I will show thee.' Will the people be kind? — 'I will show thee.' Was it north, east, south or west? — He did not know. 'He went out not knowing whither he went.' 'Get thee unto a land that I will show thee.' Who can tell the deep anxiety that appeared in Abraham's countenance and tossed in his bosom, as he walked before his father's house that night he got the command to go? Ah! brethren, this is what every converted soul has to undergo: 'Get thee out of thy country, and from thy kindred, and from thy father's house.' I will tell you what you will have to leave, if you will follow Christ. First, *you must leave the esteem of your friends.* I do not say you should leave your father's house bodily. God forbid! But you must leave their esteem. Perhaps they loved you as a friend, as a wife, as a husband; but the more they loved you they will now hate you the more. The mother hates the viper that stung her child; so will they hate you. Do not be surprised at this. 'If any man will not leave father and mother and all, for my sake and the gospel, he cannot be my disciple.' Brethren, do not think I am telling you stories. If the God of glory appears to you, you will find it true. Another thing is, *you will have to leave the company of the ungodly.* I do not say, if you are in an ungodly family you are to leave it. No, but you are not to mix with ungodly families. Another thing you will have to leave is your *idols.* Abraham did this. You must break your idols in pieces. 'Come out from among them.' 'Get thee out of thy country, and from thy kindred, and from thy father's house.' And, O brethren! you must leave them for an unseen Saviour and an unseen heaven. Remember you must walk with an unseen Saviour. Some of you will say, What will be given me? He will give you joy and peace. Remember also, 'It doth not yet appear what we shall be; but we know that when he shall appear we shall be like him.'

III.   *Abraham's promise.* Verses 2, 3: 'And I will make of thee a great nation, and I will bless thee, and make thy name great; and thou shalt be a blessing; And I will bless them that bless thee and curse him that curseth thee; and in thee shall all the families of the earth be blessed.' We have here six blessings following one another.

1.   '*I will make thee a great nation.*' God was taking him out of a great nation; but he said, 'I will make of *thee* a great nation.' So he says to all that he calls, 'I will make you one of a righteous nation' — 'I will make of thee a great nation.'

2.   '*I will bless thee.*' God did not tell him where he was going, what enemies he would meet with, what trials he would encounter, yet he said, 'I will bless thee.' This is what God says to you — If you are

willing to leave all for Christ, 'I will bless thee.' Perhaps your friends will curse thee, but 'I will bless thee.'

3. *'I will make thy name great.'* When he went from his father's house, he went where his name was not known; and, perhaps, they mocked him when he went away; but God called him 'my friend.' So perhaps it will be with you; yet God will make thy name great.

4. *'And thou shalt be a blessing.'* Abraham had been a curse by his example — he had worshipped graven images; but God said he would be a blessing. So he says to you, brethren, No doubt you have been a curse — no doubt you have led many to hell by your wicked example; yet I will make thee a blessing — a blessing to your children, a blessing to your wife, a blessing to your neighbours, a blessing to the world; the world will miss you when you die.

5. *'I will bless them that bless thee, and curse him that curseth thee.'* Abraham was to meet friends and enemies. There were some in another land that would be kind to the stranger, and there were some that would cast him out. 'Well,' says God, 'I will bless them that bless thee, and curse him that curseth thee.' God is with thee, Abraham; God is thy wall of fire. Ah, brethren! it is sweet to have God's blessing.

6. *'In thee shall all families of the earth be blessed.'* This last promise was fulfilled when out of Abraham's loins Christ was born. It cannot be performed to us in the same way; but yet it can in one way. If you are Christ's then, wherever you are, you will be a blessing.

O brethren! if you would follow Christ, count the cost. The Lord enable you to count the cost. Amen.

Sabbath Forenoon,
9th December 1842.

SERMON XIX

THE QUARREL BETWEEN ABRAHAM AND LOT

Genesis 13.7-13. *And there was a strife between the herdmen of Abram's cattle and the herdmen of Lot's cattle. And the Canaanite and the Perizzite dwelt then in the land. And Abram said to Lot, Let there be no strife, I pray thee, between me and thee, and between my herdmen and thy herdmen; for we be brethren.*

Domestic trials are not easy to bear. Most believers would like to go to heaven without a crook in their lot. I have no doubt that Jacob would have liked to have gone to heaven without the trial he had in the loss of Joseph; I have no doubt that David would have liked to have gone to heaven without the trial he had in the death of Absalom; and I have no doubt that Abraham would have liked to have gone to the better land without this strife breaking out between Lot and him. But it must not be.

The reason why domestic trials happen are — first, for the trial of our faith. Just as the jeweller puts the gold into the crucible, not to destroy the gold, but to separate it from the dross, so trials are intended by God to separate us from all dross. Another reason is to make us long for the better country. When God permits strife to rise in a believing family, it is to show you that this is not our home.

I. But let us notice this *domestic trial*, verse 7: 'And there was a strife between the herdmen of Abraham's cattle and the herdmen of Lot's cattle.' etc. You remember, brethren, how the God of glory appeared unto our father Abraham, while he was in Mesopotamia, before he dwelt in Haran; and you remember how he left his country and his father's house, to go into a land which God was to show him. Now, when Abraham came into this land, he, no doubt, thought his trials were all over. Like the meandering river winding its way to the ocean, he thought that his way would now be smooth and easy. He thought he would have no disquietude in his way to heaven; but, ah! when he heard the cry of his servant and the servants of Lot as they strove together, how changed would be his feelings? Now, this quarrel was very sinful. They were both very rich. You are told in the 2nd verse, that 'Abraham was very rich in cattle, in silver and in gold'; and then, verse 3, 'And Lot also, which went with Abram, had flocks, and herds, and tents.' They had as much of this world's goods as they knew well what to do with. If the one had been rich and the other poor, then there might have been some seeming cause to quarrel. How often is this the case in the world? — a family which was once poor gets rich, and often quarrels ensue.

Another thing that made this quarrel sinful was that *they were friends*. Lot was Abraham's brother's son. And they were near relations in the Lord. I suppose Abraham was Lot's spiritual father, and so when he left his father's house, he invited Lot to go with him; and yet they strove together, even though they were brethren. Ah! there is something peculiarly sinful in the strife of those who are related in the Lord. Some of you may think that you will never strive with those whom you have been indebted to in the Lord. It was thus with Paul and the Galatians. At one time they would have plucked out their eyes and given them to him, but they were soon removed unto another gospel, which was yet not another, and they hated him as much as once they had loved him.

Another thing that made this strife sinful was that '*the Canaanite and the Perizzite dwelt then in the land.*' There is no doubt that this is put in to show its sinfulness. When the Canaanite and the Perizzite saw Abraham every morning building his altar and slaying his lamb, and in the evening assembling his children around his tent door, and 'catechising them,' as the original means, there is no doubt they would wonder what sort of people these were; but ah! when they saw the servant's staves raised against one another, they would say, Ah, they are just like other men. It is just the same still; when Christians go to law with Christians, and when you have family quarrels, does not the world say the same? They see you go to a solitary place and there hold mysterious converse with God, and they hear you singing praise to him, and they say, Let us watch these people, and see what will become of them; and ah! when they see you strive together — when they hear your high words, what can they think? Ah! this is to sin in the sight of the Canaanite and the Perizzite.

II. *The generosity of Abraham*, verses 8, 9: 'And Abram said unto Lot, Let there be no strife, I pray thee, between thee and me, and between my herdmen and thy herdmen; for we be brethren. Is not the whole land before thee? Separate thyself, I pray thee, from me: if thou wilt take the left hand, then I will go to the right; or if thou depart to the right hand, then I will go to the left.' You may read in connection with this the 14th and 15th verses: 'And the Lord said unto Abram, after that Lot was separated from him, Lift up now thine eyes, and look from the place where thou art, northward, and southward, and eastward, and westward; for all the land which thou seest, to thee will I give it, and to thy seed for ever.' It is quite evident that Abraham was a man of peace; *that* truth was engraven on his inmost soul — 'As much as in you lies, live peaceably with all men.' Thus he did to Lot. I have no doubt but that Lot felt the sinfulness of this strife; therefore Abraham says, 'Let there be no strife, I pray thee.' But then comes the question, Who shall yield? I think it should have been Lot. God had already given the land to Abraham: 'I will give it thee.' And another reason why Lot should have yielded was, he was the younger of the two, and it was to Abraham Lot owed all he had, and surely it was becoming that the younger should yield to the elder. And another reason which worldly men would have urged was, that Abraham was the richer of the two. It is said that Abraham 'was rich in cattle, in silver, and in gold.' Just think what such men would have done in like circumstances: God has given me the land, and shall I yield it to you? Where there is might, there is right. I am quite sure this would have been the way worldly men would have acted. But observe how differently Abraham acted: verse 8, 'Let there be no strife, I pray thee, between me and thee, and between my herdmen and thy herdmen; for we be brethren. Is not the whole land before thee? Separate thyself, I pray thee, from me; if thou will take to the left hand, then I will go to the right; or if thou depart to the right hand, then I will go to the left.' Abraham yields the choice to Lot. Brethren, this 'is what it is to be a Christian, this is what Christ did. Do you remember the command to resist not evil? Matt. 5.39, 'But I say unto you, that ye resist not evil; but whosoever shall smite thee on thy right cheek, turn to him the other also.' Now, many of you do not know the meaning of this; I have been asked its meaning often; now, this is it: Abraham was smitten on the one cheek, and he turned the other also. See also 1 Cor. 6.7. 'Now therefore, there is utterly a fault among you, because ye go to law with one another: why do ye not rather take wrong? why do ye not rather suffer yourselves to be defrauded?' You will see an example of the same thing in the 9th chapter and 19th verse, 'For although I be free from all men, yet have I made myself servant unto all, that I might gain the more,' etc. My dear brethren, this is exactly what Abraham did, he suffered himself to be defrauded, he suffered himself to be a servant, that he might gain Lot. This was what Christ did himself. When they smote him on the one cheek he turned the other also. Ah, brethren, you know little of the love of Christ, if this is not in your heart. There is a great mistake, I observe, in our day; people think that to be a Christian, is to have certain doctrines in the head — to be a Calvinist; but, remember, that to be a Christian, is to have Christ in you. Abraham did not say, I will have it, for it is my right to have it. No! but he said, 'Let us separate; if you go to the right hand, I will go to the left,' etc. Ah! this is to be a Christian. It is not words that will make a Christian. It is not views that will make a Christian. It is this, and this alone.

III. I now come to the last point, and that is, to consider *the choice of Lot*, verse 10: 'And Lot lifted up his eyes, and beheld all the plain of Jordan, that it was well watered everywhere, before the Lord destroyed Sodom and Gomorrah, even as the garden of the Lord; like the land of Egypt, as thou comest unto Zoar.' And then, verse 13: 'But the men of Sodom were wicked, and sinners before the Lord exceedingly.' It is probable that Abraham and Lot were standing on the high ground near Hebron. It commands a great view, both east and west. When you look to the west, the eye stretches over a large wilderness-land of vast extent, to where the sun sets, in all its glory, in the Mediterranean; and, when you look to the east, you observe the hills of Moab, and the rich plain of Sodom, well watered every where. There was no Dead Sea with its pestiferous waters then. So that, when Lot lifted up his eyes and saw the plain, it reminded him of what his father had told him of the garden of the Lord, where our first parents were before that viper sin had entered the world. Then said Lot, that will be my land, and that will be my choice. Ah! it was rashly done. He judged by the sight of the eye. He had to leave the dwelling and the altar of Abraham. Read the 18th chapter of Genesis, and see what it was to have Abraham's prayers and council; and yet in that rash choice he bade farewell to all. He forgot Abraham's tent, he forgot Abraham's altar, he forgot Abraham's morning and evening prayers. You who have chosen the world in preference to Christ, what is there in it to make up for a believer's prayers? And then he forgot that the men of Sodom were wicked, and sinners before the Lord exceedingly. It appears that he did not go directly in, but he pitched his tent toward Sodom. O what a change! — to the men of Sodom from the tent of Abraham! O what a change from the prayers of Abraham to their swearing! A rash choice, to be repented of. And there was another thing he did not take into account, that God would destroy Sodom. When he looked on that lovely scene as the sun cast its rays over it, and on the beautiful river as it glided past, he thought it was a place well suited for him to dwell in; but ah! he did not know that there was a dark cloud behind — he forgot that Abraham had told him of the flood. Abraham had, no doubt, told him how God had destroyed the world by a flood on account of its wickedness; but yet for all that he pitched his tent toward Sodom. Ah! are there not many who go from parish to parish, and from country to country? and why? just to better their circumstances, without thinking whether they will be under a faithful ministry or not. Are there none here? — a young man, perhaps, who is leaving his father's house. What are you doing it for? Is it for a well-watered garden, or have you sought an Abraham's tent? And there are some here who are looking for partners for life? Who are you choosing? — are you leaving an Abraham's tent for a well-watered garden? Look well whom you

choose. Last of all, are there servants here choosing a place? How do
you choose? — is it for more wages? is it the fatness of the valley? or
is it for an Abraham's tent? The Lord grant that you may make the
right choice.   Amen.

SERMON XX

HIGH TIME TO AWAKE OUT OF SLEEP

Romans 13.11. *And that, knowing the time, that now it is high time
to awake out of sleep: for now is our salvation nearer than
when we believed.*

In these words, Paul tells believers that it is waking time; and I
would just tell you, dear friends, the same. It is high time for you to
awake out of sleep. There is a condition among Christians which
may be called sleeping; like the ten virgins, they slumber and sleep.
Ah! I fear there are many sleeping Christians among you. It is
waking time, believer, Do you know what o'clock it is? You do not
seem to know how near sun-rise it is.
   I will now show you what it is to be *sleeping Christians*. It is to be
one that has come to Christ, yet has fallen asleep in sin. Like the
Church at Ephesus, they have left their first love. They do not retain
that realization of the Christ's preciousness — that freshness of believing. They have forgotten the fresh grasp of a Saviour. So it is with
some among yourselves. You may have seen your sins; yet you have
lost that fresh conviction of sin you once felt so deeply. You do not
see such a beauty in Jesus. The more we look at him, just the more
we would look again. Earthly things pall upon the taste; but it is not
so with things divine — they grow sweeter the oftener you use them.
So every time you look at Jesus, he grows more precious. The rose is
sweet, yet it loses its smell; but the lovely Rose of Sharon grows
sweeter and sweeter. Earthly apples lose their taste; but the apple-
tree does not so — 'Stay me with the flagons, comfort me with
apples, for I am sick of love.' Sleepy Christians, you have lost taste
for the apples. Oh! is it not time for you to awake out of sleep?
Believer, if you sleep on, you will soon doubt if ever you have come to
Christ at all.

To awake out of sleep, then, is to see that *divine things are realities*. When you are half asleep, you see things imperfectly. Ah! you are not affected by divine realities. Now, what is it to awake out of sleep? To awake out of sleep is to see sin as it is — your heart as it is — Christ as he is — and the love of God in Christ Jesus. And you can see all this by looking to Calvary's cross. O it is an awful thing to look to the cross and not be affected, nor feel conviction of sin — nor feel drawn to Christ! O I do not know a more sad state than this! O pray that you may be wide awake! Dear friends, our life is like a river, and we are like a boat sailing down that river. We are drawing nearer and nearer to the shores of eternity. Some of you have believed for forty years. Ah! your salvation is nearer than when you first believed. Your redemption draweth nigh — the redemption of your whole soul — your complete redemption. And the time is coming when we will get it — you will be saved, and then the last stone will be put on with shoutings of 'Grace! grace! unto it.' Then will the crown be put upon your heads, for you will be more than conquerors.

Dear friends, I do not know how far the day is spent. This is a dark, dark time; but the day is breaking — the shadows are fleeing away. The river Euphrates is drying up — that shows the day is breaking. The Jews, God's ancient people, are being brought in, and that shows the day is far spent.

And it is also high time for *unconverted men to awake out of sleep*. O sinners! you are fast asleep, you are lying dormant — dead! O sleepy souls! it is high time you should awake! Do you know what angels said when they went to and fro upon the earth? They told the Lord, 'Behold, all the earth sitteth still and is at rest.' Ah! you are fast asleep. God has given you the spirit of slumber. Do you not remember the message to Amos — 'Woe to them that are at ease in Zion'? And that is the case with many of you. When you come to this house, you are in a place where Jesus has called sleepy souls, and where he has been found of very many. O sleeping souls, it is high time for you to awake! You are living in a dream. Every Christless man will find at last that he has been dreaming. Ah! the time is coming when you shall find that your following after gold is but a golden dream. And is there no pleasure in a dream? Who has not felt that there is pleasure even in dreams? But, ah! you must awake. Like a man condemned to die (and many of you are condemned already), he dreams of home, of his wife and children; of freedom and pleasure; but, ah! he awakes by the toll of the death-bell, and he finds that — behold it was but a dream! Now, unconverted men, you are taking a sleep; but, like the man, you will awake from a bright dream to a bitter reality. Dear friends, I often think when I look at your houses as I pass along, and when I look in your faces, that ministers are like watchmen — they see the fire and they give the alarm. Many of you are in danger as one in a burning house. Sometimes you wonder at our anxiety for you. Sometimes you say, 'Why are you so harsh?' O poor soul! it is because the house is on fire. O then, can we speak too harshly? — can we knock too loudly at the door of your consciences? I remember what a woman once told John Newton on her death-bed: she said, 'You often spoke to me of Christ; but Oh! you did not tell me enough about my danger.' Oh! I fear many of you will tell me the same. Oh! I fear many may reproach me on a death-bed, or in hell, that I did not tell you oftener that there was a hell. Would to God I had none to reproach me at last! God help me to speak to you plainly! It is high time to awake out of sleep, sinner: for now your damnation slumbereth not. Dear friends, it is now more than three years since I first spoke to you, though it just seems like a day since I first came beseeching you to be reconciled to God — beseeching you to come to Jesus. Every day that passes is bringing you nearer to the judgment-seat. Not one of you is standing still. You may sleep; but the tide is going on, bringing you nearer death, judgment, and eternity.

Dear friends, another reason for awaking is, *your condemnation is still getting greater and greater*. When I first came among you your guilt was not so great as now. 'Despisest thou the riches of his goodness, and forbearance, and long-suffering; not knowing that the goodness of God leadeth thee to repentance? But after thy hardness and impenitent heart, treasurest up unto thyself wrath against the day of wrath, and revelation of the righteous judgment of God.' — Romans 2.4, 5. Do any of you know that you are treasuring up wrath against the day of wrath? You are laying up in the bank. You are laying up wrath for a coming eternity. Will this not convince you that it is high time to awake out of sleep? It is time tonight to put on the Lord Jesus. It is high time, sleeper. It is the very time. Will ye not awake? Ah! I can tell you one thing — you will find it all true at last, that you have treasured up wrath against the day of wrath. Every sin is a drop of wrath; which, like a river dammed up, gets deeper and deeper and fuller, till at last it bursts forth. Oh! are there not many misers of wrath here? Do you not see that it is high time for you to awake out of sleep before you have an infinity of wrath laid up? Awake *now*, and it may be all taken away. There is one ready to take it away if ye will but apply to him. Sinner! awake then!

Another reason is, that *opportunities of awaking are passing away*. Now, I do say there are times of awaking. There is a time when the ark is passing by your houses; and if you allow it to pass, you will find one day, when you would step in, that you will be overcome by the angry waters. You remember the little man of Jericho, Zaccheus. Jesus was passing through Jericho on his way to Jerusalem to be crucified. It was the last time he was to pass that way: it was the last time Zaccheus could see the Saviour. When Jesus was to pass, lest he should be lost among the crowd, he climbed up into a sycamore tree. Jesus passed, looked up, and said, 'Zaccheus, come down; for today I must abide at thy house.' Oh! had he not come down that moment from the sycamore tree — had he not made haste to come down — he would have come down and gone to a lost eternity. Had he not that hour closed with Jesus, he would have gone to that place where there is no voice of mercy, for Jesus passed by for the last time. And I do say, sinner, if you do not come down from your sycamore tree, and receive Christ tonight, you may not be permitted tomorrow. Now is the accepted time. O come to him *now*! O you will rejoice for ever if you entertain him joyfully tonight! Sleepy sinner! now awake! It is high time to awake; for the time is at hand when there will be no Bible — no more offers of mercy. We have many precious ordinances now; but they will all come to an end too. O make haste, then, and come down, and Jesus this night will abide in your house! He is saying, 'Behold I stand at the door and knock. If any man hear my voice, and open the door, I will come in to him, and will sup with him, and he with me.' Had Zaccheus slept, he would never have seen Jesus; and if you do not awake, alas! alas! for the day comes when you shall wail because of him.   Amen.

Thursday Evening,
2nd April 1840.

SERMON XXI

THE SAVIOUR'S TEARS OVER THE LOST

Luke 19.41, 42. *And when he was come near, he beheld the city, and wept over it, saying, If thou hast known, even thou, at least in this thy day, the things which belong unto thy peace! but now they are hid from thine eyes.*

Jesus Christ is the same yesterday, today, and for ever. He is the same Saviour now that he was that day when he wept over Jerusalem. If he were on earth now as he was then. I have no doubt but that there are many here tonight over whom he would weep, as he did over impenitent Jerusalem. I would show you from these words that:

1. The gospel is what belongs to your peace.
2. There is a day of grace.
3. Christ is willing and anxious to save sinners.

I. *The gospel is what belongs to a man's peace.* 'There is no peace, saith my God, unto the wicked.' *It belongs to your peace of conscience.* Sin is the cause of all sorrow, and the very reason that you are miserable is, because you are the servant of sin. It is the gospel that first brings peace to an anxious sinner. In it Christ and his righteousness are set forth, and it is a saving sight of him that makes the burden fall off a sinner's back. Those of you who have come to Christ have peace: even in the midst of raging lusts and temptations, you have peace. When once you are under grace, you can say, 'Sin shall no more have dominion over me.' Even when there seems to be no way of escape, either on this side or on that — even when the world is spreading out the net to ensnare the soul, still, if the eye be fixed on a living Jesus, that soul can have peace. None have true peace but those that are beholding the Lamb of God which taketh away the sin of the world. Sinner, the gospel, for as much as you despise it, is what belongs unto your peace. There is no peace out of Christ — there is no peace and safety here in this world, where Satan's darts are flying so thick, but under the wings of Jesus. No doubt, many have peace who are out of Christ — they are quite happy, although living under the wrath and curse of God; but what is the reason? The secret lies in this, they are blind, insensible, spiritually dead. They do not know their own selves. They think they are safe, while, alas! they are standing on the brink of hell. Oh! sinner, that is the reason you are so happy; but there is a day coming, when the peace of the most careless carnal sinner among you will be eternally broken.

2. *In a time of trouble the gospel peculiarly belongs to your*

peace. Man is born to trouble. The past year has proved that in many of your families there have been many sicknesses, many deaths, and many last farewells among you. Who knows what will take place before this night next year? The unconverted have got no peace in the hour of trouble, — they have no anchor when the storm rages — no fountain of peace — no covert from the tempest. What an awful and miserable thing it must be, to be without peace when the storm comes. It must surely be an important thing to get into Christ, before trouble, and sickness, and death comes. In truth, the gospel does belong to your peace. All the time I have been among you, I have been offering you peace. If you get Christ, you will get peace; if you never get Christ, you will never get peace. Christ is a covert from every wind. As long as you have no sickness or trouble, you may be stout-hearted, and have a kind of peace; but ah! what will you do in the hour of your calamity? 'Can thine heart endure or can thine hands be strong in the days that I shall deal with thee?'

3. *The gospel gives peace at death.* What can give you peace, O sinner, in the hour of death? Can a neglected Bible give you peace? Will it comfort you to remember that you have lived contrary to God all your life? Will you look back with pleasure on your wicked life then? Will your merry company make you merry then? Where will all your mirth have gone to in that day? Will your money avail you in the day of wrath? What will the end be of those that obey not the gospel? Will it be peace, sinner? Ah no! At present you mock at God's people, and scorn the very thought of conversion, and do you think the end of that will be peace? You may think so. You may think these things will not make death terrible; but, oh! sinner, it is just because Satan is blinding your eyes. Sin is the sting of death; yea, these very sins which you now hug in your bosom. Your sweet cup will be poison at death. You think it sweet now; but in the end it will bite like an adder. As sure as you are sitting here tonight, as sure as this year is passing over your heads, so sure will thy sins be turned into the worm that dieth not, and the fire that is never quenched. The judgment is at hand. Does not, then, the gospel belong to your peace? Some of you will, I believe, remember in the day of your calamity, and when there is no voice of a freely preached gospel in this house, the time when the living water ran clear at your feet, and then, *then* you will confess that these things belong to your peace, when they are for ever hid from your eyes. O sinner! Christ belongs to your peace. He alone can give you peace. He took away the sting of death in his own body. He is our peace. For many a year now, I have been preaching peace to you. I have been a peace-maker. And O brethren! why is it that you will not receive it? Why is it that ye do always resist the truth? Why will ye yet despise Christ and his

gospel? O that you would be wise in time, and give heed unto those things which belong unto your peace!

II. I come now to show you *there is a day of grace*. 'If thou hadst known, even thou, at least in this thy day, the things which belong unto thy peace; but now they are hid from thine eyes.' The natural day has got its dawn, its noon, and its midnight; so, I believe, has the day of grace. Jerusalem had its dawn, when the prohpets stood and told of a coming Saviour. It had its noon, when Jesus stood and cried, 'If any man thirst let him come unto me, and drink.' And it had its midnight, when he wept over it, and said, 'If thou hadst known, even thou,' etc. The day of grace is that time during which Christ is offered to sinners. With some people that period is equal to their whole lives. They are born under the preaching of the gospel, and they live and die under it. Some divines are of the opinion that the day of grace sometimes ends before death; but whether this be true or not, one thing is certain, that there is a gradual hardening of the heart against the work of the Spirit. I have often seen this among you; you grow more hardened the longer you sit and hear the offers of salvation; you become more set upon your idols, and more inclined to follow the devices of your own hearts. I would now mention some of the seasons, which may be called days of grace.

1. *The time of youth.* I do not pretend to give a reason why it is so; but God has so ordered it in his infinite wisdom, that the period of youth is the best time for being saved. It has been observed, and it is very remarkable, that in all the great revivals that have taken place in our own and in bygone days, the most of those who have been converted were young people. Jonathan Edwards states this in his narrative of the revival in New England, and Robe states the same in his account of the revival at Kilsyth in 1742. And have we not seen it among ourselves, that while young persons have been melted and converted, those who are older have only grown more hardened in sin. O young people! improve, I entreat you, your young days. Seek the Lord while yet your hearts are young and tender. If you delay, you will grow harder, and then, humanly speaking, it will be more difficult to be saved. No doubt God can save sinners at any age; but he seems peculiarly to choose the time of youth. He loves to hear an infant sing — he loves to hear praise from the mouths of babes and sucklings, Oh then, my brethren, will you not seek him in the days of your youth? will you not call upon him while he may be found? If you let your young days pass over your heads without being saved, you will remember your misspent privileges when you are in hell, and you will bitterly mourn over them throughout all eternity.

2. *The time of a gospel ministry.* This also may be called a peculiar day of grace. God is very sovereign in giving and taking

away this. Sometimes he sends a living ministry to a place, and then a dead one. I have observed this frequently. Jerusalem had its day of faithful preaching. For many a long year did the prophets come preaching peace. Often did God send his messengers, rising early and sending them. Often did Jesus stand in the midst of the unbelieving Jews, offering them peace, preaching to them the gospel of the kingdom; then were there days of grace, but ah! they did not know it, now they are hid from their eyes. And you too who are now before me, have had your day of grace. Will you let it pass away unimproved? O sinner! will you enter upon another year with God's wrath hanging over your head? O is it not an awful thing to let year after year pass over you, and yet remain unsaved? A few hours more now will close this year, and you do not know if ever you will see the close of another one. The last enemy may have come to many of you, and you called to give in your account before this night twelve months. O sinner, strive to enter in!

3. *The time when the Holy Spirit is poured out on a place* is a peculiar day of grace. At such a time there are many pressing into the kingdom. 'The kingdom of heaven suffers violence, and the violent take it by force.' It seems easier, humanly speaking, to be saved at such a time as that. Brethren, you have had such a time, and it was an easy matter for you to be saved, that year when I was away from you; but ah! many of you let it pass by. It may indeed be said of many here, 'The harvest is past, the summer is ended, and we are not saved.' O brethren! you have been a highly favoured people; but remember these days of gospel mercies will soon be gone, never more to return, and if they leave you unsaved, O what miserable wretches must you be throughout eternity! You may never see such a time again, as you saw here in the autumn of 1839. O if you would be but wise, and know the day of your merciful visitation!

III.   I come now to shew you that *Christ is willing to save even the hardest of sinners.* 'And when he was come near, he beheld the city, and wept over it,' etc. Christ here gives two proofs that he is willing to save sinners. 1. His tears; and 2. His words. These were the tears of one who never wept but in reality; and these were the words of one who never spake but in reality. It is impossible for him to lie. 'O if thou hadst known,' he said. It was a broken wish. It shows a feeling of the greatest love and tenderness. His bowels were yearning with tenderness within him, for the love he bore to their souls. His desire was a true desire. He saw them lying in their sin. They had slain the prophets, and despised their messages. He saw that they would soon crucify himself. He saw their hands red with his own blood; and yet, for all that, he wept over them. He saw the judgments that were coming on them. He saw that they would soon lie down in hell; and therefore he wept and cried, 'O if thou hadst known, even thou, at least in this thy day, the things which belong unto thy peace! but now they are hid from thine eyes.' I believe there are some here tonight over whom Christ says the same. He sees that you have sinned against light, and against love, and that you have resisted the Holy Spirit these fifty-two Sabbaths which have now gone over your heads. He sees how you have withstood every warning, how you have resisted his ministers, how you have resisted and crucifed the Son of God afresh, how you have wounded Christ in the house of his friends; and yet he says, 'O if thou hadst known.' Perhaps, sinner, you will not turn, perhaps you will perish, and before another year has passed, you may lift up your eyes in hell, being in torments. He that cannot lie says, he would you were saved; and if you perish, sinner, your blood be on your own head. It is the very essence of the gospel that Christ is willing to save. 'He willeth not that any should perish, but that all should come to him and live.' Some will say, why did he not save Jerusalem, if he was willing? To this I answer, that you must take the gospel as you find it. It is not your business nor mine to inquire into anything of the sort. It is sufficient for us to know that he is willing to save. He said, 'If any man thirst, let him come unto me and drink.' 'He that cometh unto me I will in no wise cast out.'

Now, brethren, in conclusion, I beseech you, strive to enter in at the strait gate. Many have entered, why not you? It may be you have seen your parents, or your children, or your wife, or your husband entering in, and oh! why should not you? If you would be wise, strive to enter in. Will you let this night go by, and will you enter upon another year with an unsaved soul? You may never sit in these pews again, and yet will you despise the message still. Ye know not what you do. O brethren! it is a wonder I can stand and look upon you sitting there, with dry eyes. Bethink yourselves in time. Are you still content to remain children of wrath, enemies of God, and heirs of hell? 'O that my head were waters, and mine eyes a fountain of tears, that I might weep day and night for the slain of the daughter of my people!' Amen.

Thursday Evening,
31st December 1841.

SERMON XXII

CONVERSION

Zechariah 3.1, 2. And he shewed me Joshua the high priest standing before the angel of the Lord, and Satan standing at his right hand to resist him. And the Lord said unto Satan, The Lord rebuke thee, O Satan, even the Lord that hath chosen Jerusalem, rebuke thee: is not this a brand plucked out of the fire?

The conversion of a soul is by far the most remarkable event in the history of the world, although many of you do not care about it. It is the object that attracts the eyes of the holy angels to the spot where it takes place. It is the object which the Father's eye rests upon with tenderness and delight. This work in the soul is what brings greater glory to the Father, Son, and Spirit, than all the other works of God. It is far more wonderful than all the works of art. There is nothing that can equal it. Ah! brethren, if you think little of it, or laugh at it, how little have you of the mind of God!

Conversion may be looked at from different points. The world can notice conversion. They see a young man, perhaps, who was careless like themselves, taking to his closet. They observe a change in his speech. They see a change in his company, and they say it's a whim. There is another view of it which God's children take. They see a soul cast out into the open field to the loathing of its person, and they see Jesus, the glorious Redeemer, stooping down and binding up its wounds. They see a sister, a brother born for eternity. A third view of conversion is as a victory of Christ over the devil — 'Is not this a brand plucked out of the fire?' The world is a great battle-field. 'I will put enmity between thee and the women, and between thy seed and her seed, it shall bruise thy head, and thou shalt bruise his heel.' Satan has the world bound in strong fetters. The whole world lies in the wicked one — lies in his arms, sung to sleep with his lullaby. But there is a great One gone forth, sitting on a white horse, and having on his head many crowns, and ever and anon he is cutting the strong chains with which sinners are bound, and saying, as he does so, to Satan, 'Is not this a brand plucked out of the fire?'

I desire, dear friends, by the help of the Holy Spirit, to show you two things from these words:

1. That Satan resists every conversion.
2. That Christ is the advocate of those he saves.

I. *Satan resists every conversion.* Verse 1: 'And he showed me Joshua the high priest standing before the angel of the Lord, and

Satan standing at his right hand to resist him.' There is no doubt but that this passage describes a vision which Zechariah saw, and that Joshua represents Jerusalem. Accordingly, Zechariah saw Joshua as a sinner awakened, and coming and standing before the Lord; but he saw another standing at his right hand to resist him; not an angel of light, but an angel of darkness. Now, brethren, this describes the case of every awakened and converted soul. When God convinces a soul of sin, he brings him to stand before him — then Satan comes to resist him. Before conversion, the devil tries to keep you secure, he cries out, Peace, peace. He fills you with high notions about yourself. He fills you with pride, and with high notions about your knowledge — that you know your catechism — that you are acquainted with the doctrines of the Bible. Or he binds you with silken fetters to some unlawful attachment — to some one who is going down the broad way, and he makes you to hate the gospel. Or he brings you under the faithful preaching of the gospel, and makes you content to sit and hear it, and even delight in hearing it, thereby making you imagine you are Christ's when you know him not. But the moment Christ comes and awakens you, then comes Satan to resist you. The resistance of Satan is twofold.

1. *He resists you at the bar of God.* In ancient courts of justice the accuser stood at the right hand of the judge, and brought against the accused all his crimes. So is it with Satan. You will see this in Revelation 12.10, 'Now is come salvation, and strength, and the kingdom of our God, and the power of his Christ: for the accuser of our brethren is cast down, which accused them before our God day and night.' The same you will see alluded to in Psalm 109.6, 'Set thou a wicked man over him, and let Satan stand at his right hand.' So that you will observe, from the first moment that a spark of grace is put into your heart, Satan stands at the bar of God to accuse you. And what does he accuse you of? First, he accuses you of sin. He says, That soul is the vilest in the world. Yea, there is none like it. Or sometimes he accuses you of unbelief. That soul has denied thee. Or sometimes he accuses you of going back after you had been awakened. That soul was awakened and has gone back; even after you visited that soul, it went back.

2. *He resists you at the bar of conscience.* He says to the sinner, How can you come, you are too vile? — you are the chief of sinners, there is none like you. Or sometimes he says, It is too late; you might have been saved had you come sooner. You might have been saved had you come in youth. Or you might have been saved had you come when you were awakened, but now it is of no use to try, it is too late. Or sometimes he takes another plan. When you are awakened and stand before the angel, he stirs up corruption within you; even when

you are upon your knees he stirs up corruption in order to shut your eye from seeing the mercy seat. He stirs up the sin that is in your heart. He makes you to see its vileness in order to keep you away from Christ.

Learn two lessons from this.

1. *It is a solemn thing to be under conviction of sin.* It is true, you are seeking Christ, but it is also true that Satan is ready to resist you. Do not think you are safe because you are under conviction, remember you are not saved because you have got a sight of your sins. It is not every awakened sinner that is a saved man. And if it is a solemn thing to be awakened, what must be the danger of those of you who are not awakened, who are not seeking Christ, who are asleep over hell! You are in greater danger this day than ever you were, for you are now asleep. You are nearer hell now than ever. You may have sought pardon once, but now you have given over seeking it, and every hour is bringing you nearer hell.

2. Those of you who are under real conviction remember that *it is only Satan that resists you.* God does not resist you. Christ does not resist you. The Holy Ghost does not resist you. Remember, whoever says your sins are too many to be forgiven, it is not God, it is not Christ. It is Satan. Christ invites you to come to him. The Holy Spirit invites you, and all the friends of Christ invite you. Do not be driven back.

II. *Christ is the advocate of those he saves.* Verse 2: 'And the Lord said unto Satan, The Lord rebuke thee, O Satan; even the Lord that hath chosen Jerusalem, rebuke thee: is not this a brand plucked out of the fire?' 'If any man sin we have an advocate with the Father, Jesus Christ the righteous.' Christ is the advocate of every one he saves, and not only is he an advocate after conversion, but before, and throughout conversion. He answers Satan's objections. There are two arguments here by which he answers Satan. The first is *the free election of God.* Jerusalem was the chief city in the world for wickedness. They had sinned against light, against love, against long-suffering mercy. Yet Christ chose it. He might say, Grant that it is the chief for wickedness, yet God hath chosen it. Grant that that soul is the chief of sinners, yet the Lord is sovereign. 'I will have mercy on whom I will have mercy, and I will have compassion on whom I will have compassion.' This is the argument of Christ. Is it not strange that the very argument which troubles souls is the one which Christ uses as the reason why you should be saved? Let Satan say, you have sinned against light, against conviction, against love; still, 'the Lord that hath chosen Jerusalem rebuke thee; is not this a brand plucked out of the fire?' This shuts Satan's mouth — this is an argument which he cannot answer. The second argument Christ employs is, *the brand is already plucked out of the fire.* Christ here says, Whatever that sinner may have been, he is now plucked out of the fire. And thus all Satan's arguments are urged in vain.

All unconverted souls are in the fire. You are in the fire for two reasons.

1. *You are condemned to the fire.* 'He that believeth not is condemned already.' There is as it were a great pile of wood on which you are placed, and it is set on fire. The fire indeed has not yet reached you, though soon it will.

2. *Your hell is already begun.* Just as the children of God have their heaven begun, so you have got your hell begun. You have burning lusts, and burning passions raging within you — these are the beginnings of hell. But ah! brethren, those of you who have been brought to Christ are brands plucked out of the fire. Observe that Christ plucks the brands out of the fire, and grafts them into the living vine, that they may be made to glorify God by bearing fruit. You will be made to glorify God in one of two ways: either by bearing fruit, or by being cast, soul and body, into hell. 'For the Lord hath made all things for himself, even the wicked for the day of evil.' Oh! brethren, which do you choose? O brands in the fire! will you not cry to be plucked out of the fire? And if Christ do it, will he not have the answer to make to Satan? 'The Lord rebuke thee, O Satan: is not this a brand plucked out of the fire?'

In conclusion, I would say that this congregation may be divided into two parts; those who are brands over the fire, and those who have been plucked out of the fire. O brands in the fire! will you not cry to be plucked out of the fire? When he is plucking brands out of the fire beside you, will you not say, Lord, pluck me out of the fire? Amen.

Sabbath Afternoon,
8th May 1842.

SERMON XXIII

GRIEVE NOT THE SPIRIT

Ephesians 4.30. *Grieve not the Holy Spirit of God, whereby ye are sealed unto the day of redemption.*

The unconverted do not like to hear much about the Holy Ghost. The world cannot receive him because it seeth him not, neither knows him. Unconverted ministers do not often like to preach about the Holy Spirit. Unconverted hearers do not often like to hear about the Holy Spirit. How very foolish to many must such a command as this appear to be. If it had been said, Grieve not a father or a mother, you could have understood it, but when it says, 'Grieve not the Holy Spirit,' you do not know its meaning.

Paul is here advising Christians to let no vile communications proceed out of their mouth, and the argument he uses is one of the most wonderful that ever proceeded from the pen of man. It is, 'Grieve not the Holy Spirit, whereby ye are sealed unto the day of redemption.'

From these words, consider:

1.   The holy friendship of the Spirit.
2.   Some of the ways in which we may grieve this Friend.
3.   Apply.

I. Let me shew you *the holy friendship that subsists between the Holy Spirit and believer's soul.* It is implied in the words, 'Grieve not the Holy Spirit,' it is only a friend we can grieve. If he was an enemy he would rejoice if we fell. And this shews that he is a true friend, because when we fall the Holy Spirit is grieved. It is quite true that the infinite God does not grieve in the same sense as we do, for that would imply that he was not infinitely happy; but it is quite as true that there is something analogous between his grief and ours.

1. *The Holy Spirit comes and dwells in a believer's heart.* 'I will put my Spirit within you, and cause you to walk in my statutes, and ye shall keep my judgments and do them,' Ezek. 36.27. And so the Lord Jesus says in the 14th of John, 16th verse, 'I will pray the Father, and he will give you another Comforter, that he may abide with you for ever, even the Spirit of truth; whom the world cannot receive, because it seeth him not, neither knoweth him.' And accordingly the apostle Paul says in 1 Corinthians 6.19, 'What! know ye not that your body is the temple of the Holy Ghost which is in you, which ye have of God?' And in like manner we find God saying in Leviticus 26.12, 'I will walk among you and I will be your God, and ye shall be my people.' And, again, he says, 'This is my rest, here will

I stay, for I have desired it.' O my brethren! what an intimate friendship this is! Can any friendship be compared with this? Another friend may dwell in our neighbourhood; he may dwell in our family; but, ah! here is a friend that dwells in us. Can there be greater friendship than this? When the Lord Jesus came from heaven, and dwelt among us — when he dealt with Martha and Mary, and Lazarus — when he sat down to meat in the Pharisee's house, and permitted the woman that was a sinner to wash his feet with her tears, and to wipe them with the hairs of her head — *that* was friendship. But it was still greater friendship for the Holy Spirit to come and dwell in a clay cottage, the walls of which are covered over with leprosy; and this is the friendship of the Holy Spirit to a believing soul.

2. *The Holy Spirit teaches believing souls.* This is his great office. See John 16.12: 'I have yet many things to say unto you, but ye cannot bear them now. Howbeit when he, the Spirit of truth, is come, he will guide you into all truth.' Then 1 John 2.20: 'But ye have an unction from the Holy One, and ye know all things.' Verse 27: 'But the anointing which ye have received of him abideth in you; and ye need not that any man teach you.' etc. Now, brethren, there is no greater mark of friendship, than to teach one — to bear with a slow scholar. This is the friendship of the Holy Spirit to be believing soul. There can be no greater condescension than for a man of gigantic mind to teach a child the alphabet. It was condescension in Christ to teach the people when he sat in the boat by the side of the lake. But it is greater friendship when the Holy Spirit comes and teaches you all things; it is greater friendship when he bears with your stupidity, and when he opens your hearts to receive the truth in the love of it. This is friendship.

3. *He teaches the believer to pray;* yea, he prays in the believer. See Rom. 8.15, 'Ye have not received the spirit of bondage again to fear; but ye have received the Spirit of adoption, whereby we cry Abba, Father.' Verse 26, 'Likewise the Spirit also helpeth our infirmities' (the Greek word is very remarkable: He helps our infirmities by coming under the burden) for we know not what we should pray for as we ought; but the Spirit itself maketh intercession for us with groanings which cannot be uttered. And he that searcheth the hearts (that is the Lord) knoweth what is the mind of the Spirit, because he maketh intercession for the saints according to the will of God.' And the same thing you are taught in the little Epistle of Jude, 20th verse, 'But ye, beloved, building up yourselves on your most holy faith, praying in the Holy Ghost.' So, brethren, this is another mark of the Holy Spirit's friendship, that he not only dwells in the soul, but he teaches the soul to say, 'Abba' — he teaches the soul to 'pray

in the Holy Ghost.' It is true friendship to teach one another to pray. It is a believing mother's part to teach her little children to pray. But the Holy Spirit's love is greater than this, he not only puts the words in our mouth, but he puts the desire in our heart. It is great friendship to pray together; but oh! it is greater friendship to pray in one, and this is the friendship of the Spirit of God.

4. *He seals the believing heart.* Read the text, 'Grieve not the Holy Spirit of God, whereby ye are sealed unto the day of redemption.' And again, in the first chapter of the same book, 13th verse, 'In whom ye also trusted, after that ye heard the word of truth, the gospel of your salvation; in whom also, after that ye believed, ye were sealed with that Holy Spirit of promise.' You know, my brethren, the effect that one's habits have on others, that often the colour of the life is taken from those among whom we live. And you cannot be in the company of a holy man without receiving your impressions from him. But how much more an impression does the Spirit make: it is like the mark that the seal makes on the wax, and it is to the day of redemption, and cannot be broken, if we are sealed with the Holy Spirit of promise.

And now, brethren, let me ask, Do you know anything of this friend? The world cannot receive him; if you are of the world, you cannot receive him. Do you know anything of the Spirit making groanings within you which cannot be uttered? Nothing? Then, dear friends, you are far from God. 'The world cannot receive him, neither knoweth him.' How do you feel at the question? What! do you think it foolishness? 'The natural man receiveth not the things of the Spirit of God: for they are foolishness unto him: neither can he know them: for they are spiritually discerned.' 1 Cor. 2.14. If you do not mind these things, the reason is, you are a friend of the world, and will perish with the world.

II. *The ways in which the Spirit may be grieved.* When Christ was on the earth, we are told that on one occasion he looked round on the Pharisees, being grieved at the hardness of their hearts. Now, what Jesus then felt, the Holy Spirit feels at the sight of sin. We are told that when Christ looked on Peter, he wept. We are not told what kind of look it was, but no doubt it was one of grief — no doubt his eye said, Did I deserve this, Peter? Did I deserve that thou shouldst act thus? Have I been an enemy to thee, Peter? Have I ever offended thee, Peter? No doubt this was what his eye said.

But let me mention some of the ways in which the Spirit may be grieved:

1. *By putting the Spirit's work in the place of Christ's work.* The office of the Spirit is to glorify the work of Christ. 'He shall glorify me; for he shall receive of mine, and shall show it unto you. All

things that the Father hath are mine: therefore said I, that he shall take of mine, and shall show it unto you,' John 16.14, 15. This is the office of the Spirit. He delights not to show himself, but Christ. When the three thousand were converted on the day of Pentecost, it was the Spirit that did it; he showed them the divine excellency of the work of Christ. And why does he this? Because it gives glory to God in the highest, peace on earth, and goodwill to men. But sometimes a believer looks away from the work of Christ to the work of the Spirit in him, and he begins to rest on that as the ground of peace. Now, this grieves the Spirit. If he were a selfish Spirit, he would rejoice at this: but he is not a selfish Spirit, and, therefore, nothing grieves him so much as this. 'Grieve not the Holy Spirit of God, whereby ye are sealed unto the day of redemption.'

2. *When you do not lean all on him.* When you do not take all your holiness from him. This is the great work of the Spirit in you, to make you holy. 'Thy Spirit is good, lead me to the land of uprightness.' God promises in Ezekiel, 'I will put my Spirit within you, and cause you to walk in my statutes, and ye shall keep my judgments and do them,' Ezekiel 36.27. Now, as long as you lean on the Spirit for holiness, you and he are friends, but the moment you cease to lean on him, you grieve him. Suppose you were to cross some deep and rapid stream with one who was much stronger and abler to stand against it than you, and he said, 'Lean on me when you cross.' Now, when you came to the middle of the stream if you were to say, I cannot lean, and began to swim yourself, would you not grieve your friend? Now, this is the way in which we grieve the Spirit; for he has said, 'Even to your old age I am he; and even to hoar hairs will I carry you,' Isaiah 46.4. Now, when temptations and trials, and lusts come crowding in, if we do not lean upon the Spirit, we grieve him. Or, if we lean upon another, if you lean upon your education, your good resolutions, your past experiences. Or, suppose you run into temptation, and say, I was well brought up, I am able to resist it. In these ways you grieve the Spirit.

3. *You grieve the Spirit when you do not follow his leadings.* You remember when Christ was on earth, he said to his disciples, 'Follow me.' He would have been grieved if they had not followed him. It is so with the other Comforter; he leads us to the wilderness — he sometimes causes groanings within us. Do you resist prayer at such a time? Then you grieve the Spirit. Do you go into temptations against the strivings of your conscience? Then you grieve the Spirit. When he sees you run into temptation, he warns you — he pricks your heart, and yet you go. Ah! in this way you grieve the Spirit.

4. *You grieve the Spirit by despising ordinances.* Ordinances are the channels through which the Holy Spirit pours all blessings into

the believing hearts. Do you despise ordinances? Then you grieve the Holy Spirit. Suppose you agreed to meet a friend at a certain time; if you were not to go would you not grieve that friend? Now, this is just the way in which you grieve the Spirit, when you do not go to ordinances. How many of you come to the meeting on Thursday evenings? Are there not some who slight the friendship of the Spirit? Ah! you will yet feel the disadvantage of it to your own soul.

III. *Application.*

1. *To those here who have grieved the Spirit.* I am deeply persuaded that many here have grieved the Spirit in a remarkable manner. Does he deserve this at your hand? Has he ever been a wilderness to you, or a land of darkness? 'Do ye thus requite the Lord, O foolish people and unwise? is not he thy father that hath bought thee? hath he not made thee and established thee?' Deut. 32.6. Do ye provoke the Lord the Spirit to jealousy? Consider how ungrateful it is to grieve him. Consider what he has done for thee. Did he not convince you of sin? Has he not breathed upon your soul like the gentle gales of wind from the south? Is it not, then, ungrateful so to grieve him?

2. Consider how, in grieving the Holy Spirit, *you have lost your peace with God.* I have often told you that you cannot live in sin, and retain peace. 'There is no peace, saith the Lord, unto the wicked.' You have a guilty conscience; and a guilty conscience cannot come into his presence. Return sinner!

3. *You will go deeper into sin.* 'Without me ye can do nothing;' you cannot resist temptation — you cannot resist self — you cannot overcome sin. O unholy quenchers of the Spirit! where is this to end you? The Holy Spirit ebbs out of your heart, and leaves you like a stranded vessel, dry upon the land. Return!

4. I would say *to those who are receiving the refreshing gales of the Spirit,* grieve him not; walk softly with this friend. When he draws, run after him. Above all, follow his warnings. When he says, Do not go with this companion, go not with him. When he says, Go not into that path, go not. 'Thou shalt hear a voice behind thee saying, This is the way, walk ye in it, when ye turn to the right hand, and when ye turn to the left.' Happy souls that grieve not the Holy Spirit. Soon he shall fill that soul, and leave nothing in it but himself. Soon we shall be like him, for we shall see him as he is.   Amen.

Sabbath Evening,
2nd August 1840.

SERMON XXIV

THE TRUE PLEASANTNESS OF BEING A CHILD OF GOD

Psalm 16.6. *The lines are fallen unto me in pleasant places; yea, I have a goodly heritage.*
Proverbs 3.17. *Her ways are ways of pleasantness, and all her paths are peace.*

The words which I have read to you, dear friends, from the sixteenth Psalm, are properly and originally the words of the Lord Jesus Christ. 'The lines are fallen unto me in pleasant places; yea, I have a goodly heritage.' You will see this, if you look at the tenth verse of the Psalm: 'For thou wilt not leave my soul in hell, neither wilt thou suffer thine Holy One to see corruption.' This verse, you know, is over and over again applied to Christ in the New Testament. You know, dear brethren, that Christ, when on earth, was a man of sorrows, and acquainted with grief. He was despised and rejected of men, a man of sorrows, and acquainted with grief, and we hid, as it were, our faces from him. 'Surely he hath borne our griefs, and carried our sorrows, yet we did esteem him stricken, smitten of God, and afflicted,' Isaiah 53.4. And yet, brethren, it is quite evident that all the time of his life there was a holy joy remaining through him. Though we are never told that Christ laughed, yet it is said 'he rejoiced.' You will find evident marks of this running through the Gospels, and more through the Psalms. So that, although Christ was the surety of a guilty world — though from the womb to the cross there was a crown of thorns bound around his brow, yet he had a holy joy; yea, even in his death he could say, 'The lines are fallen unto me in pleasant places; yea, I have a goodly heritage.' As it was with Christ, so it is with his followers. You have your peculiar sorrows, believer, that the world does not know of; yet you have got a calm, upspringing well of joy, so that like our Lord, you can say — 'The lines are fallen unto me in pleasant places; yea, I have a goodly heritage.' Christ's 'ways are ways of pleasantness, and all his paths are peace.' I take those of you to witness who are believers and afflicted, is it not true, that for all your peculiar sorrows you have got a peculiar joy? Christ one day said to his disciples, 'I have bread to eat that the world knows not of.' So we have a joy that the world knows not of — a joy that all the tempests and troubles of time cannot ruffle. 'The lines are fallen unto me in pleasant places; yea I have a goodly heritage.'

I would show you from these words the true pleasantness of being a child of God. I would show you,

1. That the pleasures of the uncoverted are false pleasures.
2. That the pleasures of God's children are true pleasures.

I. *The pleasures of the unconverted are false pleasures,* because:

1. *They are not satisfying.* They pretend to satisfy, but they are not satisfying. When the devil leads you into the worldly pleasure, he says, 'Stolen waters are sweet, and bread eaten in secret is pleasant.' But when you come to taste the stolen waters, tell me, is there not something awanting. Look at Proverbs 14.3, 'Even in laughter the heart is sorrowful, and the end of that mirth is heaviness.' Ah! brethren, is it not so? You that have enjoyed most of the world's pleasures — most of its gaiety, is it not true, that 'even in laughter the heart is sorrowful, and the end of that mirth is heaviness'? Is it not true that your lips and your heart are often contrary? Is it not often true that there is a cloud of sorrow in your heart, when there is a smile on your countenance? When you are in the midst of your gaiety is it not true, that 'even in laughter the heart is sorrowful, and the end of that mirth is heaviness'? 'Whosoever drinketh of this water shall thirst again.' 'I said, Go to now, I will prove thee with mirth; therefore enjoy pleasure: and, behold, this also is vanity,' Eccl. 2.1. 'I said of laughter, It is mad; and of mirth, What doeth it?' Eccl. 2.3. Ah! brethren, as long as you are unconverted, with an eternal hell below your feet, it must, and it ever will be the case that 'even in laughter the heart is sorrowful, and the end of that mirth is heaviness.'

2. *They are short.* I told you last Sabbath, that your being was to be eternal — your history is to be for eternity. Your history on this little piece of ground is nothing compared with your history throughout eternity: it is like the tick of a clock. All the joy that an unconverted man will see is here — beyond is hell. This is what made Moses forsake the pleasures of Egypt. He was the son of Pharaoh's daughter, and he had all the pleasures he could desire. The pipe and the tabret were in their feasts; he had all the company that the world delight in; but ah! Moses found out, by the teaching of God, that the pleasures of sin are only for a season. He 'chose rather to suffer affliction with the people of God, than to enjoy the pleasures of sin for a season.' O sinner, you have pleasure, but it is only for a reason! O Christless man, you have pleasure, but it is only for a season! Look at Ecclesiastes 7.6, 'For as the crackling of thorns under a pot, so is the laughter of the fool.' You know, brethren, when you put thorns under a pot, if you did not know to the contrary, you would think they would last for a long time; but it is a bright blaze and soon over. So is the laughter of the fool. Laugh on if you will; live on with your wicked companions if you will; live on without knowing Christ, and without knowing the Father, if you will; but remember I have told

you your pleasure is short; your candle will soon be out.

3. *They are suddenly interrupted.* It is fearful to think how suddenly they are interrupted. If my heart were not made of stone, I could weep before you for things that are passing around us. Look at Psalm 73.18: 'Surely thou didst set them in slippery places; thou castedst them down into destruction: how are they brought into desolation as in a moment! they are utterly consumed with terrors.' Those of you that are unconverted are standing on slippery places. You know when a man is walking on the ice, his foot may slide, and he fall, without any warning. So it is with those of you who are unconverted. Your feet will slide suddenly. One young man who is lying this night cold and dead, was once as lively as you in the world, he sat where you sit, until the world became too sharp for him, and he forsook us and went into the world, but his feet were set in slippery places. He could hardly speak to me when I went to see him, but he shewed from his gesture, that he was consumed with terror; and then he said: Will you pray for me in the closet, and in the family, and in the church? 'Thou castedst them down into destruction, how are they brought into desolation, as in a moment.' I tell you, if you are a Christless man, your pleasures will be suddenly interrupted. You remember the rich fool in the Gospel, Luke 12.19: 'I will say to my soul, Soul, thou hast much goods laid up for many years: take thine ease, eat, drink, and be merry. But God said unto him, Thou fool, this night thy soul shall be required of thee.' O unconverted man, where would you be, if God were this night to require your soul? 'Thou are weighed in the balance and found wanting.' 'Thou fool, this night thy soul shall be required of thee.'

4. *God will judge you on account of them.* It is true that every pleasure you get apart from Christ, God will judge you on account of it. Look at Ecclesiastes 11.9: 'Rejoice, O young man, in thy youth, and let thy heart cheer thee in the days of thy youth, and walk in the ways of thine heart, and in the sight of thine eyes; but know thou, that for all these things God will bring thee into judgment.' God will bring you into judgment for every godless word, for every idle word, for every enjoyment and pleasure you get apart from Christ. O brethren! Is it true that you are living unpardoned? Is it true that you are happy — that you can enjoy social company — that you can enjoy your games — that you can enjoy your dance? Is it true, sinner, that you are happy away from God, and thinkest thou that God will not bring you into judgment? Can you throw so much contempt on Christ, on his blood, on his righteousness, on his free offer of mercy, and think that God will not bring you into judgment? You say very often, What is the harm? It is a social company — an innocent pleasure: what is the harm? I will tell you the harm, you are

despising Christ, you are despising the blood shed on Calvary, and finding your pleasures away from him, and is it not contempt of Christ to find your pleasures away from him, even supposing your pleasures had no sin in them? I do not now stop to enquire whether they are right or wrong; it is such infinite contempt of Christ, that I wonder God does not open the ground where you dance — when you have your mirth, and let you fall through into hell.

I have dwelt too long on this part of the subject, longer than I intended.

II. I come now to speak, in the second place, *on the true happiness of the children of God.* 'The lines are fallen unto me in pleasant places; yea, I have a goodly heritage.' 'Her ways are ways of pleasantness, and all her paths are peace.'

1. I observe, dear brethren, in the first place, that the joys of a believer are true *because he is forgiven.* Look at Matthew 9.2: 'They brought to him a man sick of the palsy, lying on a bed; and Jesus, seeing their faith, said unto the sick of the palsy, Son, be of good cheer, thy sins be forgiven thee.' The first reasonable joy that a sinner ever has is when his sins are forgiven him. You will not know true joy till then. You will not know solid happiness till the voice of Jesus says, 'Son, be of good cheer, thy sins be forgiven thee.' 'Daughter, be of good comfort, thy faith hath made thee whole.' There is no joy like that of being forgiven — brought out of darkness into marvellous light. There is something very heavenly in these words. 'Son, be of good cheer, thy sins be forgiven thee.' Those of you who have believed on Christ, you are forgiven. 'As far as east is distant from the west, so far hath he removed our transgressions from us.' Your sins have been already forgiven, as many of you as have believed on Christ. If you really lay hold on Christ, sinner, tonight your sins will be forgiven thee. Oh, brethren, this is happiness — this is the first sip of the cup of eternal bliss — this is peace: 'Now the God of hope fill you with all joy and peace in believing.' Rom. 15.13. O it is sweet, happy, pleasant peace! 'The lines are fallen unto me in pleasant places; yea, I have a goodly heritage.' 'Her ways are ways of pleasantness, and all her paths are peace.'

2. The joys of a believer are solid because *he is sanctified.* Every one that comes to Christ receives the Holy Spirit to dwell in their heart. It is a question, whether it be sweetest to be forgiven, or to be sanctified. I would say it was sweetest to be sanctified. 'The lines are fallen unto me in pleasant places; yea, I have a goodly heritage.' When a fresh burden of sin comes upon the conscience, the believer feels that he cannot be made happy unless he is made holy. I have often seen a young believer sunk on the brink of hell by the discovery of his sin. Who can comfort such a soul? I will tell you, 'My grace is

sufficient for thee, for my strength is made perfect in weakness. Most gladly, therefore, will I rather glory in my infirmities, that the power of Christ may rest upon me.' O these are sweet words to a soul who has begun to see the plague of his own sin. If there is such a soul here tonight, I would say, 'My grace is sufficient for thee.' Though there is a fountain of iniquity within that will never stop till you arrive among the blessed, never mind. 'My grace is sufficient for thee.' That is enough to comfort any soul. 'The lines are fallen unto me in pleasant places; yea, I have a goodly heritage.'

3. Again, the joys of a believer are solid, because *Christ will come to us in storms*. Look at Matthew 14.24-27, 'But the ship was now in the midst of the sea, tossed with the waves; for the wind was contrary. And in the fourth watch of the night Jesus went unto them walking on the sea. And when the disciples saw him walking on the sea, they were troubled, saying, It is a spirit, and they cried out for fear. But straightway Jesus spake unto them, saying, Be of good cheer: it is I; be not afraid.' Brethren, this is just a type of the way Christ cheers his disciples through the world still. If you are Christ's you will meet with storms. The world will be contrary, your own evil hearts will be contrary. But, ah! at the very time when the storm is greatest, Christ comes near the tempest-tossed ship, at the fourth watch of the night, and says, 'Be of good cheer: it is I; be not afraid.' Ah, brethren, there is peace again. 'Therefore are the lines fallen unto me in pleasant places; yea, I have a goodly heritage.' Then again, we have true and solid peace. I can't say you will have no persecution. 'All that will live godly in Christ Jesus shall suffer persecution.' But I can assure you of this, that Christ will be present; he is a 'very present help in time of trouble.' Ah! brethren, I know it is so, that if troubles are in store for the Church of Scotland, that Christ's little flock will be safe. He will come at the fourth watch of the night and say, 'Be of good cheer: it is I; be not afraid.' If the storm dashes us on the rock — the Rock of Ages, it will do us no harm. 'The lines are fallen unto me in pleasant places; yea, I have a goodly heritage.'

4. But, again, the joys of a believer are solid, because *they are eternal*. 'The path of the just is as the shining light, which shineth more and more unto the perfect day,' Prov. 4.18. The happiness of those of you who are unconverted is but for a moment. Your games, your dances, your social parties will soon be over. There are no games in hell. But brethren, the joy of those of you who are Christ's is for ever. Your peace will be eternal. It is like a river that widens in its course, until it is lost in the ocean. 'The water that I shall give him shall be in him a well of water, springing up into everlasting life,' John 4.14. Oh! brethren, surely that joy is true that shall never end.

'Mary hath chosen that good part, which shall not be taken away from her.' Luke 10.42. Every thing else can be taken away from you, your money, your friends, etc.: but if you have once embraced the Lamb of God, you have that good part which shall never be taken away from you. You are chosen to 'an inheritance incorruptible, undefiled, and that fadeth not away.' Then we can say without any fear, 'The lines are fallen unto me in pleasant places; yea, I have a goodly heritage.'

I would have you to learn from this subject, two lessons.

1. *Those of you who are Christ's should live a pleasant life in the world.* If it is true that you are pardoned — if it is true that his grace is sufficient for you, then you have good reason to live a pleasant life. Remember how you are commanded in the Bible to do everything with joy. 'The Lord loveth a cheerful giver.' God does not love the service of slaves: 'Ye have not received the spirit of bondage again to fear; but ye have received the Spirit of adoption, whereby we cry, Abba, Father,' Rom. 8.15. God commands you over and over again, that what you do, do it heartily. If you sing praise, do it heartily. If you give to the cause of Christ, do it heartily; whatever you do, do it as one who has the Spirit of God. O it is a happy thing to labour in God's service! Do not do it with that downward look that the world have on a Sabbath day. Remember that you are to suffer cheerfully. The apostles suffered with joy. You remember they had their clothes torn and their backs lacerated, yet they sang praises to God in the prison at midnight. Brethren, let us even die cheerfully. It is said of Stephen, when they stoned him, that 'he kneeled down, and cried with a loud voice, Lord, lay not this sin to their charge. And when he said this, he fell asleep,' Acts 7.60. O happy Stephen, it is more like a child falling asleep in its mother's arms, for it is said, 'He fell asleep.' And oh! how would his face shine five minutes after. He would forget all their anger; he would forget all their hard words; he would forget his suffering. If we are really to sit on the throne with Christ, why should we be like chained slaves here? Why should we not rather long to depart and to be with Christ, which is far better?

2. Last of all, learn *the utter folly and madness of those of you who are Christless.* I know that those of you who are out of Christ, think that it is we who are out of our mind; but if there is such a thing as truth in the world, I beseech you to consider whether it is you or us who are mad. I believe that you have peace — that you have joy — that you have pleasure — that you have comfort; but is it not true that you are an unpardoned sinner on the road to hell? Your peace will soon be at an end; but ours is a remarkable joy, and yet you despise it. Do you know the reasonableness of joy? We are happy, because the louder the storm, the nearer is Christ. We are happy

because we have got a happiness which God has. It is God who has made us happy. If this is madness, I would that you all had this madness. I would that this town had this madness. I would that the whole human race had this madness — then would the world be happy. Do not, then, despise this happiness. Many of you who are sitting here tonight, know that you were never brought to Christ, never washed in his blood. Yet how is it that you can live happy? Look around you, how many are dying Christless? Brethren, if you live as they did, you too will die Christless, and where he is you will never come.   Amen.

Thursday Evening,
22nd September 1842.

SERMON XXV

THE PILGRIM'S STAFF

Hebrew 13.5. *I will never leave thee nor forsake thee.*

My beloved friends, let us notice, in the first place, the history of this remarkable promise: 'I will never leave thee, nor forsake thee.' These words have been a staff in the hand of believers throughout all ages; and they will be so to you, if you lean upon them.

I. First of all, let us trace *the history of this promise.* You will notice that it is not put into this epistle for the first time — it is a borrowed promise. First of all, I think, it is borrowed from what God said to Jacob, Gen. 28.15: 'Behold, I am with thee, and will keep thee in all places whether thou goest, and will bring thee again into this land; for *I will not leave thee* until I have done that which I have spoken to thee of.' There is another place from which I think it is borrowed, 1 Chron. 28.20: 'And David said to Solomon his son, Be strong and of good courage, and do it; Fear not, nor be dismayed: for the Lord God, even my God, will be with thee: *He will not fail thee, nor forsake thee,*' etc. Now, you see, here is the promise again — 'He will not fail

---

1 This sermon was preached on Thursday evening, 24th Nov., 1842, the evening on which the author arrived from the convocation of ministers held in Edinburgh.

thee, nor forsake thee.' There is still another place where the same staff is put into a believer's hand, Josh. 1.5: 'There shall not any man be able to stand before thee all the days of thy life: As I was with Moses, so will I be with thee: *I will not fail thee, nor forsake thee.*' Now, turn back again to Hebrews, and observe how Paul brings it in — 'Be content with such things as ye have; *for* he hath said, I will never leave thee, nor forsake thee.' Now, a believer may ask this question — 'When did he say that to me?' Ah! but he said it to Jacob, and Solomon, and Joshua, and therefore it is said to you. Observe, brethren, what a blessed principle this brings out: What God speaks to one believer, he says to me. You will observe that this promise in the Old Testament is special — that is, it is addressed to one individual, but in the New Testament it is general. Some, when they read the Old Testament, say, 'This is addressed to Abraham,' or 'This is addressed to Jacob; but it is not said to me.' But what was said to Abraham, or Jacob, or Joshua, is spoken to you. The special promise to Joshua is to all believing Joshuas to the end of the world — 'I will never leave thee, nor forsake thee.' I do not know if you understand what I mean; but from this little verse we know that the special promises in the Old Testament are to all believers. God said to Abraham — 'I will bless thee, and make they name great, and thou shalt be a blessing.' So he says to all that are children of Abraham. And there is a sweet promise in the forty-third of Isaiah — 'Fear not, for I have redeemed thee: I have called thee by my name; thou art mine,' etc. That promise was special to Israel, and yet it belongs to me. And there is another sweet promise in the fifty-fourth chapter — 'For a small moment have I forsaken thee; but with great mercies will I gather thee,' etc. Now, if you were reading this promise, you might say, 'Ah! that does not belong to me.' But by turning to the thirteenth of Hebrews, we know that it belongs to all believers. There are two reasons I would give why this is true, because to some it may appear wonderful. The first is, God is the same yesterday, today and for ever — 'I am the Lord; I change not.' Ah! the unchangeableness of God explains it — 'I am the Lord; I change not.' Jesus Christ is the same yesterday, today and for ever. And there is another reason why this promise of Scripture belongs to believers now; it is that all believers are one body, and therefore whatever belongs to one, belongs to all. All believers are branches of one vine; and therefore if God say to one branch, 'I will never leave thee, nor forsake thee,' he says so to all. And therefore, for these two reasons, all the promises made to Jacob or Solomon or Joshua are made to me. And this makes the Bible not a book written for one, but a book written to me — a letter by the Lord, and directed to me: and therefore every word of divine love and tenderness that he has written in this book belongs to me.

II. And now, dear brethren, I would speak, in the second place, of *the person here spoken of* — 'I will never leave thee, nor forsake thee.' It is quite evident that it is not the language of a creature. Our parents will leave us, and our friends will leave us. These are not the words of a creature, then — 'I will never leave thee, nor forsake thee.' Observe, then, dear brethren, I entreat you, whose word it is — '*He* hath said, I will never leave thee, nor forsake thee.' It is the word of the three-one God. You may take each of the persons of the Godhead, and apply this word to him — 'I will never leave thee, nor forsake thee.' You may take it as the word of Immanuel. You remember what Christ said to his disciples — 'Lo, I am with you always, even unto the end of the world.' This is the same promise. Brethren, when the Lord Jesus comes to you, and covers you with his garment, and says, 'Fear not,' he will never forsake that soul. A mother may forsake — 'Can a woman forget her sucking child, that she should not have compassion on the son of her womb? Yea, she may forget; yet will I not forget thee.' Observe, brethren, that when once the Lord Jesus comes to a sinner to be his righteousness, he will never leave him — 'I am with you always.' Oh! it is this that makes him a friend that sticketh closer than a brother. Why will he never leave us? The first reason is, his love is everlasting love. It is not like the love of a creature — it is unchangeable. Another reason is, he has died for that soul: he has borne all for that soul. Will he ever leave a soul that he has died for?

Again, you may take these words as those of the Spirit, and then they are like those words in fourteenth of John — 'I will pray the Father, and he shall give you another Comforter, that he may abide with you for ever' — to abide with you for ever. It is the same as these words — 'I will never leave thee, nor forsake thee.' When God the Holy Spirit comes to a soul, he will never leave it. Some may often be made to say 'I think the Spirit will go away from me.' But, observe, he says, 'I will never leave thee, nor forsake thee.' David cried out in the bitterness of his soul. 'Take not thy Holy Spirit away from me.' Here is the answer — 'I will never leave thee, nor forsake thee.' God will never forsake the temple in which he dwells. He forsook the tabernacle in the wilderness, and he forsook the temple at Jerusalem; but he will never forsake the living temple.

Or, you may take these words, and apply them to God the Father. And here they come to be very much the words God gave to Abraham: he said, 'Fear not, Abram; I am thy shield and thy exceeding great reward.' He had returned from the slaughter of Chederlaomer, and of the kings that were with him. The king of Sodom came out to meet him, and said unto him. 'Give me the persons, and take the goods to thyself.' But Abraham said, 'I have lifted up mine hand unto the Lord, the most high God, the possessor of heaven and of earth, that I will not take from a thread even to a shoe latchet, and that I will not take any thing that is thine, lest thou shouldest say, I have made Abram rich.' And, immediately after, God appeared to him, and said: 'Fear not, Abram; I am thy shield, and they exceeding great reward.' This is what Asaph felt. He says, in the seventy-third Psalm, 'My flesh and my heart faileth; but God is the strength of my heart, and my portion for ever.' Ah, brethren, this is a sweet word to a poor soul who is mourning over the broken pots at his feet. This is a sweet word to those of you who are bereft — who have left houses and lands — 'I will never leave thee, not forsake thee.' This may be a sweet word to those of you who are mourning over the dead. O brethren! is this your portion? Can you look up to a three-one God, Father, Son, and Spirit, standing on these broken shreds at your feet, and say, 'Thou wilt never leave me, nor forsake me'? This is happiness. Well, well did the Lord say, 'Mary hath chosen that good part which shall never be taken away from her.' Ah, poor souls! that have chosen the world as your portion — that have chosen the portion that will be taken from you. Ah, brethren! be you wiser.

Let me mention now some of the times when we should remember these words.

1. *A time of guilt.* O the dark hour, when guilt is on the conscience, and when a frown looks down from heaven upon us. O in such an hour remember these words — 'I will never leave thee, nor forsake thee.' 'Thou hast played the harlot with many lovers; yet return unto me.' Thy redeeming God calls out, 'I will never leave thee, nor forsake thee.' 'Jesus Christ, the same yesterday, to day and for ever.' Thy redeeming God calls out, 'I will never leave thee, nor forsake thee.' 'Turn, O backsliding children, saith the Lord; for I am married unto you.' O there is a deceitfulness in sin! When Satan has got you down, he tries to make you think God has forsaken you.

2. *A time of danger.* There is no time when you may be more inclined to think God has forsaken you, than when sin and Satan are raging. There is a difference from sin raging and sin reigning, though the soul may not see it. In such a time, remember these words — 'I will never leave thee, nor forsake thee.' In a time of temptation, the believer should remember this promise. Jacob rested on it; Solomon rested on it: yea, it is a staff which has been leaned on by many believers, and you may lean on it too.

3. *When creatures leave you.* Some of you may be bereft of your substance, but remember, 'I will never leave thee, nor forsake thee.' Some of you may be called upon — some have been called upon —

to part with those who are dear to you. Some of you may be called upon to part with your teachers; but remember — and, Oh! it is hard to remember — that he that makes the creatures pleasant, still lives. Brethren, I do not know a lesson in the world that is harder to learn than this. It was God that gave me the creatures; and, now that he has taken them away, in himself I can find all that I had in them. O then! remember this — 'I will never leave thee, nor forsake thee.' Bereavements come suddenly, they come like the whirlwind; but O remember that he comes and says, 'I will never leave thee, nor forsake thee.' And, O brethren! remember that the word 'never' reaches to death — it reaches to the judgment seat. You may lay hold of that word there — 'I will never leave thee, nor forsake thee.' And when the judgment is past, these words will be the eternal solace of all those here who have believed — 'I will never leave thee, nor forsake thee.' Eternity alone will unfold the riches of this promise. He who died for us will be our eternal friend; and he who sanctifies us will for ever dwell in us; and then God, who loved us, will be ever with us. Then will we get into the meaning of his promise — 'I will never leave thee, nor forsake thee.'   Amen.

SERMON XXVI

THE OFFICE OF THE RULING ELDER [1]

1 Timothy 5.17. *Let the elders that rule well be counted worthy of double honour, especially those who labour in the word and doctrine.*

The first thing to be observed in these words is the person of whom the apostle speaks: '*The elders* that tule well.'

The second thing to be noticed, is the manner in which they execute their office: They '*rule well.*'

And the third thing is the reward: Let them be counted '*worthy of double honour*'.

1. First of all, *the persons of whom the apostle speaks,* 'The elders that rule well.' Now, it is quite obvious to every reflecting mind that there are two classes of elders spoken of here — the elders that *rule*

---

[1] This sermon was preached at the ordination of elders in St Peter's, on Sabbath forenoon, 25th December 1842.

well, and the elders who labour in word and doctrine. There are some who labour in the word and doctrine. These elders we now call pastors, but we know that in the time of the apostles they were called elders. Peter says, 'The elders which are among you I exhort, who am also an *elder*.' It is quite plain that God has set apart a class of men to be elders or ministers, and they know little of the work of a minister who thinks that they should not give themselves wholly to it. But it is quite plain that there is another class of elders here spoken of, the *elders* who rule well. It is quite plain that God has set apart a class of men not to labour in word and doctrine, but to rule the house of God. We saw lately that when Christ stood before Pilate, he said, 'My kingdom is not of this world; if my kingdom were of this world then would my servants fight for me.' Now, brethren, the ruling elder is exactly the magistrate to rule the house of God. He is not to labour in the word and doctrine, but to administer the laws of Christ's house.

2. The second thing to be noticed in these words is *the manner in which they do the work*. 'They rule well.' Paul knew quite well that there would be many who would be lazy elders, therefore Paul says they that rule well are worthy of double honour. The word in the original means, 'double reward'.

3. The third thing to be considered in these words is *the reward*. 'Let the elders that rule well be counted worthy of double honour.' You may compare this verse with the one that follows. 'For the scripture saith, Thou shalt not muzzle the ox that treadeth out the corn. And, the labourer is worthy of his reward.' From this verse many have concluded, and I think rightly, that a temporal reward was part of this double honour. The ruling elder it is supposed received a support. And our Scottish Reformers set out first of all with this practice. But there is far more meant in this double honour; it means that you should esteem them very highly for their work's sake.

I. Upon this passage I would put the following proposition:
There ought to be ruling elders in every church of Christ. It is plain that in every church of Christ we ought not only to preach according to the Word of God, but also rule according to the Word of God. And here, first of all, I desire you to notice, that so far as I can see, every church ought to have a plurality of elders. See Acts 14.23: 'And when they had ordained them elders in every church, and had prayed with fasting, they commended them to the Lord.' You will notice that in the previous part of this chapter Paul and Barnabas had been preaching the gospel at Lystra and Iconium, and Antioch, and there were a considerable number that believed on Jesus, so when they returned to them they ordained elders in every city. See

also Titus 1.5: 'For this cause left I thee in Crete, that thou shouldst set in order the things that are wanting, and ordain elders in every city, as I had appointed thee.' You will observe that Paul left Titus in the island of Crete for the purpose of ordaining elders in every city. Not one but many. Just as the 14th of Acts shows that there ought to be a plurality of elders in every church, so this shows that there ought to be a plurality in every city. See again, James 5.14: 'Is any sick among you? let him call for the elders of the church.' Here you will notice that the sick member is not to call for one elder, but many; proving that there is a plurality. Now, brethren, it is quite plain that it cannot mean that they were all labourers in the word and doctrine. The churches were so small that they did not seem more than one, it therefore follows that there ought to be elders to rule in every church.

I think this is proved from the distinction that is made between the pastor and the ruling elder. See Romans 12.4-8: 'For as we have many members in one body, and all members have not the same office; so we being many are one body in Christ, and every one members one of another. Having then gifts, differing according to the grace that is given to us; whether prophecy, let us prophecy according to the proportion of faith; or ministry, let us wait on our ministering; or he that teacheth, on teaching; or he that exorteth, on exhortation: he that giveth let him do it with simplicity; he that ruleth, with diligence; he that showeth mercy, with cheerfulness.' Now it seems quite obvious that the three outstanding officers of the Church are here spoken of: first, he that ministereth, or teacheth; second, he that giveth; and third, he that ruleth. It is quite obvious that these are not offices all in one person, for the apostle takes his illustration from the body which hath many members, and all these members have not the same office. Compare this with the 12th chapter of 1 Corinthians, verses 27-30: 'Now ye are the body of Christ, and members in particular. And God hath set some in the Church; first, apostles; secondarily, prophets; thirdly, teachers; after that, miracles; then gifts of healing, helps, governments, diversities of tongues. Are all apostles? are all prophets? are all teachers? are all workers of miracles? have all the gifts of healing? do all speak with tongues? do all interpret?' Now, this passage shews this same thing. If you lay aside apostles, miracles, and gifts of healing, which appear to have ceased, then there remains the three outstanding helps that are in the Church; first, teachers, secondly, helps; and lastly, governments. And you may observe that God has put them in; and we may therefore well say, What God hath joined together, let no man put asunder. And the third passage I would quote, is the words of the text: 'Let the elders that rule well be counted worthy of double honour, especially they who labour in word and doctrine.' Now, brethren, from these three passages it seems to be the design of the Spirit that one member of the body should preach, another rule, and a third distribute to the necessity of the saints.

I would prove the same thing from the absolute necessity of the case. If Christ's Church is to be taught well, then there ought to be pastors and teachers. If Christ's Church is to be ruled well, then there ought to be men set apart for this purpose. I remember well when I first entered upon the ministry among you. I had very inadequate views of the duty of ruling well the house of God. I thought that my great and almost only work was to pray and preach. I saw your souls to be so precious, and the time so short, that I devoted all my time, and care, and strength to labour in word and doctrine. When cases of discipline were brought before me and the elders, I regarded them with something like abhorrence. It was a duty I shrank from: and I may truly say it nearly drove me from the work of the ministry among you altogether. But it pleased God, who teaches his servants in another way than man teaches, to bless some of the cases of discipline to the manifest and undeniable conversion of the souls of those under our care; and from that hour a new light broke in upon my mind, and I saw that if preaching be an ordinance of Christ, so is church discipline. I now feel very deeply persuaded, that both are of God — that two keys are committed to us by Christ; the one the key of doctrine, by means of which we unlock the treasures of the Bible; and the other, the key of discipline, by which we open or shut the way to the sealing ordinances of the faith. Both are Christ's gift, and neither are to be resigned without sin. And I am deeply persuaded that that Church will flourish best, that is ruled best. Now, brethren, if the Church is to be ruled well, and if there was nothing in the Bible about it, I think that our Head would smile on such a thing as the appointment of elders for this work. I feel, brethren, that a minister alone is incapable of ruling the house of God well. It cannot be; if a minister is to thrive in his own soul, and be successful in his work, he must be the half of his time on his knees. And the great fault I find with this generation is that they cry that ministers should be more in public; they think that it is an easy thing to interpret the Word of God, and to preach. But a minister's duty is not so much public as private; and therefore, if Christ's house is to be ruled well, there must not only be pastors, but there must be ruling elders.

II. *The duty of the ruling elders.* But as I intend to show this in my address to them, I pass over it at present, and come to the third point.

III. *What are the qualifications* laid down in the Word of God for an elder that would rule well?

1. And the first qualification is *grace*. Brethren, if it be a qualification in a church member that he should have grace, then much more ought it to be a qualification in one who rules the Church of God. Brethren, think for a moment. How is it possible for an elder to admit any to the Lord's table, when he is but a Judas himself? How is it possible for him to excommunicate any, when he ought to be excommunicated himself? How is it possible for an elder to pray over the sick, when he ought to be taught himself to pray? Who would set a man to be a magistrate, who is a rebel against the queen? So, brethren, a graceless elder is a curse instead of a blessing.

2. A second qualification is *wisdom*. You remember it is written in the 6th of Acts concerning the deacons, that they were to be 'men of honest report, full of the Holy Ghost and wisdom'.

And, brethren, if this is a qualification required in a deacon, much more then in an elder. All Christians are not wise. You would not say that every one is fitted to be a civil magistrate; so it is true that every Christian is not fitted to be an elder. There are often questions brought before elders that are most difficult to solve, and which all are not fitted for.

3 A third qualification is that he be of *good report*. See 1 Timothy 3.7: 'He must have a good report of them that are without.' He must have a good report not only of those that are within, but also of those that are without. You must know, brethren, that an elder must mix with the world more than a pastor. Therefore it is necessary that the world see that they are men of honesty, and that their conversation is grave and serious. Brethren, there is nothing more important than this — that they should not only be esteemed by the Church, but also by the world.

4. Another qualification is they should be *public spirited men*. You know this is the qualification that is looked for in civil rulers. Now if this be true of the civil magistrate, much more so with an elder. The Master of the house did not please himself, and should not the servant imitate the Master. It is complained of by Paul, that all seek their own, and not the things of Jesus Christ.

5. And last of all, another qualification is that he should be a *prayerful man*. My dear brethren, the office of the eldership is a hard work. It is an uphill work; and, therefore, if there is a man in all the world that needs prayer, it is an elder. We are the servants of a good and mighty Master, and as long as we keep near to him he will give us strength. And he ought to be one who prays in his family as well as in secret. You may not know that an elder who does not keep worship in his family may be suspended from his office. I would

take leave to read to you the Act of Assembly, 1722, on this head: 'The General Assembly do earnestly beseech, exhort, and require elders and deacons to be faithful in the discharge of their respective offices, tender and circumspect in their walk, and punctual in their attending upon ordinances, and strict in their observances of the Lord's day, and in regularly keeping up the worship of God in their families. And the General Assembly appoints the judicators of the church to take good heed that none be admitted to, or continued in these offices, but such as are found qualified, and do behave themselves as above required.' This, then, is the law of our Church.

And he should be a social man in the prayer meeting. Every district should have its prayer meeting. O what a lovely scene would this place present, if every little district had its prayer meeting! Every elder should fan the flame that shall yet burn over Scotland.

I come now, lastly, *to the reward of the ruling elder.*

1. *Good success.* This is the chiefest reward of minister or elder. I would say with good old Philip Henry, 'I would rather see one soul saved than have thousands of gold and silver.' I have shown you, brethren, that the work of discipline has been blessed already; and if it is more exercised it will do good in time to come.

2. Another reward is, *the esteem of all good men.* It is true that the world will hate that elder most who is likest his Master; but all good men will pray for him. For my part, I would rather have the esteem of a little child of God than the esteem of princes.

3. Last of all, *there is a good reward in heaven.* When the good Shepherd shall appear, he will receive a crown of life that fadeth not away. It is not only the pastor, but the elder, that will receive a crown of life. You will be a crown of joy and rejoicing in that day.   Amen.

SERMON XXVII

THE MIGHTY CONQUEROR

Revelation 19.12. *On his head were many crowns.* Verse 17. *And he hath on his vesture and on his thigh a name written, King of kings, and Lord of lords.*

I believe, dear friends, that this passage describes the great last controversy Christ will have with this world. He has had many a controversy with it, but the last will be the greatest of all; so that it is called 'the supper of the great God'. Now, it is interesting to notice that this last conflict will be about his kingly office; not merely his controversy about his body the Church, but whether he is to be King of kings, and Lord of lords. And the final issue is already written down, verse 17: 'And I saw an angel stand in the sun: and he cried with a loud voice, saying to all the fowls that fly in the midst of heaven, Come and gather yourselves together unto the supper of the great God: that ye may eat the flesh of kings, and the flesh of captains, and the flesh of mighty men.' etc. It is interesting to notice that this great controversy, which appears to be decided at the second coming of Christ, is acted over before, in miniature, just that all believers may have an opportunity of showing what side they would be on.

Let me mention some of the many crowns that are here said to be on the head of Christ. There can be no doubt that the person on the white horse is the Lord Jesus. He is called, 'the Word of God', a name given to none other but he. You remember John, in his Gospel, says, 'In the beginning was the Word, and the Word was with God, and the Word was God.'

There are three of the crowns of Christ I would mention tonight. I do not mention the crown of creation, or the crown of providence; but I would rather speak of his mediatorial crown — the crown he has a mediator. There are three crowns he has as mediator. The first is his crown of King over all; the second is his crown over his Church; and the third is his crown over the invisible Church — King of saints.

I. *Christ has got the crown over all things to the Church.* You will see this in Matthew 28.18: 'All power is given unto me in heaven and on earth.' See also Ephesians 1.22, 'He hath put all things under his feet and gave him to be the head over all things to the church.' Now, brethren, you will observe that these two passages leave nothing that is not put under him. All power in heaven and on earth is his. And he is made head over all things to the Church; that is for the benefit of the Church.

1. *He is head over angels:* 'Let all the angels of God worship him.' We read in Revelation that the angels join in the song: 'Worthy is the Lamb that was slain, to receive power, and riches, and wisdom, and strength, and honour, and glory, and blessing.' We read in the 25th chapter of Matthew, 31st verse, that when Christ comes in his glory, all the holy angels will come with him. All the holy angels, then, are under his power. He is the head of angels. He is the confirmer of the angels.

2. And again, *he is king of devils*. It is written in Genesis: 'It shall bruise thy head, and thou shalt bruise his heel.' And you read often in the gospel, of Christ casting our devils. And remember the maniac on the other side of the sea of Galilee. When Christ commanded the devils to come out of him, they besought him to be allowed to enter into the swine, and he allowed them. How plainly does this show that Christ is king over devils. And we are told in the 68th Psalm that when he ascended up on high, 'he led captivity captive'. The word 'captivity' refers to Satan, the great captivator. And we are told the same thing in the 2nd of Colossians, 15th verse — 'Having spoiled principalities and powers, he made a show of them openly, triumphing over them' in his cross. How plainly does Christ show by this that hè is king of devils.

3. And not only is he Lord of angels and devils, *but also of men*. See Revelation 1.5: 'Jesus Christ, the faithful witness, the first-begotten of the dead, and the Prince of kings of the earth.' Ah! it is true that as a King he is mocked by many kings; but still it is true that he is 'the Prince of kings of the earth'; Assyria is the rod of his anger — the saw in the hand of the sawer.

And not only over kings, but over nations. In the Psalm we sung, it is said,

> *The floods, O Lord, have lifted up,*
> *They lifted up their voice;*
> *The floods have lifted up their waves,*
> *And made a mighty noise.*

> *But yet the Lord, that is on high,*
> *Is more of might by far*
> *Than noise of many waters is,*
> *Or great sea-billows are.*

These are just fulfilling his purpose. And the nations who are agitated like the waves of the sea, they too are but fulfilling his purpose. Just as that vast and rolling ocean with its myriads of myriads of angry waves as they rise, only fulfil his purpose. So is it with the nations of the earth, they are tossed with one political opinion after another — with one commotion after another, yet they are just fulfilling his purpose, and he will bring order out of confusion. Ah! friends, he is King of kings and Lord of lords. He is the Governor among the nations.

4. Still further, *Christ is Lord over nature, animate and inanimate*. 1. *He is Lord over inanimate nature*. Who is this that comes walking on the sea at the fourth watch? It is the Lord of all. Who is this that stands up in the little bark, and says to the raging billows, 'Peace, be still'? What manner of man is this that even the winds and sea obey

him? Ah, it is Jesus the Lord of all. He is Lord of inanimate nature.
2. And in like manner *he is Lord of animate nature*. Who is this that
commands the fig-tree to wither? It is the Lord of all. Who is this
that commands the fish to bring the silver piece to Peter? Even he
who is said, in the eighth Psalm, to have dominion over all sheep and
oxen, yea, and the beasts of the field; the fowl of the air, and the fish
of the sea, and whatsoever passeth through the paths of the sea.

Dear friends, there is a twofold lesson to be learned from this — a
lesson of comfort to the saints, and of dismay to the wicked.

1. *To the saint.* He will make all things work together for your
good. He that is thy friend, thy Redeemer; it is he that has the many
crowns on his head. You may be poor, but he is rich, and his riches
he will bestow on you. He has got all things under his feet. He is head
over all things for you; head over angels, head over devils, head over
men, head over nature, animate and inanimate. 'All things are
yours; whether Paul, or Apollos, or Cephas, or the world, or life, or
death, or things present, or things to come; all are yours, and ye are
Christ's; and Christ is God's,' 1 Cor. 3.21-23. O what a lesson of
consolation is this! There is not a wave of the sea but is thy servant,
employed to waft thee to glory.

2. And now turn we to learn *a lesson of dismay to the Christless.*
You think this way is foolishness, and more than madness; but ah!
sinner, do you know whom you despise? He is King of kings and
Lord of lords. He has got all kings, and angels, and devils, and men
under him. Ah! remember that if Christ is against thee, there is none
that can be for thee. O learn the utter foolishness of opposing Christ!
Think, if you are persecuting his members, you are opposing him.
'Saul, Saul, why persecutest thou me!' Think, if you are opposing
him, you are opposing one who has all power, and therefore able to
destroy.

II. I come now to the second crown that Christ wears — *His
crown over the visible church.* This is the kingdom that he spoke of
to Pilate — 'My kingdom is not of this world.' It is beautifully
described in the Confession of Faith: 'The catholic, or universal
church, which is invisible, consists of the whole number of the elect
that have been, are, or shall be gathered into one, under Christ, the
head thereof; and is the spouse, the body, the fulness of Him that
filleth all in all.' This is the invisible church, of which I am not now
speaking, but then follows: 'The visible church, which is also
catholic, or universal, under the gospel (not confined to one nation,
as before, under the law), consists of all those throughout the world
that profess the true religion, together with their children, and is the
kingdom of our Lord Jesus Christ, the house and family of God, out
of which there is no ordinary possibility of salvation.' Observe that

the visible church is composed of all those who profess the Christian religion, with their children. So that there are many among them who are not Christ's. Yet man is not allowed to reject them, for he cannot see the heart. So that now, you will observe that this is his kingdom over which he rules. The clearest evidence of this is in the first three chapters of Revelation. For example, the first chapter, thirteenth verse: 'And in the midst of the seven candlesticks was one like unto the Son of man, clothed with a garment down to his feet, and girt about the paps with a golden girdle.' Now, observe, the garment appears to be the robe worn by the priest; but then, the golden girdle — what do we make of it? It cannot refer to the priesthood, for the priest did not have such a thing; so that we are constrained to believe that it refers to his kingly office. I have no doubt but that this chapter is intended to represent Christ as prophet, priest, and king of his church. And to confirm this, just observe, that there are characteristics mentioned that do not appertain to the priesthood; for example, in the 2nd chapter, 16th verse, it is said, 'Repent; or else I will come unto thee quickly, and will fight against them with the sword of my mouth.' Observe, this is his kingly power. Another example is at the 23rd verse, 'And I will kill her children with death; and all the churches shall know that I am he which searcheth the reins and hearts; and I will give to every one of you according to his works.' Observe, it was not the duty of the priests to destroy men's lives, but to save them. So that here we have the kingly office of Christ. But some will say that this is the invisible church that is mentioned. But observe it is to the churches that the epistles are addressed. There were many only professors. What make you of Sardis, which had a name to live, and was dead? So that the golden candesticks represent the churches as they were, not as they ought to be. So that this shows Christ not only to be king of saints, but king over the church. Christ is the appointed King of Zion — 'I have set my king upon my holy hill of Zion.' Now, brethren, to explain this more fully, let me show you two things that he doth to this kingdom.

He appoints officers, and gives laws. This is what our Queen does. She appoints officers, and she gives laws. So is it with Christ, he appoints his ministers. He has appointed three sorts of ministers in his church. He has appointed pastors, then elders to assist the pastors, and then deacons to serve tables — to look after the poor. These are the officers he appoints over the visible church. He has given — 'Some apostles; some, elders; some, pastors and teachers.' Then he hath not only given officers, but laws. Let me mention some of the laws of the kingdom — 'Go ye into all the world, and preach the gospel to every creature.' This one of Christ's laws, and, you will observe, if any say we are not to teach and preach, they are rebelling against the Lamb. This is a law that has often been interfered with. You know ministers were forbidden to preach in a certain district some time ago. And there was a time in Scotland, when people were forbidden to attend conventicles, when Hugh McKail, and Cameron, and Renwick, were martyred for preaching the gospel. And this is the spirit that is amongst us at present; men wish to take the power out of Christ's hand. There is another law, namely, the appointment of sacraments. Christ said, 'Go and baptise all nations.' — 'This do in remembrance of me.' These commands were first given to the disciples, and are now given to ministers. There is another law. It is the law commonly called that of the keys. Christ said to Peter, and afterwards to all the disciples, — 'I give unto thee the keys of the kingdom of heaven, and whatsoever thou shalt bind on earth shall be bound in heaven: and whatsoever thou shalt loose on earth shall be loosed in heaven.' I believe that whatever we do in discipline according to the laws of Christ, it is ratified and sealed in heaven.

2. And then there are some laws for his people. One is to hear the word. 'Take heed how you hear.' Christ commands you to hear his preached word. There may come times, such as there were under the second Charles, when men will be forbidden to hear preaching. Another law is the choosing of their own office-bearers, 'Look ye out among you men of honest report, full of the Holy Ghost, and wisdom.' This is a fundamental law of Christ's kingdom. Another law is, you are to submit yourself to those who bear rule over you. There is a passage in the end of the Hebrews that speaks of this: 'Obey them that have the rule over you, and submit yourselves, for they watch for your souls, as they must give account.' Heb. 13.17.

I will not prosecute this farther; but, remember that Christ is not only King of kings, but King of his Church. This is what has been attacked in our day, and it is this which we are called upon to defend. You remember what Livingstone says: 'What would you think of the man who, when the city was beseiged, should buckle on his armour, and run to the east port, where there was no danger, while the enemy was at the west?' Now, it is Christ's kingly office that they are attacking, and it is this we ought to defend. They say Christ is not King in his Church. They say Christ has not given power to his ministers — power to ordain or refuse. Ah! friends, this is the point of the kingly office which is attacked, and it is this which you are called on to defend.

III. I come now to the third and last point: *Christ is king of his own redeemed body.* It is from this that he gets the title of 'King of saints'. 'Who shall not fear thee, thou King of saints?' There are three things which Christ does as a king to every saved soul. The first is at conversion, see Acts 5.31: 'Him hath God exalted with his right hand to be a Prince and a Saviour, for to give repentance to Israel, and forgiveness of sins.' You will notice that the office of Christ as King is to give repentance and forgiveness of sins. It is his work to say, 'Live!' Ah! friends, has he done this to you? Observe, it is not the work of man: 'He will not give his glory to another, neither his praise to graven images.' It is from his throne at the right hand of God that he sends the Spirit, and makes three thousand cry out, 'Men and brethren, what shall we do to be saved?' It is a most affecting truth I have shewn you, that you may be a member of his kingdom, and not a member of his grace. Another kingly act of Christ over his Church is to forgive sins. 'The Son of man hath power on earth to forgive sins.' Ah! dear friends, it is a kingly act to give pardon. The third work that Christ does as a King over his body is to sanctify them. It is written in Micah, 'Who is a God like unto thee, that pardoneth iniquity, and passeth by the transgressions of the remnant of his heritage? he retaineth not his anger for ever, because he delighteth in mercy,' Micah 7.18. Those whom the king pardons he subdues. Ah! dear friends, enquire if Christ is your King, by his subduing you. How happy are those of you who can say, Christ is my King! Dear friends, enquire if you are under this third crown. The third is the sweetest of all. He wears all his other crowns for this one. It is interesting to notice that in the first ages of the Church, Christians were martyred for the priestly office of Christ: at the Reformation they were martyred for his prophetical office: and it is reserved, it may be, for us to be martyred for his kingly office: it was this, you remember the Covenanters were martyred for. How necessary then, to be found on the right side!

Thursday Evening,
26th January 1843.

SERMON XXVIII

APOSTACY

Hebrews 6. 4-6. *For it is impossible for those who were once enlightened, and have tasted of the heavenly gift, and were made partakers of the Holy Ghost, and have tasted the good word of God, and the powers of the world to come, if they shall fall away, to renew them again unto repentance; seeing they have crucified to themselves the Son of God afresh, and put him to an open shame.*

There can be no doubt, dear friends, but that this is one of the most difficult passages in the Word of God. It has a depth in which an elephant may swim. Many stumble over it to their own destruction. Pray unfeignedly that we may be kept from erring in speaking from it.

There are two principal interpretations of these words which I would consider.

I. *There are some divines who believe professors are here spoken of.* They who, like the foolish virgins, have lamps and a wick, but no oil in their vessels. They who come a far way to Christ, but who do not come altogether.

I would humbly offer you three reasons why I think that this is not the right interpretation of these words.

1. It is said, they are enlightened, that they have tasted of the heavenly gift; that is, Christ, and the powers of the world to come. Now it appears to me that this is the mark of a true believer; a true believer has no more than this.

2. But I have a second objection. I do not believe that mere professors falling away cannot be renewed by repentance. You remember Simon Magus; he fell away into shameful apostasy, but what did the apostle Peter say unto him? 'Repent, therefore, of this thy wickedness, and pray God, if perhaps the thought of thy heart may be forgiven thee,' Acts 8.22. The same thing is true of Manasseh, there is little doubt but that he was a professor. He was brought up under the care of his godly father, Hezekiah, but he fell away into shameful apostasy, and set up a carved image in the holiest of all, and made his children pass through the fire to Moloch. Yet he was brought to repentance.

3. But I have a third objection. It is said, 'It is impossible for those who were once enlightened, and have tasted of the heavenly gift, and were made partakers of the Holy Ghost, and have tasted the good word of God, and the powers of the world to come; if they shall fall away, to renew them again unto repentance.' That is, it is impossible

to bring them back to saving repentance. Now this shows that they were there before. For these three reasons I feel obliged to give up this interpretation.

II. I will now give you the second interpretation which divines put upon these words. *It is that Paul is supposing a case, a case that will never happen.* Suppose 'they who were once enlightened', etc. I believe, dear friends, for the sake of warning sluggish Hebrews, and for the sake of warning you, Paul wrote these dreadful words.

Let us now go over the description here given of a true believer:

1. *They are enlightened*, verse 4. The first thing that the Holy Spirit does when he is converting a soul is to give light: 'Ye were some time darkness, but now are ye light in the Lord.' He pours a flood of light into the unconverted soul, so that it sees itself. You remember at the first creation of the world, God said, 'Let there be light, and there was light.' So it is at the conversion of a soul. The first thing that the Holy Spirit does, is to give knowledge to let us see things as they are — to let us see ourselves as we are — heaven as it is — hell as it is. This light, brethren, too, is sanctifying light. 'Beholding as in a glass the glory of the Lord, we are changed into the same image, from glory to glory.' And this is saving light: 'For this is life eternal, to know thee, the only true God, and Jesus Christ whom thou has sent.' You remember when Paul was converted, there were scales fell from his eyes, and he was enabled to see. Now this is just intended to show us what conversion is — it is as scales falling from the eyes — it is the giving of sight to the blind.

I would now put this question to you, Have you been enlightened? Can you say with the blind man, 'Once I was blind, but now I see'? Have you ever seen the wonder of this plan of salvation of Christ? On the answer of that question rests your conversion. Sometimes when a child has been awakened in a family, and begins to pray, they often ask, What fancy is this? Dear friends, it is no fancy. Such a one now sees that there is a hell — that there is a heaven — that conversion is something real. It is no mere fancy that a man may take up at pleasure. It is divine. Would to God that ye all knew it, for then ye would see that it was no fancy.

2. I come now to the second part of the description, verse 4, '*And have tasted of the heavenly gift.*' The heavenly gift is the gift of God. It is the same that is spoken of in John 1.14. 'The Word was made flesh, and dwelt among us (and we beheld his glory, the glory as of the only begotten of the Father), full of grace and truth.' Paul calls it 'the unspeakable gift' — 'Thanks be to God for his unspeakable gift,' 2 Cor. 9.15. In these words it is called 'the heavenly gift'. I suppose it is called the heavenly gift in allusion to the manna that came down from heaven. And that to taste of the heavenly gift, I

think, means to have a real experience of Christ. Those who would interpret the words as referring to professors, say it means slightly to taste; but this is not the meaning of these words, they mean to have a real experience of Christ. It is said in Hebrews 2.9, 'He tasted death for every man.' Again, in the thirty-fourth Psalm, 8th verse, 'O taste and see that the Lord is good.' That is to have a real experience of God's goodness. Have you then tasted of the heavenly gift? You know he would have been a foolish Israelite, who gathered the manna in the morning, and ground it and made it into cakes, but who never tasted of it.

3. They are *made partakers of the Holy Ghost.*' When a soul tastes the heavenly gift, then it is made a partaker of the Holy Ghost. And observe the word 'partakers'. It means sharers alike — sharers with all that are believers. And not only so, but ye are partakers also with Christ; for the Holy Ghost that dwells in Christ dwells in the believer. And you are partakers with God; 'For if sons then heirs, heirs of God, and joint heirs with Jesus Christ.' Do you, O believer, feel anything of this? You that hate believers know nothing of this. And remember, brethren, you that are not receivers of the Holy Ghost, are none of his. You may have the name! you may have the shell! you may have the outward form! but you know him not.

4. But again, *they have tasted the good word of God.*' I believe that this just means the Word of God — the Word which God has given us. It is what is spoken of in Isaiah 52.7, 'How beautiful upon the mountains are the feet of him that bringeth good tidings, that publisheth peace,' etc. It is the same word as spoken of in Isaiah 50.4, 'The Lord God hath given me the tongue of the learned, that I should know how to speak a word in season to him that is weary.' It is the same the angels spoke of when they appeared to the shepherds of Bethlehem: 'Fear not; for behold, I bring you glad tidings of great joy which shall be to all people. For unto you is born this day, in the city of David, a Saviour, which is Christ the Lord.' This is the word of God: and to taste the Word of God is to relish it — to relish it as you do your necessary food. How many taste it not! How many look round to the clock, and say, When will it be done? Ah! you have not tasted the good Word of God; and why is this? It is because you know not Christ — it is because you are on the way to hell.

5. *They live under 'the power of the world to come'.* The unconverted live under the power of this world — under the power of money — under the power of fame. Unconverted men live under the power of these things; but converted souls live under the power of the world to come: their anchor is within the veil. How is it with you? Do you live within sight of an eternal heaven or an eternal hell? My dear brethren, there is a world to come. There is a world to

come, whether you believe it or not. There is but a step between you and it. Many do not believe in a world to come at all. You that are swearers, you do not believe that there is a world to come. You that are Sabbath-breakers, you do not believe that there is a world to come. You that sell that which makes the drunkard drunken, you do not believe that there is a world to come. You do not believe there is a hell, else you could not live as you do.

Now, dear friends, I have but a moment to apply this to those whom Paul applied it to. And I would just state it simply to you, that I do not believe it is possible for a child of God to fall away and perish. They may fall, but they can never fall finally. They may fall as David did — they may fall as Abraham did — they may fall as Peter did, but they can never perish; for the faithfulness of God stands against it; the faithfulness of the Son stands against it — 'Lo, these are they which thou hast given me, and I have kept them and none of them is lost'; and the faithfulness of the Holy Spirit stands against it. Some then will ask: What is the use of these fearful words? They are to keep you from drawing back. Take an illustration: I believe that the angels can never fall, according to that passage in 1 Timothy 5.21; but they might look over the golden battlements of heaven to that place of torment, and say, *If* we had sinned, that would have been our portion. Amen.

SERMON XXIX

THE SPIRIT COMMITTED TO GOD [1]

Psalm 31.5. *Into thine hand I commit my spirit; thou hast redeemed me, Lord God of truth.*

There is something peculiarly interesting in these words; they are the words of the Lord Jesus when he hung upon the cross — he hung upon it for six long hours in bitter agony. The gall and the vinegar

---

1 This sermon was preached on Sabbath afternoon, 10th July, 1842, being the first after a severe attack of illness which the author experienced.

were bitter, but it was nothing to the wrath of God. It was at the last hour of his agony Christ said, 'Into thine hand I commit my spirit; thou hast redeemed me, Lord God of truth.' The very soul which he had made an offering for sin, he committed into the hand of God. There is something very precious in being allowed to use the same expression as Christ. There is something very pleasant in being allowed to use the words of a departed friend, and that a beloved friend. There is no friend like Christ. 'This is my beloved, and this is my friend.' There is something sweet in being allowed to use the words of Christ, in the 40th Psalm: 'Innumerable evils have compassed me about, and mine iniquities have taken such hold upon me, that I cannot look up.' There is something pleasant for a sinner to be allowed to use the words of Christ in the 40th of Isaiah, 'My way is hid from the Lord, and my judgment is passed over from my God.' In like manner it is sweet for a poor dying worm to be allowed to use the words before us.

From these words let us consider:
1. The person that speaks.
2. The person addressed.
3. The thing committed.

I. *The person that speaks.* It is an afflicted, tempest-tossed soul. Such was David, no doubt, when he wrote this Psalm. He says, verse 4, 'Pull me out of the net that they have laid privily for me.' Or, verse 8, 'And has not shut me up into the hand of the enemy,' etc. He was a poor, afflicted, tempest-tossed man. He felt that Satan and his own wicked heart were too many for him. 'Pull me out of the net that they have laid privily for me.' Such was Christ's, in that day especially, when he said, 'This is your hour, and the power of darkness.' 'Strong bulls of Basham have beset me round.' He was an afflicted, tempest-tossed soul. And, no doubt, there may be such within hearing; if so, these words are for them. They were used by the Head when he suffered for them, and he intended that they should be used by the members. Dear tempest-tossed soul, he can deliver thee. Put up this prayer, 'Into thine hand I commit my spirit; thou has redeemed me, Lord God of truth.'

II. *The person addressed.* This is the Redeemer. On the one hand there is a poor tempest-tossed believer; on the other hand there is the all-sufficient Redeemer. On the ground lies a poor tempest-tossed man; above him stands the all-sufficient Redeemer. It is to this mighty Redeemer we must go. When Christ spoke these words, he no doubt spoke to the Father, 'Into thine hand I commit my spirit; thou hast redeemed me, Lord God of truth.' Some will ask, Did Christ need to be redeemed? Ah! yes, he had our sins laid upon him, and on that account needed to be redeemed. And therefore he said, when he was at the end of the work, 'Into thine hand I commit my spirit; thou has redeemed me, Lord God of truth.' The very spirit that had been made an offering for sin. When Stephen took up the same words, he did not address them to God, but to the Redeemer; he said, 'Lord Jesus, receive my spirit.' As if he had said, 'Into thine hand I commit my spirit.' Ah! brethren, this is the only hand that can receive our spirit, none other but him who has redeemed us.

III. *What it is he commits into his hand* — 'my spirit.' The soul of man is the most precious part of man. I do not intend to speak lightly of the body, but it is not to be compared to the soul. The outer man is the setting, but the soul is the diamond. It was the spirit that was made in the likeness of God. The body will go to the dust, but not so the spirit. When free from the body it will sin no more — I mean the redeemed soul — it will be clouded no more; sin and it will be for ever separated. It was this that David committed into the hand of God. It was this that Christ committed into the hand of his Father. It is this that every poor tempest-tossed soul will commit to God. 'What shall it profit a man if he should gain the whole world, and lose his own soul?' How long will the devil deceive you, brethren? How long will you neglect the unchanging, unsatisfied spirit?

In applying these words, I desire to show you a few of those times we should commit our spirit to God.

1. *In the time of conversion.* It is the first time that ever a sinner commits his spirit into the hand of God. I think this is what Paul means when he says to Timothy, 'I know in whom I have believed, and am persuaded that he is able to keep that which I have committed unto him, against that day.' You will observe, in the Bible, that conversion is sometimes spoken of from God's part in it. Again, it is sometimes spoken of from the sinner's part in it. There is no contradiction in these two. Conversion begins first on God's part; but the Spirit works on the sinner; it produces faith in him, draws him to Jesus, and enables him to forsake sin. Dear brethren, I must speak to you seriously, and say that it is your solemn duty, as well as your sweet privilege, to commit your soul into the hand of God in conversion. In whose hand have you placed your spirit? Have you put it into the hand of the world? Was it crucified for you? Have you committed your soul into the hand of Satan, as Ahab did? He sold himself to work all manner of wickedness. What can he do for it? Can he give it peace? Can he give it joy? Can he fit it for heaven? But there are some who have committed their soul into the hand of God. There are those in this congregation who can look up to him against whom the sword of justice awoke, and say, 'Into thine hand I commit my spirit' — my poor, polluted, tempest-tossed spirit. I

would urge upon you all to commit your spirit to him. If your spirit be not committed to him, will it be saved? In a little, your spirit will return to God, who gave it, and if it be not committed into the hand of him who bore our sins, in his own body on the tree, how will you appear? Ah! but some will say, Will he receive my spirit? Ah! will he not? Did ever he say, That spirit is too vile for me — that spirit has lived too long in sin? 'This is a faithful saying, and worthy of all acceptation, that Jesus Christ came into the world to save sinners.' Chief of sinners, commit thy spirit to him.

2. To those of you who may be *tempted believers*. I say, a time of temptation is a time to put up this prayer. There are some believers who, for a long time after believing, know not what temptation is. They are like Napthali, 'satisfied with favour, and full with the blessing of the Lord.' They have eternal sunshine; but perhaps they fall when temptation comes, and they feel with Job, 'When thou hidest thy face I am troubled.' Then he goes to his knees, but he finds no comfort. He goes to the Bible, but it is a sealed book. He goes to Christian friends, but miserable comforters are they all. Now, what can he do? There is hardly such a word he can put up as this — 'Into thine hand I commit my spirit; thou hast redeemed me, Lord God of truth,' — thou hast paid thy own precious blood to redeem me; wilt thou shut me up into the hand of mine enemy? 'Pull me out of the net.' 'Into thine hand I commit my spirit; thou hast redeemed me, Lord God of truth.' There is a ray of hope springs from these words, 'Lord God of truth.' Thou hast said, 'Thy sheep shall never perish, neither shall any pluck them out of thy hand.' Thou hast said, 'The very God of peace sanctify thee wholly, and I pray God your whole soul, and body and spirit, may be preserved blameless until the coming of Jesus Christ.' Wilt thou not do all that thou hast said?

3. To those among you who may be *in affliction*. Many Christians know nothing of affliction. They are allowed to sail smoothly on; no storm comes near their little bark. They do not know what it is to write 'Ichabod' — the glory is departed — on their dwellings; or like Naomi to say, 'Call me not Naomi, call me Marah, for the Lord hath dealt bitterly with me.' Dear brethren, it is not always that you will have these days. Days of darkness and disease will come, and what is to be done? There is only one place you can go to. 'Into thine hand I commit my spirit; thou hast redeemed me, Lord God of truth.'

4. To those of you who are looking forward *to duty*. When a believer first comes to Christ, his time is all taken up about the gate, not about the way. I have been much struck with young believers. When they have been hearing a sermon, they say, How did you like

that sermon? not, What am I the better of it? But, if you are a believer, you will feel that you have as much to do with the way as with the gate. Commit thy spirit to him. O brethren, he can carry you! 'Even to hoar hairs I am he; and even to old age will I carry you.' There is none but he can carry you — before duty to guide, in duty to direct, after duty to accept. Commit thy spirit into his hand; he will guide you. 'Thou shalt hear a voice behind thee saying, This is the way, walk ye in it.'

Last of all, *to dying believers*. It was our Head that used this prayer, and it may well suit all the members. It is a solemn thing to die, because we will have to go alone. It is solemn because we are going where we never went before; all is strange and new. When we go to a throne of grace, we have been there before, and know the way; but to go *there* is dark, because we go we know not where. And then it is dark, because it is a final step. It is a solemn thing to die, because if we die wrong we cannot come back to die again. These are some of the things that make up the valley of the shadow of death. In such a time, what are we to do? Commit thy spirit into his hand. You must commit your spirit to Christ in the same way as you did in the converting hour. There is no hand that can reach across Jordan but his. There is none that can say 'Peace, be still,' but Jesus. 'Jesus Christ, the same yesterday, today, and forever.' Dear brethren, are you preparing for death? Do you not know that soon another voice will be heard here, another voice will lead the psalm? It is a hard thing for a believer to commit his spirit into the hand of Christ. What then will you do, you that are giving your soul to the god of this world? — what will you do when God says, Go to the gods which you have chosen, commit your spirit to the world you have loved?   Amen.

SERMON XXX

CHRIST THE LIFE

John 5.40. *Ye will not come to me, that ye might have life.*

There is, brethren, to my mind, nothing more affecting than just to hear of the multitudes that came around the Lord of glory, and yet were not saved by him. There were multitudes that pressed upon him as he preached by the Lake of Galilee; and they crowded round him when he preached in the house; and when he went to the mountain-side, they followed him; or, when he left the mountain-side, and came to Jerusalem, they still followed him, and he used to stand and cry, 'If any man thirst, let him come unto me and drink.' Never man spake like this man. His were choice words; and then they were delivered with such divine tenderness that the like has never been spoken since; and yet men were not saved by them. All his preaching in Galilee seems to have only converted about five hundred, of which we read in 1 Corinthians 15.6. Brethren, does it not affect your hearts to think of Christ standing in the midst of perishing sinners, and yet they would not come to him, that they might have life? My dear friends, we have the same scene before us now. You know, 'he is the same yesterday, today, and for ever.' He is still walking in the midst of the seven golden candlesticks. He is still as able to save as ever; and you will all need him. You need his arm to deliver you; and yet you will not come to him, that you might have life. Most here die unsaved — 'Many are called but few are chosen.'

I would now, dear brethren, depending on the Spirit's aid, show you:

1. The life that is in the hand of Christ.
2. The witnesses that all point you to go to Christ.
3. The reason why any are unsaved — 'Ye will not come.'

1. *The life that is here said to be in the hand of Christ* — 'Ye will not come to me, that ye might have life.' It is here implied, then, that Christ has life, and that you all stand in need of it. The life that is in the hand of Christ may be described in three ways — life judicial, life spiritual, and life eternal.

1. *Life judicial.* You know that when a man receives a pardon from government he is said to receive his life. So it is here. The word is used in the same sense in the 24th verse: 'Verily, verily, I say unto you, he that heareth my word, and believeth on him that sent me, hath everlasting life, and shall not come into condemnation; but is passed from death unto life.' In this verse, you will notice that life is opposed to condemnation, and it appears to mean justification. The same meaning may be attached to those words in the 20th chapter, 31st verse: 'These are written, that ye might believe that Jesus is the Christ, the Son of God; and that, believing, ye might have life through his name.' See also the first Epistle of John, 5th chapter, 12th verse: 'He that hath the Son hath life; and he that hath not the Son hath not life.' In this passage, life appears to be the pardon of all sin, and admission into the favour of God. And it is said in Proverbs, 'He that findeth me findeth life.' Now, Christ when he stood in the midst of the Jews, knew that they were all under the sentence of the

broken law, and he knew that he was to die for sinners; therefore he said to them, 'Ye will not come to me, that ye might have life.' In my hand there is a pardon — 'The Son of man hath power on earth to forgive sins;' yet ye will not come to me. This is true among yourselves; he is as much here present as he was then. He has suffered, the just for the unjust. He has died for sinners, and now he offers you pardon. Why are you not saved? The reason is, ye will not come to him, that ye might have life.

2. But I said that it implied *spiritual life* — the life that the Spirit begets in the soul. It is what is spoken of in the 25th verse: 'Verily, verily, I say unto you, the hour is coming, and now is, when the dead shall hear the voice of the Son of God; and they that shall hear shall live.' The same life is spoken of in Galatians 2.20: 'I am crucified with Christ; nevertheless I live; yet not I, but Christ liveth in me.' He is life. Spiritual life proceeds from the heart of Christ in the believer. See also Colossians 3.3: 'For ye are dead, and your life is hid with Christ in God.' Brethren, this life, the fountain of it, is in the heart of Christ. When Christ stood in the midst of the Jews, he knew that they were dead. He knew that their wills were dead, so that they had no will to choose him. He knew that their whole affections and spiritual beings were dead; and therefore he said, 'Ye will not come to me that ye might have life.' There was in Christ living water that might wash a thousand worlds; yet they would not come to him. It is the same with you. Christ stands and says, 'I will pour out my Spirit upon you;' but you are dead — your ear is closed, so that you do not hear the melody of a Saviour's voice; but in Christ there is life. He is ready to quicken whom he will. He is ready to make you a living soul, and yet you will not come. This is the reason why you perish — you will not come.

3. But I said that *eternal life* was implied in these words — 'Ye will not come to me that ye might have life.' These words are continually used to signify eternal life. It is said in the 25th of Matthew, 'These shall go away into everlasting punishment, but the righteous into life eternal.' And it is said in John, 'God so loved the world, that he gave his only begotten Son, that whosoever believeth on him should not perish, but have everlasting life.' And it is said in Galatians, 'He that soweth to the flesh shall of the flesh reap corruption; but he that soweth to the spirit shall of the spirit reap life everlasting.' Now, when Christ stood among the Jews, he knew that they were dead. He knew that they were walking over the fire that never shall be quenched. And, O brethren! it was this that made him cry so earnestly, 'Ye will not come to me, that ye might have life.' There is life eternal in his hand — 'I give unto you eternal life.' He was always willing to give it. Had the chief of his enemies come, they

too would have got it; but, ah! 'Ye will not come to me.' It is the same with you. Those of you who have not been born again are on the brink of destruction, disguise it as you will; but Christ has the very thing that you need. Why will you not come to him that you may have life?

II. I come now to consider *the witnesses that bear witness of him.* The *first* witness is mentioned in the 33rd verse: 'Ye sent unto John, and he bare witness unto the truth.' Compare this with the 1st. chapter of John, 6th verse: 'There was a man sent from God, whose name was John. The same came for a witness, to bear witness of the Light, that all men through him might believe.' The very purpose for which God sent John into the world was to bear witness of the Light — to bear witness of Christ. Now, the very same people were willing to hear John. Like Herod, they heard him gladly, and did many things; and yet for all that they would not come to Christ, that they might have life. They were willing for a season to rejoice in his light; and yet they refused that light itself. Ah! it is the same still. God has sent many Johns into the world to point to Christ; and though the light be dim, compared with that of John, yet we all point to that light. Many of you hear us gladly; but will you come to Christ? Ah! it is a strange thing that you are willing to hear about Christ, but yet you will not come to him. Ah! that will be your condemnation in the judgment.

There is a *second* witness mentioned in the 36th verse: 'But I have a greater witness than that of John; for the works which the Father hath given me to finish, the same works that I do, bear witness of me that the Father has sent me.' The works which the Father sent Christ to do were twofold — (1) works on the bodies of men; (2) works on the souls of men. A little before, he had cured an impotent man; and a little before that, he had cured the ruler's son. But there were other kinds of work he had come to do — I mean works on the souls of men. He had said unto a màn sick of the palsy, 'Thy sins be forgiven thee.' He said to a woman taken in adultery, 'Neither do I condemn thee.' These words bore witness of him; and yet they would not come unto him that they might have life. Brethren, I say the same to you — 'The works that I do in my Father's name, they bear witness of me.' I believe that there are none here who have not seen some converted by their side. You have seen a wife, perhaps, or a husband, or a neighbour; you have seen them live as the children of a king. Have you not seen all that? and yet you will not come to him, that you might have life. His works bear witness that he is a Saviour ready to pardon; and yet you will not commit your soul into his hand, and therefore are not saved.

Notice a *third* witness in the 37th verse — 'And the Father

himself, which hath sent me, hath borne witness of me.' The third
witness whom Christ called was the Father. The Father bore witness
to Christ in many ways. You remember at his baptism the Father
said, 'This is my beloved Son, in whom I am well pleased.' And then
the Father bears witness of Christ by his teaching sinners — 'It is
written in the prophets, And they shall be all taught of God. Every
one, therefore, that hath learned of the Father cometh unto me.'
Here you will observe that the Father is represented as the great
teacher, no doubt by the Holy Spirit. Now, in this very way the
Father bears witness of his Son. He had sent the Spirit to strive with
them; but they had resisted the Spirit. Just as Stephen says, 'Ye
stiff-necked and uncircumcised in heart and ears, ye do always resist
the Holy Ghost: as your fathers did, so do ye.' And the Father bears
witness in your consciences. He pleads with you; and yet you will not
come to Christ for all that, that ye might have life. And the Father
bears witness in times of trial and affliction: He says, 'Turn ye, turn
ye; why will you die?' O brethren! is it not sad to think that you will
not come for all that, that ye might have life?

Notice a *fourth* witness, verse 39: 'Search the Scriptures; for in
them ye think ye have eternal life; and they are they which testify of
me.' The last witness which Christ summons is the Scriptures. The
whole Bible testifies of Christ. Moses testified of him; and the
Psalms testify of Jesus; and the Gospel testifies of him. O brethren!
the whole Bible from the beginning to the end testifies of Christ. It
testifies of the way of pardon through his blood; and yet he says, 'Ye
will not come to me, that ye might have life.' You go to your Bible,
and it says, Go to Christ. But you will not come. You will go to your
minister, and yet you will not come to Christ.

Brethren, all these witnesses will rise in the judgment against you.
The ministers that have preached to you will rise up in judgment,
and say, They would not come. And those who have been converted
by your side will bear witness against you. Then the Father will bear
witness against you: he will say, 'I pleaded with you by my mercies,
and by my judgments; yet you would not come.' The very Bible will
bear witness against you in the judgment — 'Do not think that I will
accuse you to the Father: there is one that accuseth you, even Moses,
in whom ye trust.' O my brethren! what will you say in the judgment
when all these testify against you? Ah! it will only be said, you would
not have life.

III. I come now, in the last place, to consider *the reason here given
why sinners do not come to the Saviour*: 'Ye will not come to me,
that ye might have life.' Brethren, he was a true Saviour that spoke
these words. He was a wise Saviour — one who was in the beginning
with God; and yet he says, 'Ye will not come to me, that ye might

have life.' I believe that Christ could have given other reasons, why they did not come: he could have opened the book of life, and showed them that their names were never written there — that they were reprobates. But he chooses this reason — 'Ye will not come.' He stops here and says — 'Ye will not come to me, that ye might have life.' Perhaps you cannot explain why your names are not in the book of life, and yet you are invited to come. But this is not the reason why you will not come. What then is the reason? Many will not come through ignorance. Like the Jews, you go about to establish your own righteousness, and will not submit to the righteousness of God. I believe that there are many here who are as ignorant of the way of pardon as a Hindu who never heard the Gospel. 'If thou knewest the gift of God, and who it is that saith to thee, Give me to drink, thou wouldst have asked of him, and he would have given thee living water.' If you knew what a Saviour was offered you — if you knew the power of his Spirit to change the most devilish and wicked heart — you would fall down at his feet and say, 'Though he slay me, yet will I trust in him.' And there are some of you whose lust keeps you from coming to Christ. There are some of you who would take the pardon he offers — you are willing that Christ should save you from hell; but you have heard that he would save you from your sin; and this is your condemnation, that light hath come into the world, and that you love the darkness rather than the light, because your deeds are evil. You love your games, — you love your glass; and, therefore, you will not come to him that you might have life.

O my brethren! I have just to entreat you to think of two things: The first is, *How will you meet Christ in the day of judgment?* Christ will say, 'I have often gathered you as a hen gathereth her brood under her wings, and you would not.' I sent you my ministers, and you were willing for a season to abide in their light; but yet you would not come to me. I converted many by your side, and yet you would not come. My Father pleaded with you, and yet you would not come. Every page of the Bible pleaded with you, yet you would not come. O what will you say to the Lord of glory when he puts these accusations to you? And then again, *How will you feel throughout eternity, with these words ringing in your ears — 'Ye will not come to me, that ye might have life'*? When you have been a thousand years in hell, and when you look forward to an eternity of it, and think that the reason why you are there is that you would not come to Christ that you might have life. Oh! will you not say, 'Cursed ignorance! cursed folly!' O brethren! this one text will be bitter like gall and wormwood, in eternity. Oh! you will say, that it were blotted out of the Bible — that it were blotted out of my memory!   Amen.

SERMON XXXI

FAITH'S VIEW OF CHRIST

John 20.20. *And when he had so said, he showed unto them his hands and his side. Then were the disciples glad when they saw the Lord.*

When the Lord of glory left his Father's bosom, and came into this world, we are sure it was for a purpose suited to his divine nature. Christ came to make men glad. It was said of him, 'The Spirit of the Lord God is upon me, because the Lord hath appointed me to preach good tidings unto the meek,' Isaiah 61.1. Ah! sure, he must be a good Saviour that was to bind up broken hearts, and to make all men glad. Therefore, when he came, he said, 'That their joy might be full.' And you see in the verse before our text, his first words to his disciples were, 'Peace be unto you.' But the devil wants you to believe that we want to take away your mirth and joy. He is a liar, and he was a liar from the beginning. Jesus came not to destroy men's lives, but to save them; so do we. We come to break your false joy — to awaken you from your dream — before you be dashed into the burning lake. Ah! we come to give you fulness of joy that cannot wither — joy that cannot die. True, believers have sorrow; they have a poor frail body, and they may have false friends. They may have ungodly children; they have temptations and persecutions. The world knows nothing of these sorrows. But they have a joy that the world cannot give or take away. They have a joy to balance all their sorrows; they have 'joy unspeakable and full of glory'. It is a joy that will never die. It will be brighter and brighter throughout an endless eternity.

But let us consider what it was that made the disciples glad: first, what it was not, and then what it was.

I. What it was not.

1. *It was not riches.* They were all poor fishermen; none of them had nets of their own. Like their Lord, they were poor. A scribe said, 'Lord, I will follow thee, whithersoever thou goest.' Jesus said, 'The foxes have holes, and the birds of the air have nests; but the Son of man hath not where to lay his head.' When Jesus rose again, he did not give his disciples riches. Paul said he was poor; yet he possessed all things. Ah! it is not joy that riches give. You may have a little money in the bank, but it may be taken away. The bank may fail, and you lose it. Ah! riches will not profit you in the day of wrath. You remember the rich man mentioned in Luke 16. Ah! what did his riches do for him in the fire of hell? He could not get a drop of water

to cool his tongue.

2. *It was not friends that made the disciples glad.* Ah! some of you may have a family — an undivided family; or you may have friends in the world — you may have bosom companions, or lovers; but ah! these will not give you joy. The disciples did not care for friends — that did not give them joy. Notice, the doors where they were assembled, were shut for fear of the Jews. The world that hated and crucified their Master, hated them. They were like sheep in the midst of wolves; yet they were glad — their joy was not of earth. Ah, no! creature joys will soon be taken away.

3. *Their joy did not proceed from their own righteousness.* Some have all their joy from looking at themselves. Ah! that is a joy of earth — a joy that will prove false whenever the trumpet sounds; a joy that will all be dashed whenever the cry is made, 'Behold the bridegroom cometh.' Ah! is this your joy? Do you have all your joy from your looking at your own filthy polluted hearts? The disciples did not do this. Ah, no! What would they have seen there? They had once known the Lord; but they had all forsaken him in his sufferings — one of them had denied him — they were cast down — they did not know what to do; but they were glad when they saw the Lord. Ah! many of you are going to hell. Look at yourselves, and if your way be the right way, then has Christ suffered and died in vain.

4. *The disciples' joy did not flow from a sight of Christ with the bodily eyes.* Ah! some of you think, 'O if I had been there, I would have been glad,' but it was not seeing him with the bodily eye that made them glad — for two reasons: First of all, because many saw him, and only wagged the head, and spat upon him. Ah! they could look upon his nailed hands, and pierced bleeding side, and only mock. And every one in this assembly shall see him, for 'every eye shall see him'; and many shall wail because of him. It will be the beginning of eternal damnation to some of you. Second reason — It was not by seeing Christ with the bodily eye, for many have felt the same joy that the disciples did who never saw Christ with the bodily eye.

5. *The disciples' joy did not proceed from seeing their Master again.* The joy they had flowed from looking at his hands and side. It was not that he had risen and come to be with them again —it was seeing his hands and his side — 'And when he had so said he showed them his hands and his side; then were the disciples glad when they saw the Lord.'

II. What it was that made the disciples glad.

1. *It was the sense they had got that his work was finished.* When they saw his hands and his side, they saw his work was all completed. They saw the holy Lamb standing before them — he who had been

so lately pierced — with the mark of the spear still in his side. They saw the meaning of that passage in Isaiah 53.5: 'But he was wounded for our transgressions; he was bruised for our iniquities; the chastisement of our peace was upon him: and with his stripes we are healed.' When Peter looked upon him, he understood those words he afterwards wrote down — 'Who his own self, bare our sins in his own body on the tree,' 1 Peter 2.24. They saw that all the wrath due to them was poured out on Jesus; their debt was paid to the uttermost farthing, and no wonder, then, they were glad. Christ had finished the work the Father had given him to do. That prophecy in Daniel was fulfilled: 'The Messiah shall be cut off, but not for himself.' 'To finish transgression, and to make an end of sins, and to make reconciliation for iniquity, and to bring in everlasting righteousness.' Ah, brethren! it was this that made the disciples glad; they saw that all they ought to suffer was suffered for them: 'They entered into peace.' 'Then were the disciples glad when they saw the Lord.' They were to be sad no more. Ah! do not many of you look to yourselves? You do not belong to Christ. You are only glad when you look to your own righteousness. But the disciples were glad when they saw Jesus as the Lord their righteousness. It was then, and only then, that they were glad. O when will you be glad? When will you have true joy? O sinner! look to Jesus. It is only when we see that he has suffered all, and done all we had to do, that we are glad — that our joy will be full.

2. *The disciples were glad, for they saw Jesus was their living Head.* 'Because I live, ye shall live also.' 'In the world ye shall have tribulation; but, be of good cheer, I have overcome the world.' The disciples were no doubt sad — they felt a load of guilt; but now they would rejoice, for they had got a sight of him as an ever-living Saviour. Now, Peter would know how to get his proud heart subdued. Jesus was living — and he would reign till all his enemies were put under his feet. Ah! beloved! if we had a sight of a crucified, living, reigning Jesus, we would get all our enemies subdued. O look, sinner! Look, all of you! Oh! then you will have true joy. For my own part, I never knew what joy was till I felt that Jesus had died for me — that he lived for me and reigned for me. The world can give you a little joy; but here is fulness of joy. 'We that have believed do enter into rest.'

I would now apply this.

1. *You may learn from this if you are disciples.* What does your joy flow from? Does it flow from riches — from friends? The disciples' joy proceeded from a spiritual sight of the Lord Jesus. When are your happiest moments? Are they when the world prospers with you? When friends are kind — when friends and lovers

come around you? Is your joy gone when they are taken away? Ah! then, you are a disciple of the devil! 'Then were the disciples glad when they saw the Lord.' Examine again. Does it flow from your own righteousness? Does it flow from your knowledge of the Bible? — from your many prayers? Does it flow from self? Then it is not a disciple's joy. 'Then were the disciples glad when they saw the Lord.'

2. *I would exhort all present to seek a sight of Jesus.* O seek this joy! — a joy that will not pass away. Friends will be taken away — riches may flee away; but this joy will never pass away. O seek a spiritual discovery of the excellency of Christ's person and work! O it is a sweet joy! It is *that* that will be with you in death. The Author of it says, 'I will never leave thee nor forsake thee.' O let not the world keep you from looking to Jesus! It is eternal life — life eternal.

3. *To you that are seeking Christ night and day.* O how glad you will be when you find the Lord! Look away from all to Jesus. O look to him as a crucified risen Saviour! O get a sight of his beauty and his love! O dear anxious soul! seek to have joy by looking at the finished work of the Lord Jesus.

4. *To you that once had this joy, but have backslidden and lost it.* Ah! you must look again to Jesus. The disciples had it once, but they had lost it; but Jesus came to them: 'Then were the disciples glad when they saw the Lord.' Ah! we must have a spiritual discovery of his complete work, and his living power. O seek a true joy — a full joy!

Here learn all of you the *folly of self-righteousness.* Suppose the disciples had looked to themselves, what would they have seen? One had denied — all of them had forsaken him in his sufferings; but the disciples looked only to Jesus: 'Then were the disciples glad when they saw the Lord.' Look, then, to Jesus, and you will have true peace, true joy, fulness of joy — joy that the world cannot give nor take away. You that are Christ's rejoice in the Lord always, and again I say, rejoice. May God bless his own word.   Amen.

SERMON XXXII

THE LORD'S DEALINGS WITH HIS PEOPLE

Isaiah 46.3, 4. *Hearken unto me, O house of Jacob, and all the remnant of the house of Israel, which are borne by me from the belly, which are carried from the womb. And even in your old age I am he; and even to hoar hairs will I carry you: I have made, and I will bear: even I will carry and will deliver you.*

There are times in the life of a believer when he is like a traveller who has arrived at some high eminence; he can look back on the way he has gone and the way he has yet to go. So this is a passage where God tells us what he has done and what he will yet do. The history of a believer is wonderful, whether we look backward or forward. If we look back, there is election in a past eternity; and if we look forward, there is deliverance and final victory. As Christ's name is 'Wonderful,' so all the members of his body are wonderful, for they are 'men wondered at.'

The history of a believer divides itself into two parts — before and after conversion.

I. Let us consider *the past history of a believer.* Verse 3: 'Hearken unto me, O house of Jacob and all the remnant of the house of Israel, which are borne by me from the belly, which are carried from the womb.' God follows his chosen vessels before their conversion. Now, let us notice some of his providences; and the first before they are awakened is, *in preserving them.* There are some, I believe that are like John, 'filled with the Holy Ghost even from their mother's womb'; or like Jeremiah, 'before thou camest out of the womb I sanctified thee.' But this is not the way commonly, for 'we are shapen in iniquity and conceived in sin.' We are degenerate plants of a strange vine. Now those that are vessels of mercy are kept safe. God keeps them from falling into hell. They are often brought to the brink of it, it may be by a fever, or such like; but 'he sends his word and heals them.' Others are cut down; but God spares his chosen vessels. A second providence before conversion is, *God does not take away his Holy Spirit from them.* It is a wonder God does not take it away. Often they resist and grieve the Spirit, and sin against convictions. Ah, brethren! we will never know till eternity, what a mercy it was that God never took away his Spirit from us. A third mercy before conversion is, *he brings them to the place where they are awakened.* Who brought Zaccheus to the sycamore tree? It was the same hand that beckoned him to come down. Who brought the woman of Samaria to the well? The same that told her all things that ever she did. Who brought you and me to the place where we were awakened? It was he that hath 'borne us from the belly, and carried us from the womb.' — he who is the Alpha and the Omega.

A second part of the believer's history is the *time after awakening and before conversion*. Unconverted souls are Satan's property; and when Christ comes in, no wonder that Satan roars and is enraged; and so does the world — they do not like to see their companions leaving them. The tenderest parent is often enraged at his child leaving him. But let us notice what God does for them after they are awakened.

1. First of all, *he does not let them go back*. He makes them say, 'I have opened my mouth to the Lord, and I cannot go back.' — I will never, never go back. Ah! many are driven back like a ship before a stormy sea. Once they bade fair for Christ and for heaven; but they could not bear the tempest of hell and the rage of an ungodly world. But God's children are carried forward: they are carried by God from the belly — they are borne by him from the womb. Ah! you are not driven back by persecutions, nor by a tempting world. You can tell the world you have opened your mouth to the Lord, and you cannot — you will not go back. God help us to go forward!

2. *God keeps them from refuges of lies*. Some set out with great anxiety, but fall asleep, and never awake till they hear the voice, 'Come to judgment! Come to judgment! Come away!' Others take rest in outward forms, prayer, and ordinances. Some go farther still — they take rest in their feelings. These are refuges of lies; but chosen vessels are carried past these refuges of lies; and they are carried past the temptations of the world. It is a sweet thing to be carried by Jesus.

3. Another mercy is, *they are carried to Jesus* — to the Rock, the smitten Rock, to the wounded, bleeding bosom of Jesus. God never rests till he carries them to his Son — 'I drew them with cords of love.' It is God that does it. Oh! if any of you have been brought to the Rock that is higher than you, it is God that has done it. He does all, from election to coronation. O it is quite natural to be awakened, but not so to be brought to Jesus — to leave all your own righteousness, and to take the righteousness of another. O it is divine! None but God can make you do it. Ah! can you say, then, 'In the Lord have I righteousness and strength'?

II. Let us consider *the future part of a believer's history*. Verse 4: 'And even to your old age I am he; and even to hoar hairs will I carry you: I have made and I will bear; even I will carry, and will deliver you.' Here you may observe three particulars.

1. *Who is it that offers to carry them even to old age?* It is 'I am he,' — 'He.' It is the very same being that has brought us hitherto

that will carry us on till he sets us down in glory. Ah! it is a sweet truth — 'And even to your old age I am he; and even to hoar hairs will I carry you.' The future history of those of you who are come to Christ is unknown to yourselves. God in mercy hath hid it from us; but he hath carried us through the worst already; and do you think that he that has carried us thus far will let us slip now? — Ah, no! 'And even to old age I am he; and even to hoars hairs will I carry you! I have made, and I will bear,' etc. Let us notice some of the believer's trials, while journeying through the wilderness. 1. *Temptation.* It is when you are brought to Christ that you feel temptation. But, ah! you can then say, 'Rejoice not against me, O mine enemy! When I fall, I shall arise; and when I sit in darkness the Lord shall be a light unto me,' Micah 7.8. Never, till a man is brought to Christ, does Satan rage and put forth such wily temptations: 'Simon, Simon, behold, Satan hath desired to have you, that he might sift you as wheat,' Luke 22.31. As long as you are away from Christ the devil will let you pray, read the Bible, and come to the house of God, and let you think you believe; but, when Jesus comes and draws you to himself, then temptations begin. Many a believer is like to fail in the day of adversity; but, beloved, fear not. There is one who hath made and will bear — who will carry, and deliver you. 2. *There are afflictions.* Ah! there are many, many afflictions, beloved, between you and the better land. There are the afflictions of a poor, frail, dying body. There are also soul afflictions — darkness, desertions, doubting, fears. And there are family afflictions. But ah! there is a hand engaged to carry us through. It matters not the rugged mountains, if the sheep be on the Shepherd's shoulder. 3. *The time may be long.* Some may have a short fight and a sure victory — but a step to the crown. Others of you may have long, long to tarry here. This sweet promise is to you — 'And even to old age I am he,' etc.

2. Let us consider *how he will carry us.* 'Through faith.' They are 'kept by the power of God through faith unto salvation.' It is by faith you first found peace to your soul; so by faith you will be carried to the end. You came empty at first, and you found Christ; so you must come to the last. You came hell-deserving, undone, and closed with him as the Lord your righteousness; so you must come to the last. You came weak, and you found strength — you came poor, and you were made rich: so you must come to the last.

3. Consider *why he will carry us.* 1. *Because he hath said it.* And hath he said it, and will he not do it? It is impossible for God to lie. God will carry you. He hath pledged his word he will do it. 2. He will carry us *because his honour is engaged.* If we were suffered to drop from the Shepherd's shoulder, then all in heaven — all in hell — would hear of it; but, ah! no. Though we sin every day, yet he

pardons us every day — he blots out all our iniquities. 3. Another reason why he will carry us is, *because he loves us.* Ah, beloved, he love us better every day. It was said of Jesus, 'He increased in wisdom and stature, and in favour with God and man.' So it is with all that are united to him. If, when we were enemies, God loved and Jesus died for us, how much more now, being reconciled by the death of his Son! Ah, yes! he will love us — 'I have made, and I will bear; even I will carry, and will deliver you.'

I would now apply this subject.

1. *To you that are bold,* and have no fears — no doubts. Ah! rejoice with trembling. Believer, you are carried by the same hand. The nailed hand of Jesus is underneath you. Walk softly.

2. *To you that are fearful,* fear not: your Redeemer is strong. He that brought you to Christ will bring you safe to glory. He, from his throne, will put the crown upon your head — the crown of victory. He *will* do it — 'I have made, and I will bear; even I will carry, and will deliver you.' 'Greater is he that is for you, than he that is in the world.' 'Fear not, little flock: it is your Father's good pleasure to give you the kingdom.' May God bless his word.   Amen.

SERMON XXXIII

FUTURE   PUNISHMENT   ETERNAL

Mark 9.44. *Where their worm dieth not, and the fire is not quenched.*

It is very interesting to notice who they are in the Bible that speak about hell. Now, some think that speaking about hell is not preaching the gospel; and others think that simple men have no right to speak of it. Now, to them who think it is not gospel preaching, I say it is the truth — the Word of God; and to them who say it is not right to speak about it, I would have them to notice who it is that speaks most about it. Let us consider,

1.   The persons in the Bible that speak most about hell.
2.   Why these persons speak so plainly of hell.
3.   The names given to hell.
4.   The hell spoken of in the Bible is not annihilation.
5.   This eternal hell is closed in and surrounded by the attributes of God.

I. *Let us consider the persons in the Bible that speak about hell.*
And the first I would mention is David. He was a man after God's own
heart, yet he speaks of hell. He who wrote all the Psalms, the sweet
Psalmist of Israel; he who was filled with love to men, and love to God;
yet hear what he says about hell: 'The sorrows of hell compassed me
about,' Psalm 18.5. Again, 'The sorrows of death compassed me
about, and the pains of hell gat hold upon me,' Psalm 116.3. And hear
of his deliverance: 'And thou hast delivered my soul from the lowest
hell,' Psalm 86.13. And he tells us also of the fate of the ungodly that
will not accept Christ: 'The wicked shall be turned into hell, and all
the nations that forget God,' Psalm 9.17. 'Upon the wicked he shall
rain snares, fire, and brimstone, and an horrible tempest; this shall be
the portion of their cup,' Psalm 11.6. 'Let death seize upon them, and
let them go down quick into hell,' Psalm 55.15. Now, whatever you
think of the propriety of speaking about hell, David did not think it
wrong, for he sang about it.

The next person I would mention is Paul. He was filled with the love
of Christ, and he had great love to sinners. Surely that love wherewith
God loved Jesus was in Paul. He loved his enemies: notice when he
stood before Agrippa, what his feelings were, 'I would to God that not
only thou, but also all that hear me this day, were both almost and
altogether such as I am, except these bonds,' Acts 26.29. He wished
them to have the same love — the same joy — the same peace — the
same hope of glory. Now, Paul never mentions the word hell. It
seemed as if it were too awful a word for him to mention; yet hear what
he says, 'What if God willing to show his wrath, and to make his power
known, endured with much long-suffering the vessels of wrath fitted
to destruction,' Rom. 9.22. 'For many walk, of whom I have told you
often, and now tell you, even weeping, that they are the enemies of the
cross of Christ, whose end is destruction,' Phil. 3.18. 'For when they
shall say peace and safety, then sudden destruction cometh upon
them,' 1 Thess. 5.3. 'The Lord Jesus shall be revealed from heaven,
with his mighty angels, in flaming fire, taking vengeance on them that
know not God, and that obey not the gospel of our Lord Jesus Christ,
who shall be punished with everlasting destruction from the presence
of the Lord, and from the glory of his power,' 2 Thess. 1.7-9. Do not
these show you, brethren, that they that have most love in their hearts
speak most of hell?

The next person I would speak of is John, the beloved disciple. He
had leaned on Jesus' bosom at the last supper, and drawn love out of
his bosom. His character was love. You will notice how affectionately
his epistles are written. He addresses them 'beloved,' 'little children.'
Yet he speaks of hell; he calls it, seven times over, 'the bottomless pit'
— the pit where sinners shall sink through all eternity. He calls it, the

great wine press of the wrath of God, Rev. 14.19. But John has got
another name for hell, 'the lake of fire,' Rev. 20.14. It had often been
called 'hell'; but it was left for John, the beloved disciple, to call it 'the
lake of fire.'

The next person I shall mention is the Lord Jesus himself. Although
he came from God, and 'God is love,' though he came to pluck brands
from the burning, yet he speaks of hell. Though his mouth was most
sweet, and his lips like lilies, dropping sweet-smelling myrrh —
though 'the Lord God had given him the tongue of the learned, that he
should know how to speak a word in season to him that is weary';
though he spake as never man spake — yet he spoke of hell. Hear what
he says, 'Whosoever shall say, thou fool, shall be in danger of hell fire,'
Matt. 5.22. But I think the most awful words that ever came from his
lips were, 'Ye serpents, ye generation of vipers, how can ye escape the
damnation of hell?' Matt. 23.33. Again, 'Depart from me, he cursed,
into everlasting fire,' Matt. 25.41. And he speaks of it in some of his
parables too: 'The angels shall come forth and sever the wicked from
among the just, and shall cast them into the furnace of fire; there shall
be wailing and gnashing of teeth,' Matt. 13. 49, 50. And he repeats the
words of our text three times over. And could anything be plainer than
the words in Mark: 'He that believeth not shall be damned.'

II. *Let us consider, dear brethren, why these persons speak so
plainly of hell.*

1. *Because it is all true.* Christ is the faithful and true witness. Once
he said, 'If it were not so, I would have told you.' Once he said to
Pilate: 'Every one that is of the truth heareth my voice.' He himself is
'the truth.' 'It is impossible for God to lie.' When Jesus appeared on
earth, he came with love, he came to tell sinners of hell, and of a
Saviour to save from hell; and how could he keep it back? He saw into
hell, and how could he not speak of it? He was the faithful witness; so
it was with David, Paul, and John. Paul said, he had kept nothing back
— he had not shunned to declare all the counsel of God. Now, how
could he have said that, if he had not spoken of hell as he did? So must
ministers. Suppose I never were to mention hell again, would that
make it less tolerable? Oh, it is true! it is all true! and we cannot but
mention it.

2. *Because they were full of love to sinners.* They are the best friends
that do not flatter us. You know, beloved, Christ's bosom flowed with
love. Out of love he had not where to lay his head; out of love he came
to die; out of love, with tears he said, 'O Jerusalem, Jerusalem, thou
that killest the prophets, and stonest them which are sent unto thee,
how often would I gather thy children together, even as a hen
gathereth her chickens under her wings, and ye would not!' Matt.
23.37. And with the same breath he said, 'How can ye escape the

damnation of hell?' So it was with Paul: 'Knowing, therefore, the terror of the Lord, we persuade men,' 2 Cor. 5.11. Paul would weep over sinners; he says, 'For many walk of whom I have told you often, and now tell you, even weeping, that they are the enemies of the cross of Christ,' Phil. 3.18. His tears fell on the parchment as he wrote. Oh! if we had more love to you, we would tell you more about hell. They do not love you that do not warn you, poor hell-deserving sinners. O remember that love warns!

3. A third reason why they spoke so plainly of hell, was *that they might be free from blood-guiltiness*. Jesus did not want your blood laid at his door, therefore he spoke of the 'furnace of fire,' and of 'the worm that dieth not.' Ah! he says, 'How often would I have gathered you, but you would not!' God would not have bloodguiltiness laid to his charge. He says, 'As I live, saith the Lord God, I have no pleasure in the death of the wicked; but that the wicked turn from his way and live. Turn ye, turn ye from your evil way, for why will ye die?' So it was with David: 'Deliver me from blood-guiltiness, O God!' Psalm 51.14. It was fear of blood-guiltiness that made David speak so plainly. So it was with Paul; he says, 'I take you to record this day, that I am pure from the blood of all men,' Acts 20.26. So it is with ministers — we must acquit our conscience, and if you go to the judgment-seat unpardoned, unsaved, your blood will be upon you own heads. As I was walking in the fields yesterday, that thought came with overwhelming power into my mind, that every one I preached to would soon stand before the judgment-seat, and be sent either to heaven or hell. Therefore, brethren, I must warn you, I must tell you about hell.

III. *Let us consider the names given to hell in the Word of God.* And the first is 'fire'; it is taken from an earthly element suited to our capacity, as Christ takes to himself a name to suit us, as a shepherd, a door, a way, a rock, an apple tree, the rose of Sharon, etc. So when God speaks of heaven, he calls it Paradise, a city which hath foundations, golden streets, pearly gates. Now, one of these names will not describe it, nor any of them; for eye hath not seen, nor ear heard, neither hath it entered into the heart of man to conceive the things God hath prepared for them that love him. So when God speaks of hell he calls it 'a furnace of fire,' 'a bottomless pit,' 'perdition.' Now, one of these names will not do, but take them altogether, and you may conceive something of what hell is.

The first name given to hell is 'fire.' On the southern side of Mount Zion there is a valley covered over with vines — it is the valley of Hinnom, where Manasseh made his children pass through the fire of Moloch. Now, this is the name by which Christ calls it, 'a valley of fire.' And, again, he calls it 'a furnace of fire,' the walls will be fire; it will be fire above and below, and fire all round about. Again it is called a 'lake of fire.' The idea is something like a furnace of fire; it will be enclosed with burning mountains of brass. There will be no breath of wind to pass over their faces; it will be flames of fire for ever and ever. It is called 'devouring fire.' 'Who among us shall dwell with the devouring fire,' Isaiah 33.14. Compare this with Hebrews 12.29: 'For our God is a consuming fire.' It is the nature of fire to consume, so it is with the fire of hell; but it will never annihilate the damned. O it is a fire that will never be quenched; even the burning volcanoes will cease to burn, and that sun now sweetly shining upon us will cease to burn, and that very fire that is to burn up the elements will be quenched; but this fire is never quenched.

Another name given to hell in the Word of God is 'the prison.' So we learn that the multitudes that perished at the flood are shut up in this prison. Ah! sinner, if you are shut up in it you will never come out till you have paid the uttermost farthing, and that you will never do — the bars are the justice and holiness of God.

Another name given to hell is 'the pit.' Ah! it is the bottomless pit, where you will sink for ever and ever; it will be a continual sinking deeper and deeper every day. Ah! sinner, is it not time to begin and cry, 'Deliver me out of the mire, and let me not sink'? 'Let not the deep swallow me up, and let not the pit shut her mouth upon me'?

Another name given to hell in the Word of God is 'a falling into the hands of God,' 'It is a fearful thing to fall into the hands of the living God,' Heb. 10.31. 'Can thine heart endure, or can thine hands be strong, in the days that I shall deal with thee?' Ezek. 22.14. God will be your irreconcilable enemy, sinner. God, who takes no pleasure in the death of the sinner, but rather that he should live — that God, I say, will be your eternal enemy if you die Christless — if you will not believe — if you will not be saved. O what will you do, poor sinner, when his wrath is kindled?

Another name given to hell is 'the second death.' 'And death and hell were cast into the lake of fire. This is the second death,' Rev. 20.14. This is the meaning of God's threatening to Adam: 'In the day that thou eatest thereof thou shalt surely die.' Perhaps you may have stood by the bed of a dying sinner, and you may have seen how he gasps for breath — his teeth clenched — his hands clasp the bed-clothes — his breath turns fainter and fainter till it dies away. Ah! this is the first death: and is like the second death. Ah! the man would try to resist, but he finds it is in vain; he finds eternal hell begun, and God dealing with him, and he sinks into gloom and dark despair. This is the death sinners are to die, and yet never die.

Another name given to hell is 'outer darkness.' Christ calls it outer darkness. 'But the children of the kingdom shall be cast out into outer darkness,' Matt. 8.12. 'Bind him hand and foot, and take him away,

and cast him into outer darkness,' Matt. 22.13. You will see it also in 2
Peter 1.4: 'God spared not the angels that sinned, but cast them down
to hell, and delivered them into chains of darkness.' Again, Jude, 13th
verse: 'Wandering stars, to whom is reserved the blackness of
darkness for ever.' O my dear friends! this is hell — 'the blackness of
darkness,' 'outer darkness,' 'chains of darkness.'

IV. *I come now to show you that the hell spoken of in the Bible is not
annihilation.* Some people think that though they are not saved, they
will be annihilated. O it is a lie; I will show you that:

1. First of all, *by the cries of the damned.* 'And he cried, and said,
Father Abraham, have mercy upon me — for I am tormented in this
flame,' Luke 16.24. And, again, look at the words in Matt. 22.13, 'There
shall be weeping and gnashing of teeth.' Oh! these plainly show us
that it is no annihilation. In hell the multitudes will be bundled up
together in the great harvest day. 'Gather ye together first the tares,
and bind them in bundles to burn them,' Matt. 13.30. There will be
bundles of swearers — bundles of Sabbath-breakers — bundles of
drunkards — bundles of hypocrites — bundles of parents and
children; they will be witnesses of each other's damnation.

2. Hell will be no annihilation, when we consider that *there will be
different degrees of suffering.* 'It shall be more tolerable for Tyre and
Sidon at the day of judgment than for you,' Matt. 11.22. And it is said,
the Pharisees would receive 'greater damnation.' Every man is to be
judged according to his works.

3. It will be no annihilation, if we consider *the fate of Judas.* 'Woe
unto that man by whom the Son of man is betrayed; it had been good
for that man if he had not been born,' Matt. 26.24. Judas is wishing he
had never been born. I have no doubt he wishes to die, but will never
be able to die. So it will be with all here who shall go to hell — all
unworthy communicants. Ah! I tell you, if you die Christless, you will
wish you had never been born — you will wish you had never seen the
green earth or the blue sky. Ah! you will wish you had never been. O
dear brethren! better never to have had a being, than to be in hell. Ah!
there are many in hell today who are cursing the day they were born.

4. It will be no annihilation, for *it is an eternal hell.* Some weak and
foolish men think and please their fancy with the thought that hell will
burn out, and they will come to some place where they may bathe their
weary soul. Ah! you try to make an agreement with hell; but if ever
there come a time when the flame that torments your soul and body
shall burn out, then Jesus will be a liar, for three times he repeats the
words of our text, and says, it shall never be quenched. It is eternal, for
it is spoken of in words never used but to denote eternity. 'And the
smoke of their torment ascendeth up for ever and ever,' Rev. 14.11.
Ah! you see it is for ever and ever. Again, 'And the devil that deceived

them was cast into the lake of fire and brimstone, where the beast and the false prophet are, and shall be tormented day and night for ever and ever,' Rev. 20.10. Compare this with Rev. 4. 9, 10, 'And when those beasts gave glory and honour, and thanks to him that sat on the throne, who liveth for ever and ever,' etc. So you see the torments of the damned are spoken of with the eternity of God. Ah! if ever there come a time when God ceases to live, then they may cease to suffer. Again, the eternity of hell and the eternity of heaven are spoken of in the very same language. 'And there shall be no night there; and they need no candle, neither light of the sun; for the Lord God giveth them light: and they shall reign for ever and ever,' Rev. 22.5. The same words that are used for the eternity of the saints, are used for the eternity of the damned. 'They shall be tormented for ever and ever.' O sinner! if ever there come a time when the saints shall fall from their thrones, or the immortal crowns fall from their heads, then you may think to leave hell; but that will never, never be — it is an eternal hell, 'for ever and ever'; eternity will be never-ending wrath; always wrath to come. O that you were wise, that ye understood this, that ye would consider your latter end.

V. *I come now, last of all, to consider that this eternal hell is surrounded and closed in by the attributes of God.* This I shall leave, God willing, to another occasion.

I shall now apply this: First of all, *to you that are believers.* Dear brothers and sisters, all this hell that I have described is what you and I deserved. We were over the lake of fire, but it was from this that Jesus saved us; he was in the prison for you and me — he drank every drop out of the cup of God's wrath for you and me; he died the just for the unjust. O beloved, how should we prize, love, and adore Jesus for what he hath done for us. O we will never, never know, till safe across Jordan, how our hell has been suffered for us — how our iniquity has been pardoned! But, O beloved! think of hell. Have you no unconverted friends, who are treasuring up wrath against the day of wrath? Oh, have you no prayerless parent, no sister, nor brother? Oh, have you no compassion for them — no mercy's voice to warn them?

2. *To you that are seeking Christ anxiously.* I know some of you are. Dear soul, what a mercy in God to awaken you to flee from this fiery furnace! O what a mercy to be awakened to flee! — to be in earnest. Ah! your unconverted friends will tell you there is no need of being so anxious. O is there no need to flee from the wrath to come? O learn, dear soul, how precious Christ is; he is a hiding place from the wind, and a covert from the tempest. All the things in the world are like a speck of dust, all is lost for Jesus. He is all in all. He is free to you beloved — take no rest till you can say, 'He is mine.'

3. *To you that are unconverted.* Ah! you are fools and you think you

are wise; but O I beseech you, search the Scriptures. Do not take my word about an eternal hell; it is the testimony of God, when he spoke about it. O if it be true — if there be a furnace of fire — if there be a second death — if it is not annihilation, but an eternal hell — O is it reasonable to go on living in sin? You think you are wise — that you are no fanatic — that you are no hypocrite; but you will soon gnash your teeth in pain; it will come; and the bitterest thought will be, that you heard about hell, and yet rejected Christ. O then, turn ye, turn ye, why will ye die? Amen.

Sabbath, 15th July 1842.

SERMON XXXIV

GOD'S RECTITUDE IN FUTURE PUNISHMENT

Psalm 11. 6,7. *Upon the wicked he shall rain snares, fire, and brimstone, and an horrible tempest: this shall be the portion of their cup, for the righteous Lord loveth righteousness.*

Perhaps some of you may remember, about six months ago, I preached to you on the subject of an eternal hell — upon the worm that never dies, and the fire that is never quenched. There are many people that do not like to hear preaching about hell, and some people think that it is not preaching the gospel; nevertheless it is the counsel of God.

I showed you then, who they were that spoke most about hell. I showed you that David speaks of it, he who was a man after God's own heart. He says, 'The wicked shall be turned into hell, and all the nations that forget God.' Then, again, I showed you Paul was another. Although this man spent his whole life preaching the gospel, yet he spoke of 'destruction,' of being a 'castaway.' Another was John. Though he was the disciple that was filled most with love, yet he calls it 'the bottomless pit' seven times over. It is called the 'bottomless pit' because the soul will be for ever sinking in it. And we saw that he calls it what no one else does — 'the lake of fire.' And we saw that another one was Christ himself. We saw that all the apostles put together do not speak so terribly of hell as he. He says, 'How can ye escape the damnation of hell?' 'He that believeth not shall be damned.'

A second thing we inquired into was, why they speak so much about hell? And one reason was — *it is true.* Christ came to tell the truth. Brethren, if it be true, can we speak too plainly about it? If there be a hell of misery to the Christless, can we warn you too often to flee from the wrath to come? Another reason was — *it was love.* If Christ loved you less, he would warn you less. We saw that when Christ spoke about hell he wept. And Paul could not write about the enemies of the cross of Christ without tears — 'Of whom I have told you often, and tell you now even weeping, that they are the enemies of the cross of Christ.' And O, brethren! if only we could pity you more, we would tell you, even weeping. Another reason was — *that we might be free from your blood.* You remember how David cried, 'Free me from blood-guiltiness, O God!' And this is the reason why God speaks so solemnly in the Bible. He says, 'Turn ye, turn ye, why will ye die?' And Christ said, 'O Jerusalem, Jerusalem, how often would I have gathered you as a hen gathereth her brood under her wings, but ye would not!' Does he not wash his hand of your blood? And Paul says, 'I am pure of the blood of all men.'

Another subject I then opened up, was the different names by which hell is called. It is called 'fire' — 'the *gehenna* of fire.' It is called a 'furnace of fire'. In another part it is called 'everlasting fire'. We saw again it was called 'darkness.' Three times over our Lord calls it 'outer darkness.' Then again Peter calls it 'the mist of darkness.' Then again Jude calls it 'everlasting chains under darkness' — 'the blackness of darkness for ever.' In one parable of the Scriptures it is called a 'prison.' 'Agree with thine adversary quickly, lest he deliver thee to the judge, and the judge deliver thee to the officer, and thou be cast into *prison.*' And Peter speaks of 'the spirits in prison.' And in other parts it is called 'the pit' — 'Deliver him from going down to the pit.' Another name by which it is called is 'the second death' — 'the lake of fire, which is the second death.' It is called the second death because it undoes the sinner.

A fourth point was that hell was not annihilation. We saw that it was not annihilation by listening to the cries of the damned — 'I am tormented in this flame' — 'There shall be weeping and wailing and gnashing of teeth.' We saw the same thing in the parable of the tares, 'Gather the tares and bind them in bundles to burn them.' There will be bundles of liars — and bundles of drunkards — and bundles of those who have been the means of seducing one another, and of leading one another to hell. Another thing that proves that it is not annihilation is the case of Judas. It is said, 'It had been better for that man that he had not been born.' Now, if Judas was annihilated, it could have been no worse for him than if he had not been born; better not to be than to be in hell.

The last part of the subject was that hell was eternal. We saw this from the remarkable expression that 'the worm dieth not, and the fire is not quenched.' And we saw that if ever there was a time when the worm would die, and the fire be quenched, then that would be a lie. Another argument was, that hell was to be, 'for ever and ever.' And we noticed that that expression is nowhere used except to express a real eternity. It is used of the existence of God — and so it is used of the saints in glory, that they live for ever and ever. So in like manner it is used of the souls in hell.

There was another part of the subject which I had not time to enter upon, and for which reason I have chosen this text, and that was to prove that an eternal hell was consistent with all the attributes of God. 'Upon the wicked he shall rain snares, fire, and brimstone, and an horrible tempest! this shall be the portion of their cup, for the righteous Lord loveth righteousness.'

From this passage I draw these three propositions:

1.   Hell will be sudden to the wicked, 'Upon the wicked he shall rain snares, fire, and brimstone,' etc.

2.   God will punish the wicked eternally because he loves righteousness.

3.   God will justify the believer for the same reason that he condemns the wicked — 'For the righteous Lord loveth righteousness.'

I. *Hell will be sudden to the wicked.* 'Upon the wicked he shall rain snares, fire, and brimstone, and an horrible tempest; this shall be the portion of their cup.' It is quite obvious that the description here given is taken from what befell Sodom, Gen. 19. 23-25. It was a fine summer morning, the sun had just risen and was shedding his rays down upon the meandering Jordan; the women were busy about their employment, the children were sporting in the morning sun, when suddenly, darkness overcast the sky, and in a moment God rained fire and brimstone from heaven upon them. One moment they were rejoicing in the morning sun, the next they were weltering in the lake of fire. Brethren, I believe that the most of those in this congregation who will finally perish, their destruction will be sudden. It is written, 'Take heed to yourselves lest at any time your hearts be overcharged with surfeiting and drunkenness, and cares of this life, and so that day come upon you unawares.' Observe these words, 'And so that day come upon you unawares.' Compare this with the words of the text. 'Upon the wicked he shall rain snares.' Both passages are taken from the way in which the fowler catches birds; he draws in the snare suddenly, else the bird would escape. Such is the way with the wicked; the second coming of Christ will be like a snare. And, brethren, I believe, again, it is so with all you who die without finding Christ, you will perish suddenly. 'Upon the wicked he shall rain snares, fire and brimstone, and an horrible tempest; this shall be the portion of their cup.' There are many among you that do not believe that there is a hell. Though you read of it in the Bible, and are told about it, still you always put in as a salve to your conscience: 'Perhaps there is not such a place after all — perhaps it is just a bit of priestcraft got up to frighten people with.' I believe that many among you think that, and many of you will die thinking that; but, Oh! the moment you let go the last friend's hand that is grasping yours, that moment, sinner, when you find your soul in the presence of God, and when you find out for the first time that you have God to do with, that moment you will find that there is an eternal hell. 'Upon the wicked he shall rain snares, fire, and brimstone, and an horrible tempest! this shall be the portion of their cup.' O my brethren, methinks hell would not be so bad if you were counting the cost of it; but to have the eyes lifted on it in a moment — ah! you will know what the second death is then.

II. I come to the second proposition, and I desire you to attend to it, for it is what I have chosen these words for. *It is the righteousness of God which makes him punish the wicked eternally.* Verses 6, 7: 'Upon the wicked he shall rain snares, fire, and brimstone, and an horrible tempest; this shall be the portion of their cup, for the righteous Lord loveth righteousness.' I believe there is a great deal of ignorance about an eternal hell. There are many men that think God will cast sinners into hell on account of mere passion. Now, it is right to know that God did not create hell merely out of passion. Brethren, if it was passion it would pass away. But it is not from mere passionateness that he has kindled hell. And it is right that you should still farther consider that it is not that God hath pleasure in the pain of his creatures. I believe that God does not delight in the pain even of a worm. You will see this in Ezek. 18.23: 'Have I any pleasure at all that the wicked should die? saith the Lord God; and not that he should return from his ways and live?' And then, verse 32: 'For I have no pleasure in the death of him that dieth, saith the Lord God: wherefore turn yourselves, and live ye.' You will observe in this chapter that you have it put in two forms; you have it put in the interrogative form, and then you have it in the affirmative. Again, we are told, in the New Testament, that 'God will have all men to repent, and come to the knowledge of the truth.' 'He is not willing that any should perish.' And in the 17th chapter of Acts, it is said, 'God commandeth all men everywhere to repent.' These passages show that there is an essential benevolence in God, that he has no pleasure in the pain of his creatures. Speaking humanly, God would rather that the wicked should turn from his evil ways and live.

Some will ask, Why then is there a hell? The answer, brethren, and it
is an answer I desire to be written on the heart: it is that the
righteous Lord loveth righteousness. The only reason why God casts
the unbelieving into the fire that never shall be quenched is because
God is a God of righteousness, and therefore he will reign till all his
enemies are put under his feet. Perhaps, brethren, some of you will
say, why does his love of righteousness make him punish sinners in
an eternal hell? There are two answers to that: First, sin is an infinite
evil, and therefore it demands an infinite punishment. I do not know
if you understand this. The thing I was praying for in secret was that
I might be enabled to vindicate God's proceedings. Then, brethren,
sin is an infinite evil, because it is the breaking of an infinite
obligation. I suppose there are none here who will say that God is not
infinitely lovely; and therefore none will say that there is not an
infinite obligation upon us to serve him. Then, if you and I do not
this, we are breaking an infinite obligation; and if it be an infinite
evil, then it demands infinite punishment. But how can man bear
infinite punishment. If God were to put on infinite punishment, who
could bear it? Therefore it is eternal in duration: 'Upon the wicked
he shall rain snares, fire, and brimstone, and an horrible tempest,
this shall be the portion of their cup, for the righteous Lord loveth
righteousness.' I said there is another answer to this question; how is
it a righteous thing in God to punish sinners eternally? You know
you would not care what a criminal said at the bar whether his
sentence was just or not. He might probably say it was not just; but
you would believe the judge. Now, God says it is a righteous thing.
See 2 Thess. 1.6: 'Seeing it is a righteous thing with God to
recompense tribulation to them that trouble you.' You will observe it
is said: 'It is a righteous thing with God to recompense tribulation to
them that trouble you.' And how much more then will everlasting
destruction be righteous. God's whole way is equal. God, who holds
the balance in his hand, says it is a righteous thing. Dear brethren, I
pray you, in God's name, to think of this. If punishment come from
the righteousness of God, then there is no hope. If it were out of
passion, then it might pass away. Often you observe a man whose
face is red and swollen with passion, but it passes away. But ah! it is
not out of passion. If it were out of passion surely God would have
some pity when he saw the sufferings of the lost for many ages; but
ah! no. From what then does it proceed? It proceeds from the
rectitude of God. If God can cease to love righteousness, then the
fire may be quenched; but as long as he is a righteous God, that fire
will never be quenched. Oh! brethren, it is a foolish hope you
entertain that the fire will be quenched. I have seen some on their
death-bed thinking that the fire may be quenched. Ah! it is a vain

hope, sinner, God will never cease to be a righteous God. God will do anything to save a sinner; but he cannot part with his rectitude in order to save you. He parted with his Son in order that he might gain sinners, but he cannot part with his righteousness — he cannot part with his government; he would need to call good evil, and evil good first. 'Upon the wicked he shall rain snares, fire, and brimstone, and an horrible tempest; this shall be the portion of their cup, for the righteous Lord loveth righteousness.'

III. I come now to the last point, and that is *that the very same rectitude saves the believer in Jesus.* 'For the righteous Lord loveth righteousness.' I think this is the meaning of these words, 'His countenance beholdeth the upright.' The same thing is spoken of in the passage we read in Thessalonians, 'It is a righteous thing with God to recompense tribulation to them that trouble you; and to you who are troubled rest with us,' etc. The same thing we are taught in the 1st chapter of 1st John, 9th verse, 'If we confess our sins, he is faithful and just to forgive us our sins, and to cleanse us from all unrighteousness.' It is not said he is merciful, but he is just to forgive us our sins. The same thing we are taught in the 1st and 2nd verses of the 40th chapter of Isaiah, 'Comfort ye, comfort ye my people, saith your God, speak ye comfortably unto Jerusalem, and cry unto her, that her warfare is accomplished, that her iniquity is pardoned; for she has received of the Lord's hand double for all her sins.' Here God puts the pardon of Israel on rectitude. 'Her iniquity is pardoned: for she hath received of the Lord's hand double for all her sins.' Why? because in her Surety she hath received double for all her sins. Suppose, then, a sinner was to come to the Surety this night, you will observe that the sins you have committed are doubly paid. If the curse had fallen upon you, you could never have exhausted it; and therefore, upon the ground of equity, 'she hath received of the Lord's hand double for all her sins.' 'He is just to forgive us our sins.' — 'His countenance beholdeth the upright.'

My dear brethren, in impressing this subject upon you, I would speak:

1. *To those of you who are believers.* Dear brethren, you were once condemned to this hell. Over this hell you walked; but God has brought you to a Surety, where you have received of the Lord's hand double for all your sins. Prize this Surety! Ah! brethren, it is better to be saved through Christ, than even if it was possible to be saved in any other way; for not only are we saved, but God's rectitude is displayed. Prize this Surety then.

2. I would say a word *to those of you who are under concern about your soul.* I am glad that there are any concerned. Oh! that I could say all were concerned. But, dear anxious friends, this is the hell you

are going to by nature. I would say, then, see the necessity of fleeing from it. Many will say, there is no use of all that anxiety, there is no need to fear. But, dear anxious soul, if you have understood what I have been saying, you will see the necessity of a thousand-fold more earnestness. Ah! it is a fearful hell; but oh! it is more fearful to think that it is kindled by the rectitude of God. Ah! then there is need to flee. Ah! dear, dear souls, do not be turned away by the world's flattery.

3. Let me speak *to those who are careless*. My dear brethren, I have shown you a solemn truth tonight; and unless I knew that no truth in itself will convert you, I might think that you would be converted by what you have heard. I showed you that the destruction of the wicked will be sudden. Dear friends, do you think that it will be sudden? The very fact that you can sit so easily, shows that you do not believe it. Therefore, when hell comes to you, it will come like a snare. Ah! dear, careless soul, think when you go home tonight, what if it should be tonight. 'This night thy soul shall be required of thee.' Careless sinner, what would become of you if God were to shoot his darts, and rain snares, fire, and brimstone upon you? Ah! tell me, sinner, would it not embitter your eternity to think that you were told of it? Ah! you are like Lot's sons-in-law, 'he seemed as one that mocked unto them.' Ah! do you think they thought it a dream when they lifted up their eyes in hell? And oh! sinner, will it not embitter your eternity to think you had been warned to flee? The minister is free of my blood, I was warned, but I heeded not. I am the cause of my own undoing; my hands made the snare wherewith I am caught. Amen.

Sabbath Evening,
4th December 1842.

SERMON XXXV

THE ETERNAL TORMENT OF THE WICKED MATTER OF ETERNAL SONG TO THE REDEEMED

Revelation 19.3. *And again they said Alleluia. And her smoke rose up for ever.*

The first thing to be enquired into in these words is, *Who are the persons that sing this remarkable song?* There are much people in heaven: verse 1, 'I heard a great voice of much people in heaven, saying, Alleluia; salvation and glory, and honour, and power, unto the Lord our God.' They are the same people that are spoken to in the 20th verse of the chapter before: 'Rejoice over her, thou heaven, and ye holy apostles and prophets, for God hath avenged you on her.' Now, it is the same people, who, in the beginning of the 16th chapter, are described as saying, 'Alleluia, salvation, and glory, and honour, and power, unto the Lord our God.' It is 'thou heaven,' that is, ye inhabitants of heaven. They are, no doubt, the same people that John had previously seen, 'a great multitude, which no man could number, of all nations, and kindred, and people, and tongues, who stood before the throne, and before the Lamb, clothed with white robes, and palms in their hands,' Rev. 7.9. And they are described in another passage in this same book, as an hundred and forty and four thousand that stand with the Lamb on Mount Zion singing the new song. They learned it on earth, and now they sing it in heaven; so that, dear brethren, the song we are now about to consider is the song of heaven — the song that all the holy apostles, and prophets, and saints sing.

There is a second thing to be considered, and that is, *What is the matter of this song?* 'And again they said, Alleluia. And her smoke rose up for ever and ever.' The word 'Alleluia' is composed of two Hebrew words, which signify, 'Praise ye Jehovah.' Now, it is often taken to express joy. It is so in the Psalms, so no doubt it is in heaven. 'They have got songs and everlasting joy upon their heads: sorrow and weeping are for ever fled away.' It seems as if they would never weary singing it, for, 'again, they said, Alleluia.' It has another meaning, it is that of admiring praise, 'Praise ye the Lord.' It is when a person has got some glorious view of Christ — some new discovery of the character of God. Every new discovery of God's majesty bursting in on the soul, calls forth another song of praise — 'Alleluia, praise ye the Lord.'

There is a third thing to be considered, and that is, *What is the occasion of this song of the redeemed?* It is because 'her smoke rose up for ever and ever.' Observe, at the 20th verse of the preceding chapter, it is said, 'Rejoice over her, thou heaven, and ye holy apostles and prophets; for God hath avenged you on her.' And accordingly, 'thou heaven,' and 'ye holy apostles and prophets,' are described as singing 'Alleluia.' And why? Just because Anti christ is overthrown. You will observe, brethren, if you compare the preceding chapter with this when you go home, that it is the destruction of Babylon that they rejoice over. But see how the world mourned for Babylon when she fell. 'The kings and the merchants, and the ship-masters stood afar off, and would not come near for fear of her torment, but cried, alas! alas! that great city Babylon, that mighty city, for in our hour is this judgment come.' Oh! brethren, observe, when Antichrist is destroyed, then the inhabitants of heaven will begin to sing and clap their hands, 'For true and righteous are his judgments; for he hath judged the great whore, which did corrupt the earth with her fornication, and hath avenged the blood of his servants at her hand.' And when they see her smoke ascend to heaven, they will sing 'alleluia, for God hath avenged you on her.'

From this very solemn passage I draw this doctrine:

That the eternal torment of the wicked will be matter of eternal song with the redeemed.

I tried to show you last Sabbath that it was perfectly consistent with the character of God to punish sinners in an eternal hell, and now, this evening, I desire to show you, by the teaching of the Holy Spirit — for oh! brethren, it is an awful truth — that the torment of the wicked will be matter of eternal song to the redeemed.

I. First, then, *The eternal torment of the wicked will be matter of no grief to the redeemed.* However much the people of God weep over the wicked now, yet it can be shown that in heaven the torment of the wicked will be no matter of grief to the redeemed. This will appear evident if you consider the day of judgment: 'When the Son of man shall come in his glory, and all the holy angels with him, then shall he sit upon the throne of his glory; and before him shall be gathered all nations; and he shall separate them one from another, as a shepherd divideth his sheep from the goats, etc. And these shall go away into everlasting punishment; but the righteous into life eternal,' Matt. 25. 31-46. Now, brethren, no reflecting mind can consider this remarkable passage, who will be witness to the condemnation of the wicked without seeing the truth of what I have been saying. There can be no doubt but that ministers and people will stand together, and be witnesses to one another's acquittal or condemnation — that parents shall stand and be witnesses to the acquittal or condemnation of their children — that children shall stand and be witnesses to the acquittal or condemnation of their parents — that husbands shall stand and be witnesses to the acquittal or condemnation of their wives, and that wives shall stand and be witnesses to the acquittal or condemnation of their husbands. Then, dear brethren, it follows immediately from this, that it will be no grief to the righteous to see the wicked condemned. Their tears will be over, their sorrows will be past, and yet they will see them condemned, they will hear their agonizing cry — they will see their sad countenances, and yet they will not shed a tear.

The same thing is evident if you will consider the expression in the Bible that hell is to be within sight of heaven. And, as this idea may be new to some of you, I crave your attention, while I try to prove it. Turn to Luke 13.28: 'There shall be weeping and gnashing of teeth, when ye shall see Abraham, and Isaac, and Jacob, and all the prophets in the kingdom of heaven, and you yourself thrust out.' Then look at the 16th chapter, 22nd verse: 'The rich man also died, and was buried; and in hell he lifted up his eyes, being in torments, and seeth Abraham afar off, and Lazarus in his bosom.' And then look at the last chapter of Isaiah, 24th verse: 'And they shall go forth and look upon the carcasses of the men that have transgressed against me; for their worm shall not die, neither shall their fire be quenched, and they shall be an abhorring unto all flesh.' There you are told quite plainly, 'They shall go forth and look upon the carcasses of the men that have transgressed against God, whose worm shall not die, neither shall their fire be quenched.' Look also at the 14th chapter of Revelation, 10th verse: 'The same shall drink of the wine of the wrath of God, which is poured out, without mixture, into the cup of his indignation; and he shall be tormented with fire and brimstone in the presence of the Lamb.' Now, in this passage, it is quite plain, although we cannot tell how it is, that hell will be within sight of heaven, they will be tormented with fire and brimstone, in the presence of the holy angels and in the presence of the Lamb. But, brethren, you know quite well that if the eternal misery of the damned was to be an occasion of sorrow to the redeemed, it would not be; for we are told, in one of the Psalms, 'In thy presence is fullness of joy, and at thy right hand are pleasures for evermore.' And we are told in the 21st chapter of Revelation, 4th verse, that 'God shall wipe away all tears from their eyes; and there shall be no more death, neither sorrow nor crying, neither shall there be any more pain; for the former things are passed away.' You will observe, brethren, that there is to be no more pain, neither sorrow, nor crying, and yet they are to be within sight of the lost. Oh! brethren, how does this express the doctrine I stated, that the condemnation of the wicked will be matter of no grief to the redeemed. Yea, we shall give our vote that you be condemned; and not only so, but when you are condemned and cast into the lake of fire, we shall give our amen to it. Brethren, the redeemed will have no manner of grief at all for your torment.

II. I come now, secondly, to show that *the torment of the wicked will be matter of joy to the redeemed.* It will not only be no grief, but will be matter of praise. We will sing, 'Hallelujah,' when the smoke of their torment ascends up for ever and ever. Now, simply to prove this, turn with me to the 14th chapter of Exodus, 30th verse: 'Thus the Lord saved Israel that day out of the hands of the Egyptians; and Israel saw the Egyptians dead upon the sea shore. And Israel saw that great work which the Lord did upon the Egyptians; and the people feared the Lord, and believed the Lord, and his servant Moses.' Chapter 15, verse 1: 'Then sang Moses and the children of Israel this song unto the Lord, and spake, saying, I will sing unto the Lord, for he hath triumphed gloriously; the horse and his rider hath he thrown into the sea.' Brethren, this is a very full passage, and it has a deeper meaning than you would think. When Israel stood upon the shore, and saw the dead bodies of the Egyptians washed upon it, they burst forth in a song of praise to God. And in like manner, when the redeemed will stand upon the sea of glass, they will sing the same song — the song of Moses, the servant of God, and of the Lamb. And what occasioned the song of Moses? It was because the Egyptians were drowned in the Red Sea. So, in like manner, it will be with the redeemed when they see the wicked cast upon the shores of the burning lake. They will sing the song of Moses the servant of God, and the song of the Lamb. See also the 91st Psalm, 7th and 8th verses: 'A thousand shall fall at thy side, and ten thousand at thy right hand; but it shall not come nigh thee; only with thine eyes shalt thou behold and see the reward of the wicked.' Here it is as plain as words can make it: 'Only with thine eyes shalt thou behold, and see the reward of the wicked.' See Revelation 16.4: 'And the third angel poured out his vial upon the rivers and fountains of waters; and they became blood. And I heard the angel of waters say, Thou are righteous, O Lord, which art, and was, and shall be, because thou has judged thus.' Here you will observe that the holy angels praise God for pouring out his vial upon the wicked. The same thing is taught in the 18th chapter, 20th verse: 'Rejoice over her, thou heaven, and ye holy apostles and prophets; for God hath avenged you on her.' Compare this with the text: 'And again they said Alleluia, and her smoke rose up for ever and ever.' My dear brethren, from all these passages it is put beyond a doubt, that the condemnation of the wicked will be matter of joy to the redeemed, and not only at the first, but throughout eternity; for, 'Again they said Alleluia, and her smoke rose up for ever and ever.'

III. I come now, in the third place, *to enquire into the reason why the redeemed will rejoice at the condemnation of the wicked.* And I would show you first what it is not, and then what it is.

1. *It is not because they love to see human pain.* I showed you last Sabbath, that God has no pleasure in the pain of his creatures; yea, he has no pleasure even in the pain of a worm. And so it is with the redeemed. It is not because of the pain the wicked are enduring that the redeemed rejoice. You remember when Paul stood bound before Agrippa, he said, 'I would to God that not only thou, but also all that hear me this day, were both almost, and altogether such as I am, except these bonds,' Acts 26.29. I would not reckon that man my friend, who would take pleasure in the pain of a worm. Then this is not the reason why the redeemed will rejoice at the condemnation of the wicked.

2. *It is not because they will see the destruction of their enemies.* It is not because they will then see vengeance executed on their enemies. This is a devilish feeling; this is not the reason. The character of the redeemed is that they forgive their enemies. You remember the parable that our Lord told about the man who owed his master an hundred talents, and when he was unable to pay, frankly forgave him all. This is not the reason, then, why we will rejoice when we see the torment of the damned.

What is the reason, then, why the redeemed rejoice at the condemnation of the wicked? And, in one word, *it is because the redeemed will have no mind but God's.* They will have no joy but what the Lord has. I showed you last Sabbath that God must rain snares, fire, and brimstone, upon the wicked; not because he loves pain, but because 'The righteous Lord loveth righteousness.' Now, the redeemed will be of the same mind with God when they get to heaven. And God must change his nature before he can quench the fire of hell. So must it be with the redeemed — they enter into God's mind. O brethren, it is a solemn truth, and I know hardly how to speak of it; but as sure as there is a God in heaven, and as sure as there is a hell for the wicked, so surely will the redeemed rejoice over the eternal damnation of the wicked. And this is the reason: we will enter into the same mind with God. 'True and righteous are his judgments.' And when we see their torment we will rejoice and sing, Hallelujah.

From this awful subject I would have you to learn a little improvement.

Learn, *how little comfort you will have in hell.* O brethren, you will have little pity shewn you in hell: Satan cannot pity you, your companions in hell will not pity you, you will only torment one another — there will be none in hell to pity you. But oh! more than this, there will be none in heaven to pity you. God will not pity; his righteous nature demands that he rain snares, fire, and brimstone upon you. If he would cease to do this he would cease to be a righteous God. Now, he would far rather that you would all come to Christ and be saved; but if you go to hell he will have no pity on you. Christ will have no pity on you. He knocked at your door, but you would not open. He stood till his head was filled with dew, and his locks with the drops of the night. Yet, brethren, it is true, he will pity you no more. He will 'laugh at your calamities, and mock when your fear cometh.' Oh! brethren, not only will God and Christ have no pity, but your redeemed brothers and sisters will have no pity. Now they weep over you; but when that day comes, they will pity you no more. Not a tear will be shed; but on the contrary they will sing, 'Alleluia,' for the smoke of your torment will ascend up for ever and ever. Oh! brethren, this is no fancy, you will see it, and some of you will feel it too. Oh, consider! Some of you have godly parents, a godly father or mother; consider what it will be when their loved voice which you have so often heard at evening tide, address the throne of grace on your behalf — when that very voice shall say, 'Alleluia,' — when the smoke of your torments will ascend up for ever and ever. Consider you that have sat under a godly ministry, that very minister will give the word that you should be condemned. Oh! the very voice you have heard in this place, beseeching you, and if spared will beseech you in accents of love to my dying breath, — that very voice will sing, 'Alleluia,' when the smoke of your torments shall ascend up for ever and ever. Consider, I beseech you, what a precious time you have got. It is the duty of all God's children to seek your conversion; nay, God himself beseeches you to be reconciled. Jesus, who died for sinners, is waiting to wash you in his blood. The Holy Spirit is waiting to lead you to Jesus, and to sanctify you. The angels are waiting to rejoice over you, and ministers are beseeching you. Oh! what a time is this: this is the day of grace. But in a little while the redeemed will let go your hand; in a little while God will give over calling upon you to repent. Soon Jesus will laugh at your calamity; soon the Spirit will cease to strive with you, and angels will let go their hold of you. Oh! brethren, do think then, — 'Come now and let us reason together, saith the Lord.' Oh! consider; for, if you do not, we shall sing 'Alleluia,' when we see the smoke of your torment rise up for ever and ever. May the Lord bless his own word. Amen.

Sabbath Afternoon,
11th December 1842

SERMON XXXVI

THE MENTAL AGONIES OF HELL

1 Corinthians 9.27. *But I keep under my body, and bring it into subjection; lest that by any means, when I have preached to others, I myself should be a castaway.*

First, observe, *the manner in which Paul sought the kingdom of heaven.* Verse 26, 'I therefore so run not as uncertainly; so fight I, not as one that beateth the air.' Although that Paul wrote these words he had a full assurance of heavenly love. It was many years after his conversion on his way to Damascus; and I am sure, if any one had assurance of his conversion, it was the apostle Paul — 'I am in a strait betwixt two, having a desire to depart, and be with Christ, which is far better.' — 'We are confident, I say, and willing rather to be absent from the body, and to be present with the Lord.' And you remember that sweet saying — 'There is laid up for me a crown of life.' Yet for all that, Paul sought the kingdom of heaven as if he had been running a race; he was as anxious seeking it after his conversion as he had been before it. There are many people who, after conversion, sit down as if it were all over. They think they need do no more; but it was not so with Paul.

The second thing I desire you to notice from these words is, *one important effort Paul made.* It was this, 'I keep under my body, and bring it into subjection.' Paul had noticed that in the Grecian games the men who ran and wrestled were temperate in all things. Now Paul said this is what I will do in running my race. There are some Christians, I fear, who will not do so much for an incorruptible crown as the Grecian racer did for a corruptible one — 'The children of this world are wiser in their generation than the children of light.' There is too much pampering the body, and then Satan gets the advantage.

There is a third truth I wish you to notice. It is, *the reason of Paul's anxiety and care.'* Lest that, by any means, when I have preached to others, I myself should be a castaway.' I have told you, brethren, already that Paul had a very clear sight of his conversion, he knew that he was in Christ, and that none could pluck him out of his hand; yet, for all that, Paul was afraid lest he should be a castaway. Paul knew that, though he was a minister, yet, that, if he gave way to the flesh, if he lived after the flesh, he would be a castaway. He knew that many who seemed Christ's had yet fallen away. Judas he knew was a castaway. Paul felt that which I have sometimes expressed to you; if he lived after the flesh he would die. Paul knew quite well that there is an indissoluble connection between a wicked life and hell. And, oh! it was this that made him temperate in all things.

At present, I mean to speak to you principally on the meaning of the word, 'castaway'. At some previous times I have spoken to you on the subject of an eternal hell — on the worm that never dies, and the fire that is never quenched; but there is one part of the subject I have passed over, namely, the mental agonies of hell, and that is a castaway. The word castaway is supposed to be taken from workers of metals; you know there is a part of the metal which comes out of the furnace, which is called dross, which is of no manner of use, and that is cast away. It is the same word which is sometimes translated 'reprobate.' Those of you in this congregation who will be cast away, will be found to be but dross, 'reprobate silver shall men call you.'

I.   I would show you, first, that *wicked men will be cast away from Christ*. It is written, 'Depart from me ye cursed' — 'who shall be punished with everlasting destruction from the presence of the Lord, and from the glory of his power,' 2 Thess. 1.9. I say that those in this congregation who shall be found on that day to be impenitent shall be cast away; they shall be punished with everlasting destruction from the presence of the Lord. Unconverted men in this world are often very near Christ. Christ often comes to the door of unconverted men: 'Behold I stand at the door and knock,' etc. Yea, he sometimes comes so near that he stretches out his hands. 'All day long have I stretched out my hands to a disobedient and gainsaying people.' Yea, I believe that sometimes you feel Christ is near; I believe that sometimes you feel that Christ is knocking at your door. But oh! it will be a change in that day. Christ will say, depart from me — Christ will no more seek after your soul — Christ will no more knock at your door — Christ will no more stretch out his hands all day long to you; you will never hear his voice more calling on you to turn — you will never get one offer more of Christ — you will be cast away. Christ is the way to the Father — but the door will then be shut against you for ever and ever, and the shutting of the door will echo through all the caverns of hell.

II.   *The wicked and impenitent in this congregation will be cast away from God*. In one sense the wicked will never be away from God, because God fills heaven, earth, and hell. Job says: 'Hell is naked before him, and destruction hath no covering.' And it is said in Proverbs, 'Hell and destruction are before the Lord.' In one sense then, the wicked will never be away from God. It was he that kindled hell. 'The breath of the Lord, like a stream of brimstone, doth kindle it." But still, it is true, you will be cast away from God — you will be cast away from the relative enjoyments of God. 'Man's chief end is to glorify God, and to enjoy him for ever.' God says to believers, 'I will be their God, and they shall be my people.' He said to Abraham, 'I am thy shield, and thy exceeding great reward,' Gen. 15.1. Asaph sings, 'God is the strength of my heart, and my portion for ever.' Ah! this is the portion of believers; we can look up to heaven, and say, 'This God is our God, for ever and ever.' And God said to the Levites, 'Thou shalt have no inheritance among them, I am thy inheritance.' But that will not be the case with those in this congregation who will be cast away. You will be cast away from the fruition of God. The attributes of God will minister no joy to you. It is true, you cannot get far enough away from God now, you could not bear to be left alone with God for five minutes; but, oh! it will be hell for all that, to be separated from him. It will be the hell of hells to be separated from God.

You will not only be cast away from God, but *from the favour of God*. It is said, 'In thy favour is life.' Ah! child of God, say what would you sell this favour of God for? Ah! the favour of God can lighten up the pale cheek of the dying saint with seraphic brightness, and can make him rejoice, even on the scaffold, and at the stake. But, sinner, you will be cast away from the favour of God, God will send you nothing but the black cloud of his frown for ever and ever.

And you will be cast away *from the blessing of God*. God makes everything blessed to us. Our friends are blessed to us. Our food and our raiment are blessed by him; and he can make these things minister no blessedness, even though we be in possession of them, and this will be the case with those of you who will be cast away. God will take away all blessedness from you.

III.   I come to show you, brethren, in the third place, that *the wicked will be cast away by the Spirit*. It is the Spirit that is the author of joy in the unconverted, and it is he that keeps them from sin. There are three ways by which God the Spirit keeps wicked men from sin.

1.   He does so by *ordinances*. He makes them a band on their wickedness. Family worship is a great band on the wicked. The ordinance of the preached word is a great means of keeping men from open acts of wickedness. You have the terror of the law, and the sweet winning invitations of the gospel; these keep you from sin, though they may not save you.

2.   And again, brethren, the Spirit works very much through *providence*. You may notice that a wicked man would go further into sin, were he not restrained by providence. God brings poverty, so that he is not able to go into those expensive vices that he would otherwise do. And God lays sickness on him, or on his child, which keeps him from sin. Now, these things are all owing to the restraining grace of God.

3. There is a third way, that is, by *convictions*. I believe there are none here who have not had some convictions of sin. Now, God makes use of these convictions in order to restrain you; he keeps you back from going into those fearful debaucheries into which you would otherwise fall. But, oh! brethren, do you remember the Scripture? 'My spirit shall not always strive with man.' He is striving with you now; but there is a time coming when he will no more strive with you; it may not be during your life, yet it will be immediately at death. Ah! my friends, you will have no ordinances in hell — there will be no family worship in hell — there will be no singing praises in hell — there will be no preaching in hell. Some of you are weary of sermons now, but you will have none in hell; and there will be no more providences in hell — there will be no sickness in hell — and there will be no more convictions in hell; the Spirit will not strive with you in hell. O then, brethren, what an awful state you will be in, when the Spirit casts you away! Read the first chapter of Romans, and see what a man becomes when God the Spirit gives him over. Think what your families would become if the Spirit were to give them over. What a town would this be, if the Spirit were to give it over, what murders, wickedness, etc., would you hear of before tomorrow. I know a godly man in London, who, every morning, thanks God for restraining the wicked, and often at the breakfast table I have heard him say, 'Where would we have been this morning, if God had not restrained the wicked?' But, oh! when you go away from this world, the Spirit will give you over to your own heart's lusts. Then will you blaspheme God — then will you have no more any fear of losing your character. And oh! that will be misery. 'It is an evil thing and a bitter to sin against God.' It is not only 'evil' but 'bitter'. 'The way of transgressors is hard.' You say, 'Stolen waters are sweet, and bread eaten in secret is pleasant.' But you will find out that sin is the hardest master — it is an evil thing and a bitter. O you will find that the very sin you roll beneath your tongue now as a sweet morsel, will yet be your curse. The lust of drink and passion will rage within you, and that for ever. All your lusts that are now pent up in that little bosom will burst out like a volcano, and there will be nothing to subdue them. Were there no lake of fire, that would be hell enough.

IV. To be a castaway, is to be cast away *from all God's holy creatures*. Now, the state of wicked men is awful; but there are some pleasant ingredients in the cup. All God's holy creatures are anxious about you. The angels are anxious about you. If they are present here, it is to watch if a tear fall from your eye — or a prayer falter on your lips; and all redeemed men take an interest in you. We know that we were once as you are. David says, 'Rivers of water run down mine eyes because they keep not thy law.' And it is the same with God's children now. I believe there is not a child of God in this place that does not weep for you. And, my brethren, Christ has pity for men and women; and then, ministers pity you, and seek your conversion. But, oh! how different it will be when the day of grace is over. You will be cast away by the angels — they will pity you no more; they will know that the number of the elect is sealed. The redeemed will no more pity you; they will see you enter into the eternal fire, and they will not put up one prayer for you. And ministers will give up pleading for you; when Christ casts you away, we cannot hold you. When he casts you away, you will not have our invitation any more. Ah! brethren, I believe that even the devil will cast you away. Ah! it is true, he gives you now many a sweet word; he says, 'Stolen waters are sweet, and bread eaten in secret is pleasant.' But oh! then the devil himself will not bear your company. You will be cast away even by your friends, if you are beside them in hell, they will cast you from them. Oh! none in heaven or in hell will pity you. This is to be lost, this is to be 'a castaway.'

V. I have just one word more, it is *the complete misery of the unconverted.* You will be cast away *by yourself.* I believe this is what suicides try to do in this world; they try to cast themselves away from themselves; and therefore it is said of the damned, that they will seek death, but it shall flee from them. You know, dear friends, that unconverted men are often very complacent in this world. Your money gives you a great deal of pleasure; and your friends and acquaintances give you pleasure. But ah! that will not always be the case; there is a day coming when every unconverted man in this congregation would rid himself of himself if he could. You will then understand that the law of God is unalterable; you will then understand that God and you are enemies. Your understanding will be torment to you. You will eternally hate what God loves; and eternally love what God hates. And then your conscience will be like a hungry lioness in that day. God's vicegerent in the soul will cry out, and will not be quiet. And, oh! my brethren, your affections that are now so pleasant to you, they will be your torment. I believe that even hell will not take affection out of your heart; but ah! that will be your torment. Often you hear a wicked man say, 'I am a good father, I love my children'; but ah! if they are in hell it will be your torment that you brought them there; or if they are in heaven, it will be your torment that they will have no pity for you. And, brethren, your memory that is now so sweet to you, will be the worst of all. You will remember your scenes of sin — you will remember your mis-spent Sabbaths — you will remember your lying lips — you will remember your minister's voice warning and entreating you to be saved.

Memory will sting like an adder. O brethren, I believe you will loathe yourselves. You would try to tear that memory out of your bosom if it were possible. Oh! you will exclaim, 'Would that that whole soul would go out of being!' This is to be lost. You will be cast away by God — you will be cast away by Christ — you will be cast away by the Spirit — you will be cast away by all God's holy creatures — you will be cast away by devils — you will be cast away by yourself.

And now, my brethren, I would apply this to yourselves.

Those of you who are godly, learn to be as earnest as Paul was to keep under the body and bring it into subjection.

And those of you who are ungodly — those of you who are ungodly men under my ministry — Oh! if I had a voice that could reach your inmost soul, I would use it. You think I am exaggerating this; but ah! you little know. 'Who can endure the power of thy wrath?' I have not mentioned the furnace of fire; I have not spoken of God raining snares, fire, and brimstone on the wicked; but, ah! if there were no bodily agonies, what will the mental agonies of hell be? But oh! when these two meet, what will it be? Oh! what will it be to have all the wrath of God poured out on your soul and body, and yet never to annihilate you? Ah! then you will know what it is to be a castaway. O if you would not be a castaway, cleave close to God!

Finally, dear brothers and sisters, learn from this the love of Christ to you and me. He bore all that is contained in being a castaway, in order that we may be saved. Ah! poor sinner, Jesus is willing to rescue you. Many of you are old, many of you will die before the year is done. Come, then, to Christ, for oh! soon it will be too late! Soon the door will be shut for ever. May God bless his own word. Amen.

Sabbath Forenoon,
15th January 1842.

A COMMUNION SABBATH
in
ST PETER'S, DUNDEE
being the substance of the sermon and addresses
delivered on January 1, 1843, at the last
Communion season spent by the author on earth

Towards the close of the day's services, he remarked, 'God knows whether it will be the last year of my ministry among you or not.' Little was it then thought, that ere another such season came round, he would be with the general assembly and church of the first-born in heaven, — sitting at the table above, and drinking the wine new in his Father's kingdom. Such being the peculiar nature of these addresses, we hope that they will be acceptable and profitable alike to those who knew and loved the author for his work's sake, and to others who did not enjoy the privilege of his labours.

SERMON XXXVII

PAUL A PATTERN

1 Timothy 1.16. *Howbeit for this cause I obtained mercy, that in me first Jesus Christ might show forth all long-suffering, for a pattern to them which should hereafter believe on him to life everlasting.*

There are three remarkable things contained in this verse. The first, that *Paul felt himself to be the chief of sinners.* He says, 'For this cause I obtained mercy, that in me *first* Jesus Christ might show forth all long-suffering.' But the word is the very same with that in the preceding verse; but is there rendered 'the chief'; therefore Paul might have said, 'That in me the chief of sinners Jesus Christ might show forth all long-suffering,' etc. That is the first thing spoken of in this verse. There might be other sinners saved in the world; still, Paul felt himself the chief. 'Never was there a black soul washed, so black as me.' Paul was very fond of repeating this. You will observe it in another form, in 1 Cor. 15.9. Then again Eph. 3.8; and again in our text, 'I am the chief.' Brethren, these are not words of a feigned humility. Paul was writing under the direction of the Spirit. These words are words of truth and soberness. I think these words were true in two respects. First of all, I think Paul was the chief of sinners in the sight of God, although outwardly he was, touching the law, blameless. Outwardly, no man could lay any thing to his moral character; yet, he fought against God, and against Christ. Ah! brethren, there is many a one that has got a fair character who is yet an enemy and rebel against God. There are many that are as graves that do not appear, and those that walk over them are not aware of them. There are many that are like whited sepulchres that look fair to the eyes of men, but inwardly are full of dead men's bones and all uncleanness. But, further, I think Paul was the chief of sinners in his own sight. You know, brethren, if you take a very bright light into a dark chamber, it discovers the things that are there. So God took a bright light into the chamber of Paul's heart, and discovered to him the pollution that was there, and then he knew more of his own self, he felt himself the chief of sinners, and could say, 'O wretched man that I am, who shall deliver me from the body of this death?'

But there is a second thing contained in this verse: '*I obtained mercy.*' Twice over he says it. He says it in the 13th verse: 'Who was before a blasphemer, and persecutor, and injurious; but I obtained mercy.' And then, at the 16th verse, 'Howbeit for this cause I obtained mercy.' It is just like what he wrote to the Ephesians, 'By grace are ye saved.' Brethren, this is an expression that exactly suits one who is the chief of sinners. He did not say, I obtained justice — that would have been the chiefest place in hell; but, I obtained mercy. 'I was a blasphemer, and a persecutor, and injurious; but I obtained mercy.' He did not say, I obtained silver, or gold, or houses, or lands. God gives silver and gold to men who are cast into hell, but God gives mercy to none but those who are eternally saved.

There is still a third thing contained in this verse, and that is *the cause why he obtained mercy*. 'For this cause I obtained mercy, that in me first Jesus Christ might show forth all the long-suffering, for a pattern to them which should hereafter believe on him to life everlasting.' Paul felt, brethren, that he was saved to be a pattern to others. The Lord had chosen him, not because he was better than others, for he says, 'I am the chief;' but to show what the blood of Christ and the Spirit can do. I suppose there are many reasons in God why he shows mercy to any sinner. I believe that it is agreeable to all the attributes of God. I believe there is a meetness in God to show mercy to any sinner. 'It was meet that we should make merry, and be glad,' etc.; but Paul fixes on that, 'Howbeit for this cause I obtained mercy, that in me first Jesus Christ might show forth all long-suffering, for a pattern to them which should hereafter believe on him to life everlasting.' I cannot tell why others get this mercy; but, 'for this cause I obtained mercy.' You know, brethren, we understand better by pattern than any other way. Now this is what God did, he saved Paul to be a pattern to all that should hereafter believe. I might tell you for twenty years that God was willing to have mercy on sinners, and you no better; but ah! an example such as this proves that God will have mercy on sinners. Brethren, this last truth is what I mean to fix upon for a little. Let us examine why the conversion of Paul was a pattern for all who should ever believe. I think he was a pattern before conversion, at conversion, and after conversion.

I. First of all, *before conversion* Paul was a pattern to shew us that God is long-suffering. We are often told that God is long-suffering. We are told in that passage to Moses, 'The Lord God, merciful and gracious, long-suffering, and abundant in goodness and truth,' etc. And in the Psalms, 'The Lord is slow to anger, and of great kindness.' And we have many examples: it is said, 'The long-suffering of God waited in the days of Noah.' You remember how long God waited on Abraham. You remember how long God waited on Moses, when in the palace of Pharaoh. And you remember how long God had waited on all his Old Testament saints. And how long did he wait on the thief on the cross? — all his life. But the most illustrious example of long-suffering in God was in the case of Paul. It is true he was a young man; but long-suffering does not depend on that, but on how he provoked God. God found he was the chief of sinners. He was a pattern of the long-suffering of Christ. He is held up to the world's end, as a pattern and a mirror to show the long-suffering of Christ. As Christ dealt with him, so is he willing to deal with you, O sinner! I suppose when a boy at Tarsus he resisted the Holy Spirit of God. And I have no doubt that even in his own heart he learned to be a persecutor. And when he sat at the feet of Gamaliel, no doubt he heard often about him that died for sinners. No doubt Gamaliel often told the students of him who died; and that filled his heart with thoughts of persecution. And, still farther, when he saw Stephen stoned to death, he could take the clothes, and consent unto his death. Ah! it was then that he was provoking Christ to the uttermost to let him go. But no! And then when, after the death of Stephen, 'he made havock of the church, entering into every house, and haling men and women, committing them to prison.' Not content with making havock of the church at Jerusalem, he sought letters of the high priest to Damascus, that, if he found any of this way, whether they were men or women, he might bring them bound unto Jerusalem; yet even then Christ did not let him go, he followed him even to the wilderness; and, when he was about to spring upon the fold where the sheep were, Christ laid his hand upon him, that he might be a chosen vessel to bear his name to the Gentiles, and kings, and the children of Israel. And there may be some among you that may have provoked Christ in a dreadful manner. I have no doubt there are many here who have an outward decent morality, yet are provoking Christ to let them go. And, ah! my brethren, perhaps some of you are saying within yourselves, It is of no use in seeking mercy. O sinner, look to the pattern! Christ made him a pattern that none may despair.

II. I come now, in the second place, to show that Paul was a pattern *in his conversion*. He was so in three ways.

1. First, he was a pattern of *the sovereignty of God*. You are often told in the Bible that he is a sovereign God, though you do not believe it. You are often told that 'he will have mercy on whom he will have mercy.' We have also many examples of divine sovereignty in the Word of God. We have the example that God sent his Son to man, and not to fallen angels. You have also the remarkable example of God choosing Abraham out of a family that worshipped graven images. And you have another example, in what God told the Jews, — 'The Lord did not set his love upon you, nor choose you, because ye were more in number than any people; (for ye were the fewest of all people;) but because the Lord loved you.' 'Not for your righteousness do I this, be it known unto you, O house of Israel, for thou art a stiff-necked people.' And, again, God sovereignly rejected the Jews, and chose the Gentiles, and said, 'None of these men that were bidden shall taste of my supper.' And another particular example in the Word of God is, the example of Jacob and Esau. 'Was not Jacob Esau's brother, saith the Lord, yet I loved Jacob, and I hated Esau.' And before they were born, neither having done any good or evil, that the purpose of God according to election might stand, it was said, The elder shall serve the younger.' But of all the examples of divine sovereignty, Paul's was the most remarkable, because he was the chief of sinners. And, if it could reach the chiefest sinner, then it can reach to all others. Ah! my brethren, when Paul was seated at the feet of Gamaliel, what man in all the world could have said that that young Jew of Tarsus would be the man that was to save the world? Why did God take him, and not his fellow? And, brethren, if you follow him along the desert, until he came within sight of Damascus, — if you were to see him grasping the letters, that he had to Damascus, when he thought of his prey — which of you would have said, that he was to be the man whom Christ would choose? He was the chief of sinners, of all that company, yet the Lord appeared to him; the rest of them were speechless, hearing a voice, but seeing no man. It was only to Saul that he appeared. Ah! my brethren, why was this? It was that he might bear his name to the Gentiles. What was that? Just to be a

pattern to all that should ever hear the gospel, to show what divine sovereignty is. Ah! brethren, this is the pattern of divine sovereignty. There may be some here today, saying, How can he come to me? Ah! my brethren you think your heart is so hard that he cannot come to you; but, ah! he may. If Paul had been told that morning that Christ was coming to him, he would have smiled in bitter scorn, but he did come; so he may come to you. 'His way is in the sea; and his path in the mighty waters; and his footsteps not known.'

2. But, again, Paul was a pattern *of effectual calling.* We are often told, in the Word of God, about this. In the 110th Psalm, it is said, 'Thy people shall be willing in the day of thy power.' We are told, in the 65th Psalm, 'Blessed is the man whom thou choosest and causest to approach unto thee.' There are also many sweet examples, in the Word of God. There is that in Hosea, 'I taught Ephraim also to go, taking them by the arms.' We have also particular examples, in the Word of God, of effectual calling. We have the example of Lydia. It is said, 'The Lord opened the heart of Lydia, to attend unto the things that were spoken.' And we have the example of Zaccheus. Christ said to him, 'Come down, for today I must abide at thy hou,e.' But by far the most remarkable example of effectual calling was that of Paul. If you had gone round the world, you would not have found another heart more completely at enmity to God and Christ, yet he was effectually called. Ah! my brethren, if you had seen them that day when they left the gate of Jerusalem, and been asked who was most likely to receive the truth, would you not have said that Paul was the bitterest enemy that Christ had, and that he was the unlikeliest to receive the truth? And yet, when the cry came, 'Saul, Saul, why persecutest thou me? he trembling and astonished said, Who art thou, Lord?' And when the voice came again, 'I am Jesus, whom thou persecutest,' he exclaimed, 'Lord, what wilt thou have me to do?' Brethren, you often hear about effectual calling, and you read about it in your catechism; and yet, perhaps, you do not know what it is. This is it. This is what is meant by effectual calling — it is the whole powers of the mind that flow out to Christ. It is making that which was blind to see — that which was deaf to hear, and that which was dead to live. This is effectual calling, and this is God's example of it. Oh! is there a man here saying, it is not possible to turn the current of my soul to God? But he that called Paul out of darkness into his marvellous light, can do the same to you. Brethren, I believe that many of you here are dead, and are like the dry bones of Ezekiel's valley. And I believe that if you were brought to feel that Christ can turn you, that that would be the beginning of life to you. The first thing that Christ does, is to convince you that he is able.

3. Once more, under this head, Paul was a pattern of *a sinner justified by another.* He was not only a pattern of divine sovereignty, but he was a pattern of justification by another. You know, brethren, you are continually told, in the Bible, that a man is not justified by what he is, but by what another is. We have also the example of many that are justified by the righteousness of another in the Bible. We have that of Abel; we are told 'that, by faith, he offered unto God a more excellent sacrifice than Cain, by which he obtained witness that he was righteous.' We are told of Abraham, that he 'believed God,' and 'it was counted unto him for righteousness.' But by far the most eminent example of any being justified by another, is Paul. It was so for two reasons — (1) Because he was inwardly most vile; (2) And outwardly most decent. I believe that there never was a man more difficult to cover with another's righteousness than Saul, for God said he was the chief of sinners. And there was another reason, and that was, he thought himself righteous. If ever there was one that was outwardly, touching the law, blameless, it was he; he had lived a most religious life in the world. And, oh! brethren, when the righteousness of another was offered to him he said, 'I do not need it;' it was the most difficult thing to convince him of the need of another's righteousness, yet, when he was convinced he sought — he desired no other. Hear his own words, 'I do not frustrate the grace of God.' — 'I count all things but loss, that I may win Christ and be found in him, not having my own righteousness, which is of the law, but that which is by faith, the righteousness which is of God by faith.' O brethren! if that man be justified in the righteousness of another, then why may not you? If the deluge covered the loftiest mountains, would it not cover the little hills? If the sun, when it rises, casts a mantle of beauty over the snowy Alps, will it not cover and cast a beauty over the lesser hills? If this righteousness can cover Paul, then it can cover any other. This is good news to the vilest wretch before me. If the Pharisee found righteousness in another, then may you. Brethren, many of you may have heard that there is a way of righteousness through another, and yet, perhaps you did not understand it. This is it — this is a pattern of it.

III. And now, brethren, I meant to show you, in the third and last place, that Paul was an example *after conversion,* but that I shall merely touch upon. I said, brethren, that Paul was a pattern before conversion, at conversion, and now I would show you that he was a pattern after conversion. he was a pattern after conversion in this respect: *That he became the chief of saints, and the first of apostles.* You are often told in the Scriptures that the gospel makes men holy, and we have many examples of it in the Word of God; but by far the greatest example was that of Paul. He might well say like one of old,

'I am not the man I was.' Paul often reminds us of one who had been in heaven, — 'Our conversation is in heaven.' He looked to God as a reality, to heaven as a reality, to hell as a reality, and then he says, 'We walk by faith.' He says, 'I am persuaded, that neither death nor life,' etc. Brethren, that is a pattern to you, to show that conversion makes a man a new creature. Ah! is there any one here thinks that you have been called — that you are converted, and yet living in sin? You do not answer to the pattern. He was a pattern in all he did, he was a pattern in all his labours, he was like his Lord, he travelled by sea and land to preach the gospel. Before conversion, he laboured hard to destroy men, but now he labours hard to save men. He is a new creature.

My dear brethren, from all this, let us learn two lessons:

1. The first is by the way, but it should not be omitted. If there be any great sinner in this congregation that is saved, you are saved to be a pattern, a pattern to your family, a pattern to your friends, a pattern to the world. I believe, brethren, that wordly men are often scandalised to see notorious sinners saved. It is hard to say who is the chief of sinners: it is not those that are open sinners that are the chiefest. Paul was no drunkard, no swearer, and yet he says, 'I am the chief.' But, remember, if you are saved, it is not for your own ease — God forbid.

2. One lesson more, brethren, and I am done. What you have heard this day makes some of you inexcusable for not coming to the Saviour. If the chief of sinners found mercy, why have you not found it? There are many, many in this congregation who know they are not saved — that they are not washed. Now, sinner, I say if Paul who was the chief of sinners was brought to Christ, and not only saved, but made the chief of saints, why may not you? O brethren! I believe that Mary Magdalene, and Manasseh, and Paul will rise up in the judgment and condemn you — they will lift up their blood-red hands and say, We, we found mercy, — why have not you? Oh! what will you answer? Paul will say, I had a harder heart than you, yet Christ made me willing in the day of his power, — and why not you?

ADDRESS AT FENCING THE TABLES

In conformity to the custom of our fathers, it is now my duty, brethren to put a fence around the Lord's table. And I would say in one word that all should come to the Lord's table who are saved like the pattern. If you can look back to the time when Christ found you, and if you can see divine sovereignty in your conversion, and if you are righteous in the righteousness of another, then, as it was said, 'Who can forbid water that these should be baptized?' etc.; so, brethren, we can say in like manner, who can forbid wine and bread to those who have received Christ as well as we? I can say to all this congregation who have been saved according to the pattern that they are not only welcome by me, but by Christ — 'Eat, O friends, drink, yea, drink abundantly, O beloved.'

Let me, dear brethren, lay before you one or two texts of Scripture that will show you, if you will be honest with yourself, whether you are a saved soul or not — Phil. 3.3 (last clause): 'And have no confidence in the flesh.' My brethren, if you have been saved — if you have been taught of God — if you have been made to come to the Lord, then you are one that has no confidence in the flesh. You have no confidence in a fleshly righteousness. You do not look to your past life for righteousness. You do not look to your conversion for righteousness. You do not look to the work of the Spirit in you for righteousness. This is the mark of every child of God: if you lack this mark, you are none of his; if your peace flows from looking at yourself; it is not divine.

A second mark, brethren, you will find in the 6th chapter of Hebrews, 18th verse (last clause): 'Who hath fled for refuge to lay hold upon the hope set before us.' Ah! brethren, that was the way with the pattern. Paul fled for refuge to lay hold upon the hope set before us. Have you done this? Are you one of those that have fled for refuge to lay hold upon the hope set before us? Now, brethren, it cannot but strike you that there are many persons that have no confidence in the flesh, yet have not fled to Christ. Now, you will observe that both of these are necessary; both are necessary if we would come rightly to the Lord's table. I now put it to you in the name of my Master, whose I am and whom I serve, Have you fled for refuge to lay hold on the hope set before you? Have you fled out of Sodom, and into Zoar? Have you fled to Christ, the hope set before us? If not, brethren, you may come to the Lord's table, but you will find no good there — you will not find a feast of fat things — you will not find wine upon its lees.

Another mark is in the 1st chapter of John, 12th verse: 'but as many as received him, to them gave he power to become the sons of God, even to them that believe on his name.' Ah! brethren, I put the question, Have you received him? At the Lord's table you are to receive broken bread and poured out wine. The meaning of that is, I receive him that was broken for sinners. Is it then true, have you received him? Do not mistake, brethren — a mistake on this matter is vital. They that receive him will be saved; they that receive him not will be lost. They that receive him may come to the Lord's table; they that receive him not ought not to come. It is not, my brethren, an unmeaning service. If you receive the bread and wine unworthily then, brethren, Satan hath filled your heart to lie unto the Holy Ghost. It is false as hell — there cannot be a more complete and more blasphemous falsehood. But have you received him? Are you saying, Thou art willing and I am willing; thou art willing to be mine, and I am willing to be thine; I am polluted — thou art the fountain; I am empty — thou art fullness; I am nothing — thou art all? Are ye willing to be a blot, a stain? Are you willing to lie down at his feet, to allow him to be all? Do you believe this? Then you are welcome to the Lord's table. It is not I that bid you; it is he that made it; he is come, and calleth for you.

Once more, Psalm 119.5: 'O that my ways were directed to keep thy statutes.' Brethren, this is a simple verse, but it is the breathing of the new creature; never did an old creature breathe this from his inmost soul. Can you say that? Do you breathe an entire devotedness to him? Have you given up every sin for him? Some of you may say, God forbid that I should part with every sin. It is but a little one; I cannot part with my money, I cannot part with my pleasures, I would come to the Lord's table. Well, you may come, but you come uninvited; nay, you come against the Master's will. None are invited but those who want complete devotedness to him. Is it so with you? Some soul may say, 'O that my ways were directed to keep thy statutes.' I am vile, but thou knowest it will be heaven to me to be like thee. Is it so? Then the master says, 'Come.' He says to you what he said to the disciples, 'Come and dine.' Amen.

TABLE SERVICE, BEFORE COMMUNICATING

My dear friends, if you have received Christ, he welcomes you now to his table. He says, 'Eat, O friends, drink, yea drink abundantly, O beloved.' And you should say to him, 'Let my beloved come into his garden and eat his pleasant fruit.' 'This is a faithful saying, and worthy of all acceptation, that Christ Jesus came into the world to save sinners, of whom I am chief.' Ah! brethren, this should be the very word upon your tongue, when you take the bread and wine — you ought to be remembering your sins — 'I am chief.' Even in heaven, at the table there, we will remember our sin, though we shall have no grief on account of it. We shall be conformed to his image. Much more ought we to remember them there. Eat bitter herbs with your passover lamb. Remember that you are the chief. I believe, if you are truly following God, you have seen more sin in yourself than ever you saw in another. Ah! brethren, I protest to you, that when I have the most solemn thoughts of these things, when I have most thoughts of heaven, and of hell, it is then that I see most the meaning of these words, 'I am the chief.' And you will notice, brethren, that he does not say, 'I was the chief,' but 'I am the chief.' It is not only that you had such a nature, but you have it yet.

It is not only that you grieved the Holy Spirit, but you do it now. Ah! it was this that grieved Paul. But Christ came into the world to save sinners. That is what the broken bread says, that is what the poured out wine says. He died for sinners. There is a voice rises from the communion table that says, Christ saves sinners. The bread broken and the wine poured out, are lively witnesses that he has died. The bread was first broken that night in which he was betrayed, and then after supper he took the cup, and gave thanks, and said, 'this cup is the new testament in my blood, which is shed for you.' These are lively emblems to shew he came to die. O! he did not come in his chariot as a king: he saves us by dying. The couch he lay down on was a rocky sepulchre. This is a faithful saying, you may stake your eternity on it. It is a saying that never failed yet, with any that laid grip upon it. Brethren, it is worthy to be received, it is not only faithful, but worthy. Your eternal weal or woe depends on it. It is 'worthy of all acceptance'. It is worthy to be received with the will, the affections, the mind, the conscience. He came into the world to work out a righteousness, and now he reigns above. Ah! brethren, have you received this faithful saying? Then you are welcome, and the Lord meet with you, and may he come to you in the breaking of bread. 'Twas on that night,' etc.

AFTER COMMUNICATING

I said to you, brethren, that you would remember your sins in heaven. I said to you, too, that you would look back upon them all, and yet not be sad; and what is the reason, brethren, that we will not be sorry for our past sins in heaven? The reason is that we will be with Christ, and he has died. 'And I looked, and lo, a Lamb stood on the Mount Sion, and with him an hundred forty and four thousand, having his Father's name written on their foreheads.' Brethren, the happiness of heaven is that we will be with the Lamb, not that we will be beyond the reach of fear; but that we will be with the Lamb. Therefore, Paul says, 'I have a desire to depart and to be with Christ, which is far better.' 'We shall be like him, for we shall see him as he is.' You will notice in the whole Scriptures that it is Christ that is the happiness of heaven. 'I saw them on the Mount Sion with the Lamb.' And oh! it is this that makes your little cottage like heaven. To have the Lamb with you is to have the essence of heaven with you. And you will observe they have the Father's name on their foreheads:

now, I will tell you what that means. It is to be like the Father. Christ is the likeness of the Father; now they will be not only inwardly, but outwardly like him. O brethren, this is our joy on earth. 'Be ye merciful, as your Father which is in heaven is merciful.' It is the heaven of heavens to be like the Father. You know the Bible tells us some have got the whore's forehead, their sin is written on their forehead. O brethren, the happiness of heaven is to have him formed in us. And it is said, 'I heard the voice of harpers harping with their harps.' Brethren, observe the employment of heaven. The company in heaven are to be like Christ, and the employment of heaven is to sing the new song. Oh! shall we ever sing the new song. Oh! shall we ever sing the song of Moses and of the Lamb? Brethren, I believe we shall. I think it can hardly be possible when I think of this heart, when I think, O brethren, of that, I say, And shall we ever sing the new song — shall we ever sing when the wicked lie dead at our feet? Ah! brethren, I believe that we shall. At the beginning of another year let us raise up our Ebenezer and say, 'He will bless us still.' 'The Lord shall keep thy soul, he shall preserve thee from all ill.' 'God is faithful, who also will do it.' O brethren, if we are to sing the new song, let us do it now.

> O sing a new song to the Lord,
> For wonders he hath done;
> His right hand and his holy arm,
> Him victory hath won.

If we are to sing the new song in heaven, let us sing it at Calvary. If we are ever to sing the new song, let us do it now, let our spikenard send forth a sweet smell. The Lord go with you and keep you. Amen.

CONCLUDING ADDRESS, AFTER THE DAY'S SERVICES

Suffer, dear brethren, one word more of parting exhortation. You may read in the 8th chapter of Romans, 13th verse: 'For it ye live after the flesh, ye shall die; but if ye through the Spirit do mortify the deeds of the body, ye shall live.' Brethren, I think a goodly number of you have this day got the peace of God that passeth knowledge. It is not like the world's peace — 'Not as the world giveth give I unto you.' It is a peculiar peace, heaven-sent, calm, unruffled by the trouble of this world, sanctifying peace. But ah! brethren, the peace of a believer is not always uninterrupted. If you are his children you will also have the warfare of his children.

1. Observe, dear brethren, first of all, that you have 'flesh' as well as 'spirit'. You have an old man as well as a new man. Brethren, perhaps some of you would like to forget that you have an old heart,

and while the king is sitting at his table you would like to forget that you have a nature opposed to him in you. But, ah! it is not good for the soul to be without knowledge. Then carry away this lesson — It is good to rejoice with joy unspeakable and full of glory, yet, remember, you have a law, a law of sin and death. 'They that are Christ's have crucified the flesh with its affections and lusts.' 'The flesh lusteth against the Spirit, and these two are contrary the one to the other, so that we cannot do the things that we would.' 'In me, that is in my flesh, dwelleth no good thing.' It is called in Colossians, 'members' — 'Mortify your members.' And in Romans it is called a body of sin and death, a complete body. Observe, brethren, that if you are come to Christ, you have not only got the new law written in your heart, but you have got the complete law of sin written on your body. O brethren, never forget this 'sin that dwelleth in you'. Remember that sin will dwell in you till you die. It is good to know this. A believer that does not know this is unarmed. Remember, let indwelling sin keep you at the feet of Christ, not from him.

2. There is a second thing I want you to carry away: 'If ye live after the flesh ye shall die.' Oh! my beloved, if you are really Christ's you will be kept by the power of God through faith unto salvation. It is quite true that if the great Shepherd has laid his hand upon you, none will pluck you out of his hand. But yet, listen, brethren, it is equally true, 'if you live after the flesh you shall die.' A wicked life and hell are linked together. My brethren, there is an indissoluble connexion fixed in the purpose of God between a wicked life and an eternal hell, and you cannot separate them. Remember, if you live after the flesh, you shall die. If sin get the upper hand and reigns in you, then you are on the way to hell. If you live after the flesh, you will prove that your experiences were all delusion. Oh! are there not among us fearful monuments of this? Are there not those that once sat down at the same table with us, and now they live after the flesh, and will die? 'It had been better for you not to have known the way of righteousness, than, after you have known it, to turn from the holy commandment delivered unto you.' O my brethren, I earnestly entreat your attention to this. In the judgment day you will not be asked, What did that man think? but, What did he do? It is quite true, brethren, that all who are savingly united to the Lord Jesus will be saved and go to heaven; but they will be saved in a way of holiness. There is no path but that of holiness that leads to heaven. 'If ye live after the flesh ye shall die.' Remember, sin will be in the vessel with us: but it will be fettered. But if sin is at the helm, then the vessel will break upon the rocks.

3. One word more. 'If ye through the Spirit do mortify the deeds of the body, ye shall live.' My dear brethren, this is to be your

constant duty, to mortify the deeds of the body. You will notice it is also slow, it is a putting off the old man with his deeds; it is a mortifying the deeds of the body; that is a slow death. Mortification is a slow death, so with sin in the soul. I believe that no sin will die till we be dead; but, brethren, we are every day to be mortifying the deeds of the body. How are we to do this? It is through the Spirit — this is the secret of gospel holiness; never forget it. The world tries sometimes to mortify the flesh, but not through the Spirit; but do you through the Spirit mortify the deeds of the body. What is the meaning of this? It is to let the Spirit always manifest himself — there is no other way. Brethren, if you do not keep the Spirit on the throne, then sin will reign. Let the Spirit teach you. Let the Spirit keep you always at Gethsemane. O there is nothing like a pacified conscience — pacified through the blood of Jesus! Try to be always at Gethsemane. You know, brethren, there is a wind in foreign countries that blights vegetation. Such is the wind that blows over Calvary and Gethsemane to the lusts of the flesh, it is withering to them.

But it is not only through the teaching of the Spirit, but also through the indwelling of the Spirit, that the deeds of the body are to be mortified. In the 8th of Romans, Paul says, 'If Christ be in you, the body is dead, because of sin; but the Spirit is life, because of righteousness.' The only way to put out the fire, is to let in the water of the Spirit. Brethren, you think your planning will do it; but, no, there is nothing between you and deepest fall into sin, but the Spirit. Ah! many do not believe this; they say, my principles, my good name, my resolutions will keep me; but, ah! brethren, remember, there is no power but the Spirit dwelling in your soul, that will keep you from sin. There are many here may say, 'I will never go back to sin, I will never go back to the world' — and, I believe, you are honest in saying so; but stop a little, when your soul is far from Christ, when you do not have that sense of his presence that you now enjoy, and see what you will do. Ah! brethren, we are but worms, and they are the happiest worms who do least. Then, brethren, we must be sanctified entirely through the Spirit. If there be not an Almighty hand behind me, I cannot go to the Lord Jesus, I cannot keep myself from any sin.

And, last of all, if it be so, brethren, that it is by the Spirit we are to be sanctified, then do not grieve the Spirit of God — do not resist him. Now, I would just tell you one way of grieving the Spirit — entering into, what I would call the outward eddy of temptation. Now, this is just the same with temptation, — if you enter into the outer circle of temptation, you will grieve the Spirit. There are many Christians who would not go into temptation; but they go to the outer circle. Ah! how many have fallen there, and why? I will tell you why — they grieve the Spirit. He is easily grieved. He is like the dove, easily driven away. 'If you then, through the Spirit, do mortify the deeds of the body, you shall live.' Oh! then, see that you are wholly Christians — that you give yourselves wholly up to him. It is good, at such a time as this, on the first day of this year, to devote yourselves to him. But, oh! it is not enough that you should profess with your lips. There are many that profess, but do not.

Dear friends that did not sit down at the Lord's table: Some, I think, kept away on account of their guilty conscience. I do entreat you to think that the harvest is coming, when it shall be said, 'Gather the tares, and bind them in bundles, to burn them.' God is calling you to turn now, and you will not turn. But, ah! when that day comes, you will remember you were warned. Dear friends, is it not a solemn thing not to sit down at the Lord's table? Is it not a solemn thing to say, 'I do not take the bread and wine, because I do not take Christ'? If you do not acknowledge him, you make a solemn profession that you are not his. Ah! my heart's desire and prayer for you is, that you may be saved. God wants you to turn and live; your opportunity for being saved is going past, — it will be far less if you let this day pass without your soul being saved. Dear brethren, let this solemn day move you. God said to Moses, 'It shall be the beginning of months to you.' Oh! if you are saved, this will be the beginning of years to you.

Now, dear brethren, 'I commend you to God, and to the word of his grace, which is able to sanctify,' etc. I commend you to the Lord, on whom you have believed — to whom could I commend you, but to him? The Lord be with you through this year. God knows whether it will be the last year of my ministry among you or not; but I would leave you with him, because I know that 'he that hath begun a good work in you will perform it until the day of Jesus Christ.' I would leave you with the Lord. 'Have respect unto the work of thy hands.' The Lord bless this day's service. Amen.

As was customary with Mr M'Cheyne, on such solemn occasions, to leave texts for meditation, the following were at this time suggested:

With those of you who are seeking Christ: Psalm 50.15. With those of you who are God's children: Acts 14.22 (last clause). With those of you who are Christless: Rom. 2.4.

HYMNS

THE HOLY SCRIPTURES

Laden with guilt and full of fears,
    I fly to thee, my Lord,
And not a glimpse of hope appears,
    But in thy written Word.

The volume of my Father's grace
    Does all my griefs assuage;
Here I behold my Saviour's face
    Almost in every page?

This is the field where hidden lies
    The pearl of price unknown:
The merchant is divinely wise
    Who makes the pearl his own.

Here consecrated water flows,
    To quench my thirst of sin;
Here the fair tree of knowledge grows,
    Nor danger dwells therein.

This is the judge that ends the strife,
    Where wit and reason fail:
My guide to everlasting life,
    Through all this gloomy vale.

O may thy counsels, mighty God,
    My roving feet command;
Nor I forsake the happy road
    That leads to thy right hand.

INVITATION TO THE YOUNG

'I love them that love me; and those that seek me early
shall find me.' Prov. 8.17.

Come, while the blossoms of thy years are brightest,
    Thou youthful wanderer in a flowery maze;
Come, while the restless heart is bounding lightest,
    And joy's pure sunbeams tremble on thy ways;
Come, while sweet thoughts, like summer buds unfolding,
    Waken rich feelings in the careless breast —
While yet thy hand the ephemeral wreath is holding,
    Come and secure interminable rest.

Soon will the freshness of thy days be over,
    And thy free buoyancy of soul be flown;
Pleasure will fold her wing, and friend and lover
    Will to the embraces of the worm be gone;
Those who now bless thee will have passed for ever;
    Their looks of kindness will be lost to thee;
Thou wilt need balm to heal thy spirit's fever,
    And thy sick heart broods over years to be!

Come, while the morning of thy life is glowing,
    Ere the dim phantoms thou art chasing die —
Ere the gay spell, which earth is round thee throwing,
    Fades like the crimson from a sunset sky.
Life is but shadows, save a promise given,
    Which lights up sorrow with a fadeless ray.
O, touch the sceptre! — with a hope in heaven —
    Come, turn thy spirit from the world away;

Then will the crosses of this brief existence
    Seem airy nothings to thine ardent soul.
And shining brightly in the forward distance,
    Will of thy patient race appear the goal;
Home of the weary! where, in peace reposing,
    The spirit lingers in unclouded bliss:
Though o'er its dust the curtained grave is closing,
    Who would not early choose a lot like this?

A HYMN OF PRAYER

'O God of Israel, hear my prayer!
 Let me thy richest blessings share;
 Thy blessings shall my portion be;
 Oh! let that blessing rest on me!

'If shining suns my path attend,
 And all their cheering influence lend;
 Thy blessing still I'll most desire,
 To that my highest hopes aspire.

'Or, if affliction's storm shall low'r,
 I'll trust thee in the darkest hour;
 On thee I'll rest my anxious mind,
 And in thy blessing comfort find.

'Preserve me from the snares of sin,
 And ever keep my conscience clean:
 Till all the cares of life shall cease,
 And, blessing thee, I die in peace!'

Thus pious Jabez often prayed,
 Reclining on Jehovah's aid;
 And all who seek the Lord shall find
 The God of Jabez still as kind.

O children! who assemble here,
 With holy love and humble fear,
 Like him present the fervent prayer,
 And in God's richest blessing share!

A HYMN OF PRAISE

O could we speak the matchless worth —
O could we sound the glories forth,
  Which in our Saviour shine;
We'd soar and touch the heavenly strings,
And vie with Gabriel, while he sings
  In melody divine.

We'll sing the precious blood he spilt,
The ransom that atones our guilt,
And saves our souls from hell:
We'll sing his glorious righteousness,
In which all pure and spotless dress
  Our souls with him shall dwell.

We'll sing the characters he bears,
And all the forms of love he wears,
  Exalted on his throne:
In loftiest songs of sweetest praise,
We would to everlasting days
  Make all his glories known.

Well — the delightful day will come,
When Christ our Lord shall bring us home,
  And we shall see his face:
Then with our Saviour, Brother, Friend,
A blest eternity we'll spend,
  Triumphant in his grace!

THE BARREN FIG-TREE

Within a vineyard's sunny bound,
An ample fig-tree shelter found,
    Enjoying sun and showers —
The boughs were graceful to the view,
With spreading leaves of deep green hue,
    And gaily-blushing flowers.

When round the vintage season came,
This blooming fig was still the same,
    As promising and fair;
But though the leaves were broad and green,
No precious fruit was to be seen,
    Because no fruit was there.

'For three long years,' the Master cried,
'Fruit on this tree to find I've tried,
    But all in vain my toil;
Ungrateful tree! the axe's blow
Shall lay thy leafy honours low!
    Why cumbers it the soil?'

'Ah! let it stand just one year more,'
The dresser said, 'till all my store
    Of rural art I've shown;
About the massy roots I'll dig,
And if it bear, we've gained a fig —
    If not, then cut it down.'

How many years hast thou, my heart,
Acted the barren fig-tree's part,
    Leafy, and fresh, and fair:
Enjoying heavenly dews of grace,
And sunny smiles from God's own face —
    But where the fruit? ah! where?
How often must the Lord have prayed
That still my day might be delayed,
    Till all due means were tried;
Afflictions, mercies, health, and pain,
How long shall these be all in vain,
    To teach this heart of pride?
Learn, O my soul, what God demands
Is not a faith like barren sands,
    But fruit of heavenly hue;
By this we prove that Christ we know,
If in his holy steps we go —
    Faith works by love, if true.

'THEY SING THE SONG OF MOSES'

Dark was the night, the wind was high,
  The way by mortals never trod;
For God had made the channel dry,
  When faithful Moses stretched the rod.

The raging waves on either hand,
  Stood like a massy tott'ring wall,
And on the heaven defended band
  Refused to let the waters fall.

With anxious footsteps, Israel trod
  The depths of that mysterious way;
Cheer'd by the pillar of their God,
  That shone for them with fav'ring ray.

But when they reached the opposing shore,
  As morning streaked the eastern sky,
They saw the billows hurry o'er
  The flower of Pharoah's chivalry.

Then awful gladness filled the mind
  Of Israel's mighty ransomed throng;
And while they gazed on all behind,
  Their wonder burst into a song.

Thus, thy redeemed ones, Lord, on earth,
  While passing through this vale of weeping,
Mix holy trembling with their mirth,
  And anxious watching with their sleeping.

The night is dark, the storm is loud,
  The path no human strength can tread;
Jesus, be Thou the pillar cloud,
Heaven's light upon our path to shed.

And oh! when life's dark journey o'er,
  And death's enshrouding valley past,
We plant our foot on yonder shore,
  And tread yon golden strand at last.

Shall we not see with deep amaze,
  How grace hath led us safe along?
And whilst behind — before we gaze,
  Triumphant burst into a song!

And even on earth, though sore bested,
   Fightings without, and fears within;
Sprinkled today from slavish dread,
   Tomorrow, captive led by sin.

Yet would I lift my downcast eyes,
   On Thee, Thou brilliant tower of fire —
Thou dark cloud to mine enemies —
   That hope may all my breast inspire.

And thus the Lord, my strength, I'll praise,
   Though Satan and his legions rage;
And the sweet song of Faith I'll raise,
   To cheer me on my pilgrimage.

'THE TIME IS SHORT'

The time is short! — the season near,
   When death will us remove,
To leave our friends, however dear,
   And all we fondly love!

The time is short! sinners, beware,
   Nor trifle time away;
The word of 'great salvation' hear,
   'While it is called today.'

The time is short! ye rebels, now
   To Christ the Lord submit;
To mercy's golden sceptre bow,
   And fall at Jesus' feet.

The time is short! ye saints rejoice —
   The Lord will quickly come:
Soon shall ye hear the Bridegroom's voice,
   To call your spirits home.

The time is short! it swiftly flies —
   The hour is just at hand,
When we shall mount above the skies,
   And reach Emmanuel's land.

SOME OTHER
CHRISTIAN FOCUS PUBLICATIONS
TITLES

The Beauties of Boston
by Samuel McMills

Ourselves
by Brownlow North

The Days of the Fathers in Ross-shire
by John Kennedy D.D.

An Exposition of the Westminster Confession of Faith
by Robert Shaw

Help for the Young
Matthew Henry

Paterson on the Shorter Catechism

Bible Stories
by Carine MacKenzie
Gideon
Ruth
Peter
Mary